THE DISC ADVANTAGE: HARNESSING PERSONALITY FOR A WINNING ORGANIZATIONAL CULTURE

by Matthew Snyder

DISCLAIMER

The information provided in this book, "The DISC Advantage: Harnessing Personality for a Winning Organizational Culture," is intended for general informational and educational purposes only. While the DISC model offers valuable insights into personality and behavior, it should not be considered a definitive or absolute assessment of individuals or teams.

The authors and publisher are not liable for any outcomes or consequences resulting from the use of the information presented in this book. Readers are encouraged to consult with qualified professionals, such as human resources specialists or organizational consultants, for specific advice and guidance tailored to their unique situations.

The DISC model is one of many tools available for understanding personality and behavior. It is not a substitute for professional judgment or expertise. The authors and publisher make no warranties or guarantees, express or implied, regarding the accuracy, completeness, or effectiveness of the information contained in this book.

Any references to specific companies, organizations, or individuals are for illustrative purposes only and do not constitute endorsements or recommendations.

By reading and using the information in this book, you acknowledge and agree to the terms of this disclaimer.

FORWARD

The Unseen Force: How to Harness Personality for a Thriving Organizational Culture

There's an invisible force that profoundly shapes your success: your organizational culture. It's not just about perks or office layouts; it's the very DNA that determines how your team functions, innovates, and ultimately achieves its mission.

In this book, we're about to demystify this force. We're going to take you on a journey through real-world experiences and proven strategies to not just create a winning culture, but to engineer one that *attracts*, *retains*, and *ignites* the very best talent.

Why This Book is Different

You'll find no generic platitudes or one-size-fits-all solutions here. Instead, we'll dive deep into the powerful DISC personality framework – the secret weapon that allows you to understand your team members on a fundamental level.

Imagine being able to tailor your hiring process, communication styles, and even reward systems to resonate with each individual's unique motivations and strengths. That's the power DISC puts in your hands.

What You'll Discover

- **The "Why" of Winning Cultures:** Uncover the undeniable link between a vibrant culture and your

bottom line.
- **Decoding Your Culture Code:** Learn to assess your current culture, pinpoint areas for improvement, and articulate the ideal culture you aspire to.
- **Leadership as Culture Architects:** Discover how your leadership style can make or break your cultural aspirations.
- **Building Your Dream Team with DISC:** Master the art of hiring for personality fit and skill alignment.
- **Creating a Culture of Engagement and Growth:** Learn how to onboard, recognize, and nurture your team members in ways that truly resonate.
- **Sustaining a Winning Culture:** Develop strategies to measure, adapt, and ensure your culture thrives for the long haul.

Who This Book Is For

Whether you're an HR professional seeking to revolutionize your talent management practices or an organizational leader hungry to cultivate a high-performing team, this book is your roadmap. It's for those who are ready to move beyond theory and into the realm of actionable, results-driven strategies.

Get Ready to Transform Your Organization

By the time you turn the final page, you'll be equipped with a toolkit of practical insights and a newfound understanding of the human element that drives success. You'll have the power to not just create a winning culture, but to cultivate an environment where your team thrives and your organization flourishes.

Are you ready to unlock the full potential of your team? Let's get after it.

With best wishes for your unwavering success,

Matthew Snyder

https://managemax.properties/

CHAPTER 1: THE WHY OF WINNING CULTURES

Unlocking The Secret Sauce Of Thriving Companies

Organizational culture isn't just about beanbag chairs and free kombucha—though those can be nice perks. It's the beating heart of a company, the invisible force that shapes how people think, act, and make decisions. Think of it as a company's unique vibe, the unwritten code that guides everything from brainstorming sessions to how they treat customers.

Imagine culture as the operating system running in the background of your company's computer. Just like Windows or macOS, it dictates how everything functions, from employee morale and retention to innovation and, yes, even cold, hard cash. When a company's culture aligns perfectly with its mission and values, it's like turbocharging an engine—everything runs smoother, faster, and more efficiently.

But here's the kicker: culture isn't set in stone. It's a living, breathing entity that evolves over time. It's shaped by everything from the CEO's leadership style to watercooler gossip, from market trends to the collective energy of your team. And that's the good news—because it means you can *choose* to shape your culture instead of letting it shape you.

The Payoff: Why Culture Matters

Let's be real—a killer culture isn't just about being a "good" company. It's a serious competitive edge. In today's cutthroat market, where talent is gold dust and rivals are lurking around every corner, a company with a magnetic culture attracts and keeps the best people. And those rockstar employees? They're the ones who drive innovation, create raving fans out of your customers, and ultimately, boost your profits.

Don't just take our word for it. The data backs it up: companies with strong cultures consistently outperform their peers in employee engagement, productivity, customer satisfaction, and even stock prices.

Take, for example, McKinsey & Company, one of the world's leading management consulting firms. While known for its demanding work environment, McKinsey also encourages a culture of mentorship, continuous learning, and collaboration. This investment in their employees' growth and well-being translates into high employee engagement and retention rates, essential in a field where knowledge and expertise are paramount. Their ability to attract and retain top talent allows McKinsey to consistently deliver exceptional results for its clients.

Your Choice: Winging It or Winning It

Every company has a culture, whether they realize it or not. But you have a choice: let your culture develop haphazardly ("culture by default") and hope for the best, or take the reins and consciously shape it ("culture by design").

Ignoring culture is a risky game. Left unchecked, it can turn toxic, leading to high turnover, plummeting morale, and missed opportunities galore. But when leaders invest time and energy into building a positive culture, the rewards are immense. Engaged employees, happy customers, and a thriving business—that's the trifecta of success.

Empowering Leaders: Your Culture Toolkit

This book is your ultimate guide to becoming a culture maestro. We'll give you the tools, strategies, and inspiration to transform your workplace into a vibrant, high-performing hub. Imagine a company where creativity flows freely, collaboration is the norm, and innovation is baked into the DNA. Picture employees who love coming to work and customers who can't wait to tell their friends about your brand.

That's not just a dream—it's your future. By understanding the science of culture, mastering the art of intentional design, and following the practical steps we lay out, you'll create a workplace that's not just successful but also deeply meaningful.

This journey might not always be easy, but it's one of the most rewarding adventures a leader can take. This is about more than just making money; it's about leaving a legacy. Are you ready to unleash your company's full potential?

Unmasking Your Company's Hidden Culture: A Deep Dive

Forget those cliché images of ping pong tables and nap pods. We're going beyond the surface to uncover the *real* organizational culture—the hidden currents that shape how your company truly operates. Think of it like an iceberg: you see the tip—the office layout, dress code, maybe a few inside jokes—but there's a whole world beneath the surface that drives everything.

A. Cracking the Cultural Code

To decipher this code, let's explore the two layers of the cultural iceberg:

- **The Tip of the Iceberg: Visible Elements**

These are the obvious aspects of culture that you can see and feel. It's the office vibe—open and collaborative spaces or rows of cubicles? It's the dress code—suits and ties or jeans and T-shirts? It's the rituals and celebrations—Friday happy hours or company-wide volunteer days? It's even how people talk and make decisions—are meetings formal and hierarchical, or is everyone encouraged to speak their mind?

- **Beneath the Surface: Hidden Elements**

This is where the real magic (or mayhem) happens. It's the company's core values—what truly matters, beyond the glossy marketing slogans. Is it innovation, teamwork, integrity, or something else? It's the unspoken assumptions that guide behavior—what does "success" look like here? How do people deal with conflict? And it's the unwritten norms that govern everything from how feedback is given to who gets invited to important meetings.

Your Company's Unique DNA

Just like people, every company has a distinct personality shaped by its culture. This is your company's cultural DNA—the unique blend of values, beliefs, and behaviors that makes it tick. It influences who you hire, who you attract as customers, and ultimately, how successful you'll be. Understanding your company's cultural DNA isn't just about putting a label on it—it's about unlocking its potential to drive your company forward.

B. The Birth of a Culture: It's Not an Accident

Culture doesn't just appear out of thin air. It's shaped by a complex web of influences, with leadership at the helm.

- **Leadership's Ripple Effect**

Leaders are like cultural DJs, setting the tone for the entire organization. Their words, actions, and decisions reverberate through the company, influencing how everyone else behaves. When leaders walk the talk and model the desired values, employees are more likely to follow suit. But when there's a disconnect between what leaders say and what they do, it creates a toxic breeding ground for cynicism and disengagement.

- **The Stories We Tell (and the Ones We Don't)**

Company lore, founder stories, tales of triumph and failure—these narratives are more than just anecdotes; they're powerful tools for shaping culture. They transmit values, create a shared sense of purpose, and even give employees a script for how to act in different situations. But beware of the unspoken stories—the ones about who gets promoted and why, the real reasons behind decisions—because they can reveal the true culture lurking beneath the surface.

Systems and Processes: The Backbone of Your Culture

Your company's systems and processes aren't just administrative details—they're the backbone of your culture. Think of them as the bones that give your culture structure and support its every move. Every system, from how you hire and onboard new employees to how you evaluate performance and reward success, plays a crucial role in either reinforcing or undermining your company values.

- **Alignment is Key**

Imagine a company that preaches teamwork and collaboration, but its performance reviews focus solely on individual achievements. That's a recipe for cultural whiplash! When systems and processes don't align with your values, it creates confusion, frustration, and resentment among employees. The key is to intentionally design your systems and processes to support your desired culture.

- **The Unseen Consequences**

Misaligned systems can have ripple effects you might not even realize. A company that claims to value innovation might unknowingly stifle it with endless bureaucracy and a fear of failure. Or a company that wants to attract top talent might unknowingly push them away with an outdated promotion system that favors seniority over merit.

- **Culture is a Constant Work in Progress**

Culture isn't a one-and-done deal. It's constantly evolving, just like your business. As you grow and change, your systems and processes need to keep up. Regular check-ins and adjustments are essential to ensure they're still serving your cultural goals.

This book is your guide to aligning your systems and processes with your cultural aspirations. By focusing on attracting the right people and building systems that support them, you can create a workplace where everyone is pulling in the same direction. When your systems and processes work hand in hand with your values, you unleash a powerful engine for success.

The Roi Of Culture: Where Good Vibes Meet Great Returns

Forget the fluffy stuff—a positive workplace culture isn't just about kumbaya moments and office dogs (though those are awesome). It's a financial powerhouse that can supercharge your bottom line in ways you might not expect. Let's dive into the cold, hard data that proves how a killer culture translates to real-world results.

A. The Quantifiable Impact: More Than Just Warm Fuzzies

1. Employee Engagement and Retention: The Turnover Antidote

Employee turnover is a silent killer for companies. Replacing a single employee can cost a pretty penny—think 50% to a whopping 200% of their annual salary. High turnover disrupts everything, from productivity to morale. It's like constantly training new recruits for a game they'll quit before halftime.

But here's the secret weapon: engaged employees. They're not just clocking in and out; they're invested in the company's success. And guess what? A Gallup study found that highly engaged teams are a whopping 21% more profitable. Companies with strong cultures often become magnets for talent, boasting lower turnover rates and employees who are genuinely happy to be there. That's a recipe for cost savings and a workforce firing on all cylinders.

To measure this magic, track metrics like the Employee Net Promoter Score (eNPS), send out pulse surveys, and keep a close eye on retention rates and tenure. The numbers don't lie.

2. Productivity and Innovation: The Culture-Fueled Rocket

Want your team to crank out brilliant ideas and get things done faster? Look no further than your company culture. Research has shown time and time again that positive work environments are like rocket fuel for productivity. When employees feel valued, supported, and empowered, they're not just working harder—they're working smarter.

And that's not all. A culture of trust and collaboration is a breeding ground for innovation. When people feel safe to share their ideas and take risks, that's when the real magic happens. To gauge your culture's impact on productivity, track metrics like output per employee and revenue per employee. For innovation, keep tabs on the number of new ideas generated, patents filed, successful product launches, and how quickly you can bring those new products and services to market.

3. **Customer Satisfaction and Loyalty: The Employee-Customer Love Connection**

Happy employees lead to happy customers—it's a simple equation with powerful results. When your team loves their jobs, that enthusiasm spills over into every customer interaction. They go the extra mile, solve problems with a smile, and create those "wow" moments that turn customers into raving fans.

And the financial impact? Huge. It costs way more to acquire a new customer than to keep a happy one coming back for more. So, by building a culture that prioritizes employee engagement and exceptional customer service, you're not just boosting morale—you're boosting your bottom line.

Keep an eye on customer satisfaction surveys (like the Net Promoter Score), retention and churn rates, repeat purchase rates, and customer lifetime value. These metrics tell the story of how your culture is translating into loyal, high-value customers.

4. Financial Performance: The Proof is in the Profits

A strong culture isn't just good for the soul—it's good for the wallet. Study after study shows that companies with kick-ass cultures rake in higher revenue growth, fatter profit margins, and happier shareholders. Your culture can even affect your stock performance!

Think of it this way: a positive culture isn't just a fluffy expense; it's an investment that pays off big time. It's a magnet for top talent, a driver of innovation, and a key ingredient in building a brand that people love. All of that translates to long-term, sustainable growth and a competitive edge that's hard to beat.

So, crunch the numbers. Look at your revenue growth, profit margins, return on assets (ROA), return on equity (ROE), and even your stock performance. These are the hard facts that prove a great culture isn't just good for the soul—it's good for business.

B. Case Studies: Where Culture Meets Cold, Hard Cash

Let's take a closer look at a few companies that have cracked the code, proving that a well-crafted culture can be a company's most valuable asset.

Zappos: The Customer Service Champions

Zappos, the online shoe and clothing retailer, isn't just known for its vast selection of footwear—it's legendary for its fanatical devotion to customer service. But this isn't just a random act of kindness; it's a carefully cultivated culture where employee happiness is paramount. Zappos invests heavily in training, benefits, and creating a positive work environment where employees feel valued and empowered to go the extra mile for customers.

This culture of empowerment has paid off in spades. By

putting their employees first, Zappos has seen a dramatic reduction in customer service costs. Why? Happy employees are more efficient, more effective at solving problems, and less likely to burn out. Plus, Zappos' delighted customers have become their biggest advocates, spreading the word and driving sales through the roof. It's a win-win-win: happy employees, happy customers, and a happy bottom line.

LEGO: Building a Brighter Future, One Brick at a Time

Remember when LEGO was on the verge of bankruptcy? It's hard to believe now, but in the early 2000s, the iconic toymaker was facing a crisis. Dabbling in too many unrelated ventures had diluted their brand, and the rise of digital entertainment threatened to leave them in the dust.

But LEGO didn't just throw in the towel. Instead, they did something radical: they went back to basics. They rediscovered their core values of creativity, imagination, and playful learning, and they infused those values into every aspect of their company culture.

The results were nothing short of spectacular. LEGO's profitability and revenue skyrocketed as they reconnected with their core audience and released hit products like the LEGO Movie franchise. The company's brand image was revitalized, attracting new generations of LEGO lovers. This incredible comeback proves that a strong culture isn't just a nice-to-have; it's the foundation for sustainable growth and success.

These case studies are just a glimpse into the transformative power of culture. They show that when you invest in your people and create a workplace where they thrive, the financial rewards are undeniable. Culture isn't just about creating a feel-good atmosphere; it's a strategic imperative that can make or break a company's success.

Culture Clash: The Epic Battle Between "Default" And "Design"

Your company's culture is like a choose-your-own-adventure story, and you're holding the pen. Will you let the tale unfold haphazardly, accepting whatever twists and turns fate throws your way ("culture by default")? Or will you seize control, crafting a narrative that aligns with your company's values and aspirations ("culture by design")? The choice you make could mean the difference between a blockbuster success and a box office bomb.

A. Real-World Examples: Cautionary Tales and Inspirational Sagas

- **Culture by Default: The Corporate Horror Story**

Picture this: a company where fear and intimidation reign supreme, where unethical practices are swept under the rug, and employees are treated like cogs in a machine. Sounds like a nightmare, right? Unfortunately, it's the reality many workers have faced in companies like Enron, where a toxic culture of greed and deceit ultimately led to the company's spectacular implosion.

Or consider Uber's recent fall from grace. The ride-sharing giant's "bro culture" became infamous for its tolerance of harassment, discrimination, and cutthroat competition. The consequences were devastating: mass resignations, a tarnished reputation, and a company scrambling to pick up the pieces.

These are extreme cases, but they serve as chilling reminders that when leaders neglect culture, things can go very wrong. Even in less dramatic scenarios, a lack of intentional culture-building can create workplaces where employees are disengaged, uninspired, and just plain unhappy. And that's a recipe for high turnover, plummeting productivity, and missed opportunities.

- **Culture by Design: The Hollywood Blockbuster**

Now, imagine a company where creativity flows like champagne, collaboration is the norm, and employees are empowered to take risks and chase their wildest ideas. That's the kind of culture you'll find at Pixar Animation Studios.

Ed Catmull and John Lasseter, the visionaries behind Pixar, didn't leave culture to chance. They meticulously crafted an environment that encouraged risk-taking, collaboration, and a relentless pursuit of excellence. Their "Braintrust" model, where directors and peers provide honest feedback on works in progress, has become legendary for its ability to elevate storytelling and push creative boundaries.

Netflix is another shining example of culture by design. Their "Freedom and Responsibility" philosophy gives employees unparalleled autonomy and ownership over their work. This radical trust has fueled a culture of innovation and accountability, propelling Netflix to the forefront of the entertainment industry.

B. The Cost of Neglect: A High Price to Pay

Neglecting culture isn't just a missed opportunity—it's a costly mistake. When leaders fail to take charge, they risk unleashing a domino effect of negative consequences:

- **Misalignment:** A chaotic symphony of conflicting priorities, unclear expectations, and a disconnect between stated values and actual behaviors.
- **Conflict:** A breeding ground for interpersonal drama, fueled by mistrust, resentment, and a lack of collaboration.
- **Missed Opportunities:** A stagnant company struggling

to attract top talent, adapt to change, and innovate.

C. The Power of Choice: Your Culture, Your Way

But here's the empowering truth: you have the power to write a different story. You don't have to be a victim of circumstance; you can be the architect of your company's culture. By being intentional about the kind of environment you want to create, you can unlock a world of possibilities.

Think of it like building a dream home. You wouldn't just throw up some walls and hope for the best, would you? You'd carefully consider the layout, the materials, the design elements that reflect your personality and lifestyle. The same goes for your company culture.

Start by defining a clear vision for the kind of culture you want to create. What values are non-negotiable? What behaviors do you want to encourage? Then, roll up your sleeves and start building. Develop a culture code, create rituals and symbols that embody your values, and make sure your systems and processes are aligned with your vision.

This is where the real journey begins. The path to a thriving culture is paved with deliberate choices, bold experiments, and a willingness to adapt and evolve. It's a continuous process of learning, refining, and strengthening the cultural fabric of your organization.

In the upcoming chapters, we'll go deeper into the how-to's of culture transformation, providing you with the tools and strategies to turn your vision into reality.

Case Studies: When Culture Makes Or Breaks A Company

Ready for some real-life drama? Buckle up, because these company transformations prove that culture isn't just a buzzword—it's the secret sauce that can either propel a company to legendary status or send it spiraling into oblivion.

General Electric: The Rise and Fall of an Empire

General Electric, once an industrial titan, found itself mired in complacency and bureaucracy. It was like a dinosaur lumbering through the modern age, missing out on opportunities left and right. Enter Jack Welch, the CEO who became as famous (or infamous) for his management style as GE was for its appliances.

Welch was a force of nature, a man on a mission to shake up GE's sleepy culture. He introduced a controversial "rank and yank" system, essentially firing the bottom 10% of performers each year. While this boosted short-term profits and sent GE's stock price soaring, it also created a culture of fear and intense competition. It's a classic example of a double-edged sword: Welch's tactics delivered impressive results in the short term, but some argue that his relentless focus on immediate gains ultimately compromised GE's long-term sustainability.

Microsoft: The Phoenix Rises from the Ashes

In the early 2010s, Microsoft was stuck in a rut. Internal competition was fierce, innovation was stifled, and morale was at an all-time low. It was like a once-great sports team that had lost its spark.

But then came Satya Nadella, a new CEO with a vision for a different kind of Microsoft. He championed collaboration, empathy, and a "growth mindset" where learning and development were prioritized. This cultural shift was like a breath of fresh air. Suddenly, Microsoft was back in the game, innovating with products like the Surface and Azure cloud platform. Employee engagement soared, and top talent flocked to the company. Nadella's cultural transformation breathed new life into Microsoft, proving that even giants can change their stripes.

Southwest Airlines: Where Fun and Profitability Fly High

When you think of Southwest Airlines, you probably think of their quirky in-flight announcements and friendly flight attendants. That's no accident. Southwest has built its entire brand around a "fun-LUVing" culture that values employees like family.

This isn't just about creating a feel-good workplace; it's a strategic advantage. Happy employees are more engaged, more productive, and more likely to go above and beyond for customers. That translates to happy customers, who keep coming back for more, driving up profitability. Southwest consistently ranks high in customer satisfaction and employee engagement, proving that fun and profit aren't mutually exclusive.

Patagonia: The Planet-Saving, Profit-Making Machine

Patagonia isn't just an outdoor apparel company; it's a mission-driven brand with a cult following. Their commitment to environmental sustainability and social responsibility isn't just a marketing gimmick—it's woven into the fabric of their culture.

This purpose-driven approach has earned Patagonia a stellar reputation, attracting loyal customers who share their values. Their "Worn Wear" program, which encourages customers to repair and reuse their clothing, has become a symbol of their commitment to sustainability. Patagonia proves that doing good and doing well can go hand in hand.

The Takeaway: Your Culture, Your Destiny

These case studies show that culture isn't just some abstract concept—it's the lifeblood of your organization. When you intentionally shape your culture, you're not just creating a better workplace; you're building a sustainable competitive advantage. So, ask yourself: what kind of story do you want your company to tell?

Your Culture, Your Call

This chapter has been a whirlwind tour of the incredible power of culture. We've seen how it's not just a fluffy feel-good factor, but a driving force behind employee engagement, innovation, customer satisfaction, and even cold, hard profits. We've marveled at companies like Zappos, Microsoft, and Southwest Airlines, who've turned their unique cultures into gold mines. And we've shuddered at the cautionary tales of those who ignored culture, only to watch their empires crumble.

One thing is crystal clear: culture isn't something that just happens. It's a choice. You can either let it evolve haphazardly, hoping for the best, or you can seize the reins and intentionally craft a culture that propels your company to greatness. It's the difference between being swept along by the current or charting your own course to success.

Calling All Captains: Chart Your Course

Leaders, the ball is in your court. The culture of your organization is your responsibility, your legacy. You're not just the CEO, the CFO, or the COO—you're the Chief Culture Officer. Embrace that role! Become the architect of a workplace where people are excited to show up every day, where innovation thrives, and where customers become lifelong fans.

Don't wait for a crisis to force your hand. Start now. Take a good, hard look at your current culture. What's working? What's not? Where do your values align with your actions, and where do they clash? Once you've got a clear picture, you can start building the culture you envision.

But remember, culture isn't just about setting a vision—it's about investing in your people. Give them opportunities to grow, create a sense of belonging, and support an environment where everyone feels safe to speak their minds. When you build a culture of trust, respect, and psychological safety, you're not just creating happy employees—you're unleashing their full potential.

And don't forget: culture is a living thing. It needs to adapt and evolve as your company grows and changes. Stay curious, experiment, and be willing to iterate. Think of it as tending a garden—you need to constantly nurture it, prune it, and adapt to the changing seasons.

The Adventure Awaits: Building Your Dream Culture

The journey to build a winning culture is an adventure, not a destination. In the following chapters, we'll dive into the nitty-gritty of how to make it happen. We'll talk about defining your core values, aligning your systems and processes with those values, communicating your culture in a way that sticks, and measuring your progress.

We'll also tackle the challenges of sustaining a positive culture over time and share strategies for keeping the momentum going, even when faced with setbacks. Think of it as a treasure map to guide you through the uncharted territory of cultural transformation.

So, are you ready to embark on this exciting journey? Get ready to unleash your inner cultural architect and build a workplace that not only thrives but leaves a lasting legacy. The adventure awaits!

Your Turn: Imagine The Possibilities

Now it's your turn to step into the role of cultural visionary. Take a moment to dream big and imagine the transformative power of culture within your organization.

The "What If?" Challenge:

Challenge yourself to brainstorm at least three "What If?" scenarios for your workplace. These scenarios should be bold, ambitious, and focused on creating a more positive, engaging, and productive culture. Don't be afraid to think outside the box and push the boundaries of what's possible.

Here are a few examples to get you started:

- What if we built a culture of radical candor and transparency, where everyone felt safe to speak their truth, challenge ideas, and give honest feedback? How would this impact communication, problem-solving, and innovation?
- What if we made employee well-being a top priority, offering flexible work arrangements, mental health resources, and opportunities for personal growth? How would this affect productivity, retention, and overall happiness?
- What if we celebrated failures as learning opportunities, encouraging experimentation and risk-taking? Could this lead to breakthroughs and unexpected successes?
- What if we actively sought out diverse perspectives and created an environment where everyone felt included, valued, and empowered to contribute their unique talents? How would this enhance our creativity, problem-solving, and ability to connect with a wider audience?

Remember, there are no wrong answers here. The goal is to ignite your imagination and spark new ideas for how you can intentionally shape your organization's culture.

Take It Further:

- Share your "What If?" scenarios with colleagues and leaders within your organization. This can open up a dialogue about cultural aspirations and potential improvements.
- Start small. Choose one of your scenarios and explore ways to implement it, even in a limited way. Experiment, learn, and iterate to see what works best for your organization.
- Celebrate successes. As you make progress towards your cultural goals, recognize and celebrate those wins. This will reinforce positive change and build momentum for further transformation.

By embracing the "What If?" challenge, you'll be taking the first step towards creating a workplace culture that not only supports your business goals but also inspires and empowers your people to achieve their full potential.

Test Your Knowledge!

1. Briefly describe the "Iceberg Analogy" in the context of organizational culture.
2. Name three visible elements of organizational culture.
3. Name two hidden elements of organizational culture.
4. Explain how a company's culture can be its "unique DNA."
5. What are two ways leaders influence organizational culture?
6. How can stories and symbols shape a company's culture?
7. Give an example of how a misaligned system or process can undermine the desired culture.
8. Why is it essential to regularly review and update systems and processes in relation to culture?
9. Name one company that exemplifies "culture by design" and explain why.
10. What are the potential consequences of neglecting organizational culture?

The answers are below

Test Your Knowledge! Answer Key:

1. The Iceberg Analogy compares organizational culture to an iceberg, where the visible aspects (behaviors, artifacts) are just the tip, while the majority (values, assumptions, beliefs) are hidden beneath the surface.
2. Dress code, office layout, rituals, ceremonies, logos, communication styles. (Any three)
3. Values, assumptions, beliefs, norms. (Any two)

4. A company's culture shapes its unique identity, how it operates, and the types of employees and customers it attracts, much like an individual's DNA shapes their unique traits.
5. Leaders influence culture through their actions, communication, and the values they prioritize and model.
6. Stories and symbols transmit values, create shared experiences, and reinforce the company's identity and purpose.
7. Rewarding individual achievement in a collaborative culture could undermine the emphasis on teamwork.
8. Culture is dynamic and evolves over time, so systems and processes need to be updated to ensure continued alignment with the desired culture.
9. Pixar: They intentionally created a culture of creativity, collaboration, and risk-taking through practices like the "Braintrust" model.
10. Neglecting culture can lead to misalignment, conflict, missed opportunities, low morale, high turnover, and even company failure.

CHAPTER 2: DECODING THE CULTURE CODE: THE KEY TO SUCCESSFUL RECRUITMENT AND RETENTION

The Culture Conundrum – Cracking The Code To Attract, Engage, And Retain Top Talent

In the cutthroat arena of today's talent wars, your company culture isn't just a perk; it's your secret weapon. Forget the buzzwords; we're talking about the living, breathing essence of your organization. It's the invisible force that shapes how employees think, feel, and perform, impacting everything from groundbreaking ideas and skyrocketing productivity to happy customers and a thriving bottom line.

A. The Importance of Culture Fit

Culture fit isn't just about a candidate nodding along to your mission statement or enjoying the free kombucha on tap. It's a deep-seated alignment – a symphony of values, work styles, and personality that harmonizes with your company's unique vibe and ethos.

The Employee's Viewpoint

When employees find their cultural groove, the magic happens:

- **Engagement and Satisfaction:** Work transcends the mundane. It becomes a source of passion, purpose, and a sense of belonging to something bigger. Imagine employees who are genuinely excited to come to work each day, ready to give it their all.
- **Performance and Productivity:** It's not just a warm fuzzy feeling; it's science. Studies consistently show that when employees feel aligned with their company's values, they're more motivated, innovative, and laser-focused on results.
- **Retention and Loyalty:** Culture fit is the ultimate retention strategy. Employees who feel valued and connected to their workplace are less likely to jump ship, saving your company the hassle and expense of constantly replacing and training new hires.

To help you understand and measure this vital alignment, we've included a sample survey and interview guide in the appendix at the end of this book. These tools will help you tap into your employees' perspectives and uncover potential areas for growth.

The Company's Vantage Point

A thriving culture isn't just a warm and fuzzy perk; it's a tangible competitive advantage that sets you apart from the pack:

- **Attracting Top Talent:** A positive, well-defined culture is like a beacon in the talent jungle, drawing in high performers who not only have the skills you need but also

share your passion and purpose.
- **Building a Dream Team:** When employees are on the same wavelength, collaboration flows effortlessly, problems become puzzles waiting to be solved, and the team consistently delivers exceptional results.
- **Igniting Innovation and Agility:** A healthy culture is a breeding ground for innovation. When employees feel safe to experiment, take calculated risks, and challenge conventional thinking, the possibilities are endless.

B. The High Cost of Misalignment

Ignore culture fit at your peril. When employees and company values clash, the consequences can be devastating.

Cautionary Tales: Real-World Examples

The corporate graveyard is littered with the tombstones of companies that failed to prioritize culture fit: Some survive and live to fight another day, other's aren't so fortunate. A few recent examples:

- **WeWork's Rise and Fall:** WeWork's meteoric rise was fueled by a charismatic leader and a culture of excess and hype. However, this culture masked unsustainable business practices and a lack of financial discipline. As the company's true financial situation was exposed, investors fled, the CEO resigned, and the company's valuation plummeted.
- **Retail Rout: Sears' Slow Decline:** Once a retail titan, Sears suffered a slow and painful decline as its bureaucratic culture stifled innovation and alienated employees. A lack of investment in customer service and an outdated business model further exacerbated the problem, leading to plummeting sales and the eventual bankruptcy of the company.
- **Financial Fallout: Wells Fargo's Scandal:** Wells Fargo's reputation was severely damaged when it was

revealed that employees, under immense pressure to meet sales targets, had opened millions of unauthorized accounts for customers. This unethical behavior, driven by a culture that prioritized profits over integrity, led to billions of dollars in fines and a loss of customer trust.

The Domino Effect: A Downward Spiral

Cultural misalignment isn't just an HR issue; it's a business cancer that can metastasize throughout your entire organization. The initial symptoms might be subtle – a drop in morale, increased absenteeism, missed deadlines – but if left untreated, they can quickly escalate into a full-blown crisis.

1. **Disengagement and Exodus:** When employees feel a stark disconnect between their values and the company's culture, their enthusiasm wanes, and their productivity plummets. This sense of disillusionment can quickly escalate into an exodus of talent, leaving your company scrambling to fill critical roles.
2. **Overburdened and Burnt Out:** As valuable team members depart, the remaining employees are often left to shoulder the burden of their colleagues' workloads. This can lead to burnout, resentment, and a further decline in morale, creating a breeding ground for more departures.
3. **Compromising on Quality:** In a desperate attempt to fill vacancies, companies may lower their hiring standards, bringing in individuals who lack the skills, experience, or cultural alignment needed to thrive. This not only fails to solve the problem but can actually exacerbate it, as these new hires struggle to integrate and contribute effectively.
4. **Customer Dissatisfaction: A Chain Reaction:** The ripple effects of a disengaged workforce extend beyond your office walls. Frustrated and overworked

employees are less likely to provide exceptional customer service. Their negativity can seep into their interactions with clients, resulting in miscommunications, delays, and a general decline in customer satisfaction.
5. **Financial Fallout:** As customer satisfaction dwindles, so does revenue. This financial strain can lead to budget cuts, layoffs, and even more pressure on the remaining employees, creating a vicious cycle that can be difficult to escape.
6. **The Death Spiral:** If left unchecked, this downward spiral can be catastrophic, culminating in the potential demise of the company.

C. Breaking the Cycle and Building Your Competitive Advantage

Fortunately, this bleak scenario is not inevitable. By acknowledging the critical importance of cultural alignment and taking proactive steps to nurture a positive and supportive environment, you can break this destructive cycle and transform your culture into a powerful competitive advantage.

Uncovering Your Current Culture: A Journey Of Self-Discovery

Embarking on the journey of building a stronger workplace begins with a deep dive into the present. It's about peeling back the layers to uncover the often-hidden values, behaviors, and norms that form the unique DNA of your company's culture. This section equips you with tools for introspection and in-depth analysis, guiding you toward valuable insights that will illuminate your path forward.

A. Self-Reflection: Look Within

Before we embark on formal assessments, let's turn our gaze inward. Your own experiences and perceptions within the organization offer a crucial starting point for understanding your company's culture.

Cultural Inventory:

- *Exercise:*
    1. Take a moment to distill your current company culture into five words or phrases. Do these words spark joy and pride? Or do they hint at underlying unease or discontent?
    2. Now, dream big. What does your ideal workplace look like? Capture that vision in five words or phrases.
    3. Compare your two lists. Where do they diverge? Where do your aspirations align with reality? This exercise can unearth hidden desires for change and illuminate potential areas for growth.

Values Check:

- *Exercise:*

1. Reflect on your personal values. What principles guide your compass? What aspects of a work environment do you hold dear?
2. Hold your personal values up against your company's stated values. Are they in harmony? Or do they clash? If they're misaligned, consider the impact on your engagement, sense of fulfillment, and overall happiness at work.

Storytelling:

- *Exercise:*
    1. Reflect on a significant event in your workplace – a moment of triumph, a challenging project, a memorable interaction.
    2. Share this story, weaving in the details, emotions, and actions that made it meaningful.
    3. Analyze the story. What hidden values or beliefs does it expose? What unspoken rules or norms were at play? Does your story paint a picture of a supportive and collaborative environment, or one marred by competition and distrust?

A Word of Caution: Tempering Idealism with Reality

It's easy to idealize your company's culture, especially if you're in a leadership position. But your perspective is just one piece of the puzzle. Your experience may not reflect the reality for every employee.

Consider a company that boasts about its commitment to employees, yet allows a rogue middle manager to run rampant with hardly any oversight, instilling fear in their subordinates. This stark contrast between words and actions exposes a deep-seated cultural hypocrisy, eroding trust and undermining morale.

To ensure you're not blinded by your own biases, here are a few tips:

1. **Acknowledge the Gap:** Recognize that your ideal culture and the reality on the ground may not be in perfect sync. This is natural and simply a starting point for improvement.
2. **Seek Diverse Perspectives:** Don't just listen to your own voice. Actively seek feedback from employees at all levels, departments, and locations. Encourage open and honest communication, even if it's critical.
3. **Look for Disconfirming Evidence:** Challenge your assumptions by actively seeking out information that contradicts your initial impressions. If you believe your company is highly collaborative, for example, look for instances where teamwork might be lacking.
4. **Compare with External Benchmarks:** Research how other successful companies in your industry cultivate their cultures. How does your company stack up? What can you learn from their practices?
5. **Consider Historical Context:** How has your company culture evolved over time? What events or changes have shaped it? Understanding this historical context can shed light on why your culture is the way it is today.
6. **Utilize Anonymous Feedback:** Create a safe space for employees to share their honest opinions without fear of repercussions by using anonymous surveys or feedback mechanisms.

Remember, the goal of this exploration is not to paint a perfect picture, but to gain a clear-eyed understanding of your company's cultural strengths, weaknesses, and areas for improvement. This knowledge will empower you to build a culture that truly supports your employees and propels your company towards greater success.

B. Deeper Dive: A Comprehensive Culture Assessment

While self-reflection is a valuable starting point, a truly in-depth understanding of your culture requires a deeper dive involving a variety of perspectives and tools.

Surveys:

A well-designed survey is a powerful tool for gathering quantitative data about your company's culture. It provides a broad overview of how employees perceive various aspects of their workplace experience.

- **Employee Engagement Surveys:** These surveys assess overall employee satisfaction, commitment, and alignment with company values. They often explore topics like job satisfaction, relationships with colleagues and managers, opportunities for growth, and overall perception of the company culture. By measuring employee engagement, you can identify areas where your culture is thriving and areas that need attention.
- **Culture-Specific Questionnaires:** These surveys take a deeper dive into specific cultural dimensions, such as collaboration, communication, innovation, decision-making processes, leadership styles, and more. They allow you to tailor your assessment to the specific aspects of your culture that you want to understand better.

Considerations for Effective Surveys:

- **Anonymity and Confidentiality:** Guarantee that employees can respond honestly without fear of repercussions. This is crucial for getting accurate and unfiltered feedback.
- **Question Types:** Use a mix of quantitative (e.g., Likert scale ratings) and qualitative questions (e.g., open-ended responses). Quantitative data provides a broad overview of trends, while qualitative feedback offers deeper insights into individual experiences and perceptions.
- **Thorough Analysis:** Don't just skim the surface of

the survey results. Analyze the data carefully to identify patterns, themes, and potential areas of concern. Look for discrepancies between different groups of employees (e.g., departments, levels) to uncover hidden cultural dynamics.

Interviews:

While surveys provide valuable quantitative data, interviews offer a deeper, more nuanced understanding of your company's culture. They allow you to explore individual perspectives, experiences, and emotions in greater detail.

- **Structured Interviews:** These interviews use a standardized set of questions, ensuring consistency across participants and making it easier to compare responses. They can be particularly effective for gathering information on specific cultural aspects, such as leadership styles, decision-making processes, or communication norms.
- **Informal Conversations:** While less structured, informal conversations can be incredibly insightful. They provide a safe space for employees to share their stories, opinions, and feelings more openly. These conversations can reveal unspoken tensions, hidden values, and the emotional impact of the culture on employees.
- **Target Audience:** To get a well-rounded picture, include a diverse group of employees in your interviews. Talk to individuals from different levels, departments, and locations. Don't just focus on high performers or those in leadership positions; front-line employees often have valuable insights that can be overlooked. Avoid cherry-picking interviewees or coaching them on the "right" responses. Your goal is to gather honest, unfiltered feedback.

Observations:

Observation is a powerful tool for understanding your company culture in action. It's about paying close attention to the everyday interactions, behaviors, and artifacts that reveal your company's cultural norms and values.

- **Workplace Walkthroughs:** Take a leisurely stroll through your office space, but do it with an anthropologist's eye. Observe the physical layout, decor, communication styles, and overall atmosphere. What messages do these elements convey about your company's values and priorities? Does the space feel collaborative and inviting, or decaying, sterile, and hierarchical?
- **"Culture Walks":** These are more focused observations where you intentionally seek out specific behaviors, interactions, and artifacts that reveal cultural norms and values. Observe how colleagues greet each other, how meetings are conducted, and what kind of language is used in conversations. Pay attention to posters, slogans, awards, and other visible symbols of your company's identity. What stories do these elements tell about your culture? In a moment, the book will present you with more detailed guidance on this important culture review recommendation.
- **Objective Lens:** It's crucial to approach your observations with an objective lens. Avoid jumping to conclusions or making assumptions based on limited information. Simply observe, document your findings, and analyze them later to draw meaningful conclusions.

By combining these self-reflection exercises, comprehensive assessments, and insightful frameworks, you'll gain a deeper understanding of your company's current culture. This knowledge is the foundation for building a workplace that attracts, engages, and retains top talent.

Crack The Code: Your Workplace Is Talking!

Your workplace is a living, breathing organism with its own unique personality and hidden language. It's more than just desks, walls, and the hum of computers; it's a dynamic ecosystem where stories unfold, rituals take place, and unspoken rules reign. Your office is a silent narrator, whispering secrets about your company's culture—and it's time to start listening.

Embark on a Cultural Safari

A "culture walk" is your ticket to decoding these hidden messages. You'll uncover the subtle cues and clues that reveal the true essence of your organization's values, norms, and unspoken beliefs.

Your Guide to Decoding the Workplace Wilderness

As you embark on your cultural safari, here's your guide to navigating the terrain:

- **Habitat & Habit:**

    - **Layout and Design:** Open floor plans buzzing with collaborative energy? Or a maze of closed-door offices hinting at hierarchy? The very architecture of your space can reveal your company's approach to teamwork, communication, and power dynamics.
    - **Decor & Branding:** Are the walls adorned with vibrant murals that inspire creativity, or do minimalist white walls project a more buttoned-up vibe? Is the company logo omnipresent, or are personal touches encouraged? The aesthetics of your workplace are a visual feast, offering clues about your company's personality and the image it wants to portray.

- **Cleanliness & Orderliness:** Is your office a well-oiled machine of organization, or does it resemble a post-apocalyptic wasteland of clutter? The state of your environment speaks volumes about your company's attention to detail, efficiency, and overall professionalism.

- **Interactions: The Dance of Culture:**

  - **Greetings & Conversations:** Observe the subtle dance of social interaction. Are greetings warm and inviting, or curt and formal? Do conversations buzz with shared interests or stick strictly to business? These interactions are the building blocks of relationships and offer glimpses into the level of camaraderie and trust within your team.
  - **Body Language: The Unspoken Truth:** Smiles, frowns, eye contact, posture – these nonverbal cues often speak louder than words. Do your colleagues exude energy and enthusiasm, or do their hunched shoulders and averted gazes suggest stress and disengagement? Body language can unveil unspoken emotions and attitudes.
  - **Meetings: Collaboration or Command:** Are meetings lively forums for brainstorming and debate, or are they dominated by a few voices? How are decisions made – through a democratic process or by executive fiat? The dynamics of your meetings reveal a lot about your company's leadership style and decision-making processes.
  - **Conflict Resolution: The Art of Disagreement:** How do disagreements play out in your workplace? Are conflicts addressed openly and respectfully, or do they simmer beneath the surface? The way your company handles conflict is a litmus test for its tolerance of diverse opinions and its commitment to creating a safe and inclusive environment.

- **Language: The Cultural Dictionary:**

    o **Jargon & Acronyms:** Does your workplace sound like a foreign language with its own alphabet soup of acronyms and buzzwords? While industry-specific jargon has its place, inclusive language builds a sense of belonging, whereas exclusive language can create barriers and alienate newcomers.
    o **Tone:** Is the overall tone of communication positive, supportive, and encouraging? Or does negativity and cynicism permeate the airwaves? The tone of your workplace can have a profound impact on morale and productivity.
    o **Stories & Legends:** Every company has its folklore – tales of legendary successes, epic fails, and larger-than-life personalities. These stories aren't just water cooler fodder; they transmit values, reinforce beliefs, and shape the company's identity.

- **Artifacts: The Tangible Expression of Culture:**

    o **Awards & Recognition:** What kind of achievements are celebrated – individual heroics or team triumphs? The types of awards and recognition programs reflect the behaviors and outcomes your company values most.
    o **Mementos & Photos:** Take a peek into personal workspaces. Do desks and walls showcase family photos, quirky knick-knacks, or inspiring quotes? These personal touches offer a glimpse into the diverse personalities and values that make up your workforce.
    o **Dress Code:** Is your office a sea of suits, a haven for hoodies, or somewhere in between? Your dress code speaks volumes about your company's formality, creativity, and overall vibe.

Beyond Observation: Deeper Engagement for Deeper Insights

- **Talk to People:** Don't be a silent observer. Strike up conversations with employees across different departments and levels. Ask open-ended questions about their experiences, what they value most about the company, and what they wish could be different. These conversations can reveal nuances and emotions that may not be apparent through observation alone.
- **Document Your Findings:** Keep a detailed record of your observations, notes from conversations, and any photos or videos that capture the essence of your culture walk. This documentation will serve as a valuable reference point as you analyze your findings and develop action plans.

Reflection and Action: Turning Insights into Impact

After completing your culture walk, take time to reflect on your observations. What patterns or themes emerged? Were there any surprises that challenged your initial assumptions? How do your findings align (or misalign) with your company's stated values and goals?

Use these insights to pinpoint areas where your culture can be strengthened or enhanced. Share your observations with colleagues and leaders to spark meaningful conversations and collaborative action. Remember, a culture walk is not a one-time event; it's an ongoing process of discovery and refinement. By regularly engaging in this practice, you can ensure that your company culture remains vibrant, aligned with your goals, and a true reflection of your organization's values.

Dreaming Big: Crafting A Company Culture That Sizzles

Your company's culture is its unique fingerprint – a blend of values, beliefs, and behaviors that shape how your team interacts, innovates, and thrives. This is the secret sauce that makes your workplace irresistible to top talent. In this section, we'll embark on a journey to envision and articulate the cultural DNA that will not only attract the best and brightest but also keep them engaged, inspired, and fiercely loyal.

But before we dream big, let's take a reality check. Included in the appendix of this book is a handy Organizational Culture Self-Assessment. This tool will help you take stock of your current cultural landscape, pinpointing strengths to amplify and areas ripe for a little TLC.

A. The DNA of Dream Companies: What Sets Them Apart

Ever wondered what makes companies like Google, Apple, Patagonia, or Zappos the envy of the working world? It's not just the ping-pong tables and endless kombucha (though let's be honest, those perks are pretty sweet). I had a front-row seat to this phenomenon during my MBA years, when I was fortunate enough to sit down with Tim Cook, then a senior vice president at Apple, in their Silicon Valley headquarters. Even back then, he spoke passionately about Apple's unwavering commitment to a culture of teamwork, relentless pursuit of excellence, and a mission that went beyond just making cool gadgets. It was obvious that this cultural DNA was a key ingredient in their recipe for attracting and retaining top talent.

Fast forward to today, and Cook, now CEO, continues to champion this vibrant culture, and Apple's success story is a testament to its power. So, take a note from one of the greats:

don't dismiss the "soft and fuzzy" stuff we're talking about in this book. These aren't just feel-good concepts; they're the very building blocks of a thriving company culture. And trust me, investing in your culture will pay off in tangible, bottom-line results.

So, what exactly is this cultural magic that sets these companies apart? It's their unique DNA – a potent combination of values, behaviors, and practices that, together, create a workplace that people dream of joining and never want to leave. Let's unravel this DNA and discover the secrets to building a company culture that sizzles.

- **Strong Values: The North Star:** These companies aren't just paying lip service to values; they live and breathe them. Their values aren't empty slogans on a motivational poster; they're the guiding principles behind every decision, every interaction, every project.
- **Transparency: The Trust Elixir:** Open and honest communication is the lifeblood of these organizations. Information flows freely, feedback is encouraged, and everyone feels safe to speak their mind. This creates a culture of trust, where employees feel valued and empowered to contribute their best.
- **Employee Development: Fueling the Fire:** Top-performing companies know that investing in their people is the smartest investment they can make. They provide ample opportunities for learning, growth, and advancement, encouraging a culture where employees are constantly challenged and inspired to reach their full potential.
- **Recognition and Rewards: The High-Five Factory:** From shout-outs in company-wide meetings to bonuses and promotions, these companies make sure their rock stars feel appreciated. Recognizing and rewarding exceptional performance, both individually and as a team, creates a culture of motivation and a sense of shared

accomplishment.
- **Work-Life Balance: The Happy-Healthy Combo:** Burnout is the enemy of innovation. These companies champion work-life balance, encouraging employees to take time off, prioritize their health, and recharge their batteries. Because they know that a well-rested, happy employee is a productive one.
- **Purpose-Driven: More Than Just Money:** It's not just about profits; it's about making a difference. These companies have a clear sense of purpose – a mission that goes beyond the bottom line. This shared purpose gives employees a sense of meaning and fuels their passion for their work.

B. Values Clarification: Building Your Cultural Foundation

Building a magnetic culture starts with identifying the core values that will be the bedrock of your organization.

- **Values Clarification Exercise:**
    1. **Brainstorm:** Gather your team and let the ideas flow! What values resonate most with your company's mission and vision? What qualities do you admire in your employees? What kind of impact do you want to make on the world?
    2. **Prioritize:** Not all values are created equal. Rank them in order of importance. What are the non-negotiables that define your company's DNA? What are the aspirational values you strive to embody?
    3. **Discuss and Refine:** Get everyone on the same page. Have open and honest conversations with key stakeholders – leaders, employees, even customers – to reach a consensus on your core values.
    4. **Define Behaviors:** Don't let your values be just words on a page. For each value, define the

specific behaviors and actions that bring it to life. This will help your team understand how to embody these values in their everyday work.

C. Crafting a Cultural Manifesto: Your Declaration of Independence

A cultural manifesto is more than just a document; it's a declaration of your company's cultural identity. It's a rallying cry that unites your team around a shared vision and set of values. This is your company's constitution – a guiding light for decision-making, behavior, and communication.

Don't worry, we've got you covered. You'll find a template for crafting your own Cultural Manifesto at the end of this book, ready to spark your creativity and help you articulate your company's unique spirit.

D. Visioning Workshop: Your Cultural Brainstorming Bonanza

A truly magnetic culture isn't just handed down from on high; it's co-created by everyone in the company. A visioning workshop is your chance to tap into the collective wisdom and imagination of your team. It's a vibrant, interactive experience where leaders and employees come together to dream up the ideal workplace culture – together.

This workshop isn't just about pie-in-the-sky dreaming; it's about translating aspirations into actionable plans. Here's how to unleash the creative power of your team:

- **Brainstorming Blitz:** Kick off the workshop with a brainstorming session that's all about generating a dazzling array of ideas. Encourage everyone to think big, be bold, and let their imaginations run wild. What would make your workplace truly exceptional? What values, behaviors, and rituals would cultivate a sense of belonging, purpose, and joy?

- **Storytelling Time:** Invite participants to share personal anecdotes and experiences that exemplify the desired culture. These stories are powerful tools for illustrating abstract values and bringing them to life. They can be funny, inspiring, or even cautionary tales – the key is that they spark conversation and generate a shared understanding of what a thriving culture looks like.
- **Prioritization Power-Up:** Not all ideas are created equal. Work together to rank the most important cultural attributes. This helps to focus your efforts and ensure that your cultural transformation initiatives are aligned with your team's collective vision.
- **Action Planning: From Dreams to Reality:** Now it's time to turn those inspiring ideas into tangible actions. Break down the vision into concrete steps. What initiatives can you launch to nurture collaboration, spark innovation, or enhance employee well-being? Assign ownership of each action item, set timelines, and create a roadmap for bringing your dream culture to life.

E. Crafting a Compelling Employee Value Proposition (EVP): Your Talent Magnet

Your Employee Value Proposition (EVP) is the secret sauce that sets your company apart from the competition. It's the unique blend of rewards, benefits, and experiences you offer your employees in exchange for their talent and dedication. This is a magnet, attracting top talent and keeping them engaged, motivated, and loyal.

A strong EVP is more than just a competitive salary and a generous benefits package. It's about creating a holistic employee experience that aligns with your ideal culture and speaks to the hearts and minds of your ideal candidates.

Key Ingredients of an Irresistible EVP:

- **Compensation and Benefits:** Of course, a fair and

competitive salary is essential. But don't forget about the other perks that make a real difference – comprehensive health insurance, retirement plans, stock options, flexible work arrangements, generous parental leave, and more.
- **Career Development Opportunities:** Top talent craves growth and development. Offer robust training programs, mentorship opportunities, tuition reimbursement, and clear career paths to show your employees that you're invested in their future.
- **Work-Life Balance:** In today's fast-paced world, work-life balance is more important than ever. Demonstrate your commitment to employee well-being by offering flexible schedules, encouraging time off, and promoting a healthy work environment.
- **Company Culture and Values:** This is where your cultural manifesto comes to life. Showcase your company's unique personality, values, and mission. Highlight the aspects of your culture that make your workplace a truly special place to be.
- **Meaningful Work:** People want to feel like their work matters. Give your employees the opportunity to contribute to something bigger than themselves, to make a difference, and to use their skills and talents to their fullest potential.

By crafting a compelling EVP that aligns with your ideal culture, you're not just attracting top talent – you're building a workforce that is engaged, motivated, and passionate about your company's mission. It's a win-win for everyone involved.

Nurturing Your Cultural Ecosystem: A Continuous Journey Of Growth

Building a vibrant company culture isn't a one-and-done project; it's a thrilling expedition of growth and evolution. Culture is a living, breathing ecosystem, constantly adapting and thriving through careful nurturing. In this section, we'll unveil the secrets to weaving your culture into the fabric of everyday life, developing a growth mindset, and ensuring your values remain the compass guiding your organization's journey.

A. Onboarding for Culture: The Art of the First Impression

Forget about dry paperwork and yawn-inducing introductions. Onboarding is your chance to roll out the red carpet and immerse new hires in the heart and soul of your company – its culture. It's your opportunity to create an unforgettable first impression that leaves them feeling excited, inspired, and eager to contribute.

- **Cultural Immersion:** Don't just tell, show! Turn onboarding into an immersive experience that showcases your company's unique personality. Weave cultural elements into every interaction – from the warm welcome message and engaging orientation materials to introductions to their team members, social events that spark camaraderie, and even the design and décor of your workspace. Let your values and norms shine through in every corner, creating an instant sense of belonging.

- **Values in Action:** Move beyond abstract value statements and bring them to life with vivid, real-world examples. Show new hires how these values guide decisions, shape interactions, and influence everyday work. Share stories of employees who embody these values, turning them into relatable role models and inspiring newcomers to embrace them.

- **Mentorship and Buddy Programs:** Pair new hires with seasoned employees who can act as their guides, offering support, answering questions, and sharing insider knowledge about the unwritten rules and nuances of your workplace. These mentors or buddies can help newcomers quickly acclimate to the environment and feel like valued members of the team.

- **Feedback Loop:** Your onboarding process isn't a static script; it's a dynamic conversation. Regularly seek feedback from new hires to understand their experience and pinpoint areas for improvement. This iterative approach ensures that your onboarding program remains fresh, relevant, and perfectly aligned with your evolving culture.

B. Continuous Feedback and Development: The Growth Mindset in Action

In a thriving company culture, growth isn't just an option; it's a way of life. It's about nurturing a mindset where learning, development, and continuous improvement are the norm, not the exception.

- **Feedback Culture:** Forget the dreaded annual review. Cultivate a workplace where feedback is an ongoing, open dialogue, flowing freely and constructively in all directions. Encourage regular conversations between peers, managers, and employees, building trust and transparency. Make feedback a natural part of your team's rhythm, not a stressful once-a-year event.
- **Learning Opportunities:** Invest in your employees'

growth like you would a prized stock portfolio. Offer a diverse menu of learning opportunities – from formal training programs, workshops, and conferences to online courses, tuition reimbursement, and mentorship programs. Empower employees to take charge of their development, and watch them blossom.
- **Career Paths and Growth:** Show your employees a clear path to the summit. Map out career paths, create opportunities for advancement, and encourage lateral moves or skill diversification. When employees see a future for themselves within your company, their engagement and loyalty will skyrocket.

C. The Cultural Crossroads: Innovation or Stagnation?

Every company faces a pivotal decision: will you be a daring innovator or a risk-averse follower? This choice isn't merely a matter of preference; it's a strategic imperative that will shape your company's destiny.

Risk-Taking Rebels vs. Process Protectors: Which Path Will You Choose?

Companies often find themselves at a cultural crossroads, pulled between the allure of innovation and the comfort of stability. This tension is especially evident as companies grow and mature.

- **Risk-Taking Rebels:** These are the trailblazers, the rule-breakers, the ones who aren't afraid to color outside the lines. They thrive on taking calculated risks, embracing failure as a learning opportunity, and pushing the boundaries of what's possible. Startups and entrepreneurial ventures often embody this spirit, as they're fueled by the founder's passion, vision, and relentless pursuit of growth.
- **Process Protectors:** These organizations value stability, predictability, and adherence to established procedures.

They prioritize risk mitigation and often have a more hierarchical structure with clearly defined roles and responsibilities. While this approach can bring a sense of order and efficiency, it can also stifle creativity and hinder innovation.

The Cultural Tug-of-War

As companies evolve, their cultures often undergo a subtle but significant shift. The entrepreneurial fire that ignited their early success can gradually give way to a more cautious, process-driven approach. This isn't necessarily a bad thing – as companies grow, they need to establish systems and processes to ensure stability and scalability.

However, this transition doesn't have to mean the death of innovation. The key is to strike a balance between risk-taking and stability, ensuring that the entrepreneurial spirit remains alive and well.

Preserving the Founder's Mindset

Companies that successfully maintain their innovative edge often do so by intentionally preserving the founder's mindset. This means embracing a culture that values:

- **Empowerment:** Giving employees the autonomy to make decisions, experiment with new ideas, and take ownership of their work.
- **Agility:** Being responsive to change, willing to pivot quickly, and embracing new technologies and approaches.
- **Learning and Growth:** Creating a culture of continuous learning, where mistakes are seen as opportunities for growth, not reasons for punishment.
- **Collaboration:** Supporting a collaborative environment where diverse perspectives are valued and employees feel comfortable sharing ideas and challenging assumptions.

By keeping the founder's spirit alive, companies can create a culture that promotes both stability and innovation, ensuring their continued success in a rapidly changing world.

C. Performance Management: A Cultural Mirror

Your performance management system is more than just a tool for evaluating employees; it's a reflection of your company's culture. It should not only measure individual achievements but also reinforce the values, behaviors, and norms you want to cultivate.

- **Values-Based Evaluation:** Don't just focus on the numbers. Assess employees based on how well they embody your company's core values. This could include factors like collaboration, initiative, customer focus, integrity, and continuous improvement.
- **360-Degree Feedback:** Gather feedback from a wide range of sources – peers, managers, subordinates, and even clients – to create a comprehensive picture of an employee's performance. This approach provides a more holistic view than traditional top-down evaluations, revealing strengths and areas for development that might otherwise go unnoticed.
- **Ongoing Conversations:** Ditch the dreaded annual performance review in favor of regular, ongoing conversations about goals, progress, and development. This builds a more supportive and collaborative environment where feedback is seen as a tool for growth, not a judgment.
- **Recognition and Rewards:** Don't just reward the top performers; recognize and celebrate employees who exemplify your company's values. This could include acknowledging acts of kindness, collaboration, innovation, or going the extra mile for a customer. By aligning your rewards with your values, you reinforce the behaviors you want to see more of.

D. Cultural Audits: The Pulse Check on Your Cultural Health

Cultural audits are regular check-ups for your company's health. Just as we visit the doctor to ensure our bodies are in tip-top shape, regular cultural audits give you a snapshot of your company's well-being, highlighting what's working and where there's room for improvement.

- **Regular Assessments:** Don't wait for a cultural crisis to strike. Instead, schedule routine check-ups, ideally once or twice a year. This proactive approach allows you to keep a finger on the pulse of your culture, identify emerging trends, and address potential issues before they snowball.
- **Data Collection: The Cultural Detective's Toolkit:** To get a complete picture of your cultural landscape, use a variety of tools and techniques. Gather quantitative data through employee surveys to measure satisfaction, engagement, and alignment with values. Complement this with the rich qualitative insights gleaned from interviews, focus groups, and keen observations of everyday interactions and behaviors.
- **Analysis and Action: Turning Data into Transformation:** Don't let your data gather dust. Analyze the findings from your surveys, interviews, and observations to uncover hidden patterns, identify areas of strength, and pinpoint opportunities for growth. This is not a solo mission; involve key stakeholders from across the organization to gain diverse perspectives and build a shared understanding of your cultural landscape. Armed with this knowledge, you can then develop targeted action plans to address any weaknesses and amplify your strengths.

Additional Considerations: The Secret Ingredients of a Thriving Culture

While audits and assessments provide valuable insights, there are other essential ingredients for cultivating a thriving company culture:

- **Leadership: The Cultural Architects:** Leaders set the tone, embody the values, and inspire others through their words and actions. Their behavior is a powerful ripple that can either elevate or erode the cultural fabric. Ensure your leaders are not just managers but cultural ambassadors who champion your values and lead by example.
- **Communication: The Cultural Lifeline:** Open, honest, and transparent communication is the lifeblood of any healthy culture. Regularly communicate your company's values, mission, and cultural expectations through a variety of channels – town halls, newsletters, intranets, social media. This creates a shared understanding and reinforces the importance of your cultural DNA.
- **Flexibility and Adaptation: The Art of Evolution:** Culture is not static; it's a living, breathing entity that must evolve alongside your organization. As your company grows and changes, be prepared to adapt your approach, refine your practices, and embrace new ideas. This flexibility ensures that your culture remains relevant, engaging, and responsive to the needs of your employees and your business.
- **Celebration: The Fuel for Cultural Growth:** Recognize and celebrate the individuals and teams who embody your company's values. Publicly acknowledge their achievements, share their stories, and create rituals that reinforce positive behaviors. By celebrating success, you create a sense of pride and belonging that fuels further growth and innovation.

By actively nurturing and maintaining your cultural ecosystem through these strategies, you create a self-sustaining engine that attracts, engages, and retains top talent, propelling your organization towards enduring success. Remember, your culture is your greatest asset – invest in it wisely, and it will reward you tenfold.

Cultural Transformations: When Companies Rewrite Their Dna

These aren't just stories of change; they're sagas of resilience, reinvention, and the raw power of culture to transform a company's destiny. These real-world examples illuminate how deliberate shifts in values, behaviors, and leadership can rewrite an organization's genetic code, propelling it toward unprecedented success.

Adobe: From Boxed In to Boundless Creativity

Once synonymous with shrink-wrapped software and perpetual licenses, Adobe found itself at a crossroads as the digital world embraced cloud computing and the subscription model. This wasn't just a change in business strategy; it was a call for a cultural metamorphosis.

With a bold leap, Adobe transformed into the Creative Cloud, a vibrant ecosystem of software and services. It wasn't just about technology; it was about reinventing themselves as a company that thrives on agility, innovation, and an unwavering focus on customer needs. The investment in cloud infrastructure, the reimagining of product development, and the overhaul of marketing and customer engagement weren't just tactical moves; they were cultural shockwaves that shook the company to its core.

- **Key Takeaways: The Adobe Blueprint for Change**
    - **Adapt or Become Extinct:** Adobe's story is a stark reminder that even industry giants can't rest on their laurels. Embracing change and adapting to evolving market dynamics is crucial for survival.
    - **Innovation as a Way of Life:** The shift to a subscription model demanded a culture where experimentation, risk-taking, and relentless

improvement weren't just buzzwords, but the heartbeat of the company.
- **Leadership's Guiding Light:** Bold leadership and a crystal-clear vision were the compass that steered Adobe through this transformative journey.

Domino's Pizza: The Dough-lightful Comeback Story

From a punchline about mediocre pizza to a tech-savvy innovator, Domino's staged a comeback that's nothing short of legendary. Their once-complacent culture, resistant to change, had led to plummeting sales and a reputation that was, well, less than cheesy.

But Domino's didn't crumble; they listened. They embraced customer feedback, threw out the old recipe book, and whipped up a whole new flavor profile. They invested in technology – online ordering, GPS tracking, and all the digital bells and whistles – transforming themselves into a pizza powerhouse of the 21st century. But perhaps the most crucial ingredient in their recipe for success was a new culture of transparency and accountability, empowering employees to take ownership of their work and deliver a pizza experience that truly delivered.

- **Key Takeaways: The Domino's Recipe for Reinvention**
  - **The Customer is King (or Queen):** Domino's transformation is a testament to the power of truly listening to your customers and prioritizing their needs.
  - **Embrace Change as Your Pizza Topping:** The company's willingness to ditch outdated practices and embrace new technologies was the secret sauce that catapulted them back to the top.
  - **Transparency and Accountability: The Dynamic Duo:** By creating a culture of openness and ownership, Domino's transformed its employees into passionate brand ambassadors, delivering not

just pizza, but an experience that keeps customers coming back for more.

Harvard Business School: The Evolution of an Ivory Tower

Even institutions as prestigious as Harvard Business School (HBS) are not immune to the winds of change. While revered for its academic rigor, HBS had a reputation for encouraging a cutthroat, individualistic culture.

In recent decades, HBS has embarked on a multi-faceted cultural evolution. The school has made concerted efforts to increase diversity and inclusion, resulting in a more representative student body, faculty, and staff. Recognizing that collaboration is the cornerstone of success in today's interconnected world, HBS has also promoted a more team-oriented approach. Furthermore, the school has woven ethics, social responsibility, innovation, and entrepreneurship into its curriculum and research, reflecting a broader societal shift towards values-based leadership and sustainable business practices. Even the pandemic played a role, accelerating HBS's adoption of online learning and expanding its reach beyond the hallowed halls of its campus.

- Key Takeaways: Lessons from the Ivory Tower
    - **The Never-Ending Quest for Knowledge:** Even the most established institutions must embrace continuous learning and adaptation to remain relevant and meet the evolving needs of their students and society.
    - **The Power of Collaboration:** In today's complex world, the ability to collaborate effectively is more critical than ever. HBS recognizes this and has made it a core pillar of its educational philosophy.
    - **Values at the Core:** By integrating ethics, social responsibility, and sustainability into its curriculum, HBS is preparing future leaders to navigate the complexities of the modern business landscape with

integrity and a commitment to creating a positive impact on the world.

These stories are a testament to the transformative power of culture. They show that cultural change isn't just possible; it's essential for long-term success. It's a journey that requires a long-term commitment, visionary leadership, and a willingness to adapt and evolve.

Your Cultural Odyssey

None of this is a one-and-done scenario. These reviews and strategic cultural decisions need to be repeated regularly to have the desired impact. As your company grows, markets shift, and employee expectations transform, your culture must evolve alongside them, becoming a dynamic, resilient, and ever-adapting force.

The journey to a truly thriving culture requires a compass and a map. It demands regular check-ins, a healthy dose of self-reflection, and a willingness to listen to the heartbeat of your organization – your employees. By engaging in open dialogue, gathering feedback, and refining your strategies, you ensure that your culture remains vibrant, energized, and perfectly aligned with your goals. This is not a sprint to the finish line; it's a lifelong journey of discovery, refinement, and constant evolution.

Your Toolkit for Cultural Transformation: Unleash the Magic

To equip you for this exciting adventure, we offer a treasure chest of resources:

- **Books and Articles: A Literary Feast:** Feast on a curated collection of insightful reads on organizational culture, leadership, and change management. Glean wisdom from seasoned experts and ignite your imagination with their stories and strategies.
- **Websites and Online Resources: The Digital Oasis:** Dive into a vast online oasis of reputable websites, blogs, and communities devoted to cultivating vibrant company cultures. Stay ahead of the curve by staying informed about the latest trends, research, and best practices.
- **Consultants and Experts: Your Cultural Sherpas:** Sometimes, you need a guide to navigate unfamiliar

terrain. Don't hesitate to seek out experienced culture consultants or coaches who can offer invaluable insights and accelerate your cultural transformation efforts.

- **Templates and Tools: Your Practical Playbook**: Put theory into practice with our downloadable templates for crafting compelling cultural manifestos, conducting insightful employee surveys, and more. These practical tools will streamline your efforts and empower you to take action.
- **Training Programs: Skill-Building for Cultural Success:** Invest in your team's growth by providing targeted training programs on leadership development, communication skills, and conflict resolution. These essential skills are the building blocks of a healthy, productive, and harmonious workplace.

The Call to Adventure: Be the Hero of Your Cultural Story

You have the power to shape your company's culture. It's time to step into your role as a cultural architect, a visionary leader who can transform your workplace into a thriving ecosystem.

- **Embrace Your Power:** Don't wait for someone else to take the lead. Seize the reins, take ownership of your culture, and inspire others to join you on this transformative journey.
- **Embrace Experimentation:** There's no one-size-fits-all formula for cultural success. Dare to experiment, try new things, and learn from both your triumphs and your stumbles. The journey is just as important as the destination.
- **Embrace Continuous Improvement:** Remember, culture building is an ongoing adventure. Celebrate your victories, learn from your setbacks, and never stop striving for a better, more vibrant workplace.

The Ripple Effect: Your Cultural Impact Spreads Far and Wide

The investment you make in your company culture is an investment that pays dividends for years to come. A thriving culture has a ripple effect that extends far beyond the walls of your organization, impacting individuals, your company, and even society as a whole.

- **Individual Impact:** A positive, supportive culture develops a sense of purpose, belonging, and well-being, leading to happier, healthier, and more fulfilled employees.
- **Organizational Impact:** A strong culture ignites a fire of innovation, fuels productivity, and creates a sustainable competitive advantage that sets you apart from the crowd.
- **Societal Impact:** When companies prioritize creating positive work environments, they contribute to a more equitable, inclusive, and fulfilling world of work for all.

Final Thoughts: The Power to Shape Your Destiny

Your culture is not just a set of values; it's the beating heart of your organization. It's the invisible force that shapes your destiny, propelling you towards greatness or holding you back. Embrace the opportunity to nurture, mold, and evolve your culture into a powerful engine for success.

But remember, culture doesn't exist in a vacuum. It's shaped, nurtured, and ultimately embodied by the leaders within your organization.

In our next chapter, **Leadership: The Culture Architects**, we'll dive deep into the pivotal role leaders play in cultivating and sustaining a thriving company culture. We'll explore different leadership styles, their impact on culture, and provide actionable tips for leaders to embody and communicate your organization's values, driving your cultural evolution forward.

CHAPTER 3: LEADERSHIP: THE ARCHITECTS AND CHAMPIONS OF GROWTH-ORIENTED CULTURE

Introduction

The year is 2008. The global economy is in freefall, and the once-mighty automotive industry teeters on the brink of collapse. Yet, amidst the wreckage, one company manages to defy gravity, not just surviving but soaring. That company was Ford, and their secret weapon wasn't a flashy new model or a brilliant engineering feat. It was something far more fundamental: a radical transformation of their company culture.

Alan Mulally, Ford's then-CEO, inherited a company riddled with infighting, paralyzed by fear, and mired in a toxic blame-game culture. He knew that to save Ford, he had to overhaul more than just their assembly lines—he had to revolutionize the very DNA of the organization.

Mulally's "One Ford" plan was a bold declaration that transparency, collaboration, and accountability would become the company's new bedrock. He didn't just preach these values from the C-suite; he lived them, sparking a chain reaction that ignited enthusiasm and transformed the entire company from the inside out.

The results were nothing short of astonishing. Ford not only dodged bankruptcy but emerged from the crisis stronger, more innovative, and ready to conquer the road ahead. Their phoenix-like rise is a testament to the raw power of a positive, growth-oriented culture.

But Ford's story isn't just a historical anomaly; it's a beacon of hope, a testament to what's possible when leaders dare to reimagine their company's culture. It highlights the undeniable truth that culture isn't just a feel-good frill or a "nice-to-have" perk. It's the lifeblood of an organization, the beating heart that propels engagement, ignites innovation, and ultimately determines a company's fate.

This book is your roadmap to creating that kind of culture—a vibrant ecosystem where employees aren't just cogs in a machine but valued contributors who are empowered to push boundaries, take calculated risks, and unleash their full potential. Your company's culture is its unique personality—a vibrant tapestry woven from shared values, beliefs, behaviors, and norms. A positive culture acts like a magnet, attracting top talent and building a sense of belonging and purpose that drives extraordinary results.

But make no mistake, crafting this kind of culture isn't magic; it's intentional leadership. Leaders are the architects of this transformation, shaping the cultural landscape through their every action, decision, and word. They are the living embodiment of the company's values, setting the tone from the top and inspiring others to follow suit.

In the following chapters, we'll dive deep into the art and science of cultural leadership. We'll explore the nuances of different leadership styles and how they influence the workplace. We'll dissect real-world examples of companies that have mastered the cultural game. And most importantly, we'll arm you with a practical toolkit of strategies, tactics, and frameworks to build a workplace where innovation isn't just a buzzword, it's a way of life.

Leaders As Culture Carriers: Embodying, Transmitting, And Adapting To Change

Leadership isn't just about spreadsheets and strategy sessions. It's about sculpting the very essence of a company – its culture. Leaders are the master artisans of this cultural masterpiece, responsible for designing the blueprint and meticulously overseeing its construction. They're not mere figureheads; they're active participants, breathing life into the values, norms, and behaviors that pulse through the organization's veins.

Leadership Role Modeling: Setting the Tone from the Top

Imagine leaders as conductors of a grand symphony orchestra. With a flick of their wrist or a nod of their head, they set the tempo, the mood, and the overall tone of the performance. Similarly, leaders in the workplace orchestrate the cultural symphony through their actions, communication style, and interactions. They are the ultimate tone-setters, influencing the emotional climate and establishing the behavioral standards that permeate the organization.

When leaders embody the company's values in every fiber of their being, they become a powerful model for others to emulate. The contagious energy causes a ripple effect that starts at the top and spreads throughout the ranks. When employees witness their leaders' genuine passion, commitment, and unwavering belief in the company's mission, it sparks a fire within them. This shared enthusiasm fuels productivity, creativity, and a collective sense of purpose, propelling the company towards greater heights.

But it's not just about charisma or inspiring speeches. Effective leadership requires a deep understanding of the desired culture, a willingness to continuously learn and adapt, and a steadfast commitment to holding both themselves and others accountable for living the values. It's about walking the talk, every single day.

Culture Carriers: Transmitting Values through Every Decision

Leaders are not just figureheads; they are the living embodiment of the company's culture. Every decision they make, every action they take, and every word they utter sends a message about what's valued and expected within the organization. From resource allocation to hiring and promotion decisions to how conflicts are resolved, leaders' choices can either nurture or erode the cultural foundation they seek to build.

Transparency and open communication are the lifeblood of cultural transmission. When leaders articulate the company's values, explain their reasoning behind decisions, and provide regular feedback, they promote trust and understanding among employees. This transparency isn't just about being nice; it's about creating a shared language and common understanding around the company's culture, ensuring everyone is rowing in the same direction.

But it's not just about the big pronouncements or formal announcements. Leaders can weave cultural values into the very fabric of the workplace through symbols, rituals, and even language. The office layout, dress code, the way meetings are conducted, and the words and phrases used in everyday conversations can all subtly reinforce or undermine the desired culture. By paying attention to these seemingly small details, leaders can create a more cohesive and consistent cultural experience for everyone.

The Ripple Effect of Leadership: A Cascading Influence

Leadership isn't confined to the corner office. Its influence ripples outward, touching every corner of the organization. It's like a stone dropped into a pond, creating concentric circles that spread far and wide. This phenomenon is rooted in social learning theory, which tells us that people learn by observing and imitating the behavior of those around them, especially those in positions of power.

So, when employees see their leaders modeling honesty, integrity, and a willingness to take risks, they're more likely to embrace those same qualities. But the opposite is also true. Negative behaviors, such as micromanagement or a lack of integrity, can spread like wildfire, poisoning the cultural well.

It's important to note that this ripple effect isn't always uniform. Different teams or departments may develop their own micro-cultures, often influenced by their direct leaders. This means that creating a cohesive company culture requires alignment and consistency across all levels of leadership. It's a symphony, not a solo act.

Culture Storytelling: Weaving a Tapestry of Shared Identity

Stories are the threads that weave together the rich tapestry of an organization's culture. They take abstract concepts like "innovation" or "collaboration" and make them tangible, relatable, and memorable. But not just any story will do; the most effective stories are those that are authentic, grounded in real experiences, and told with passion and conviction.

When leaders share personal anecdotes about challenges they've faced, obstacles they've overcome, or valuable lessons they've learned, it resonates with employees on a deep level. These stories not only illustrate the company's values in action but also humanize the leaders themselves, making them more approachable and inspiring.

Over time, a collection of these stories forms a powerful narrative that binds employees together and reinforces the desired culture. This shared narrative creates a sense of belonging, purpose, and continuity, even as the company grows and evolves.

Flexibility and Adaptation: Evolving with the Times

Culture is not a static monument; it's a living, breathing organism that must adapt to survive. As the business landscape shifts, new technologies emerge, and employee expectations change, the company's culture must evolve in tandem to remain relevant and effective.

Leaders play a crucial role in this process of cultural evolution. They must be open to new ideas, willing to experiment, and agile enough to pivot when necessary. By embracing change and supporting a culture of continuous learning and improvement, leaders can ensure that their company's culture remains a wellspring of strength and competitive advantage.

Case Study: The Goldman Sachs Culture of Apprenticeship and Mentorship

A prime example of a thriving culture can be found at Goldman Sachs, the global powerhouse of investment banking, securities, and investment management. While known for its demanding and results-oriented environment, Goldman Sachs also deeply invests in its people, developing a culture of apprenticeship, mentorship, and continuous learning.

New hires are immediately immersed in an apprenticeship model, paired with seasoned mentors who offer guidance, support, and access to challenging opportunities. This approach not only accelerates professional development but also builds a strong sense of community and belonging from day one.

Goldman Sachs goes beyond traditional mentorship by emphasizing sponsorship. Senior leaders actively champion high-potential employees, advocating for their career advancement, providing access to key networks, and creating opportunities for them to shine.

The firm's commitment to continuous learning is evident in its extensive training and development programs. These programs equip employees with the skills and knowledge they need to excel while reinforcing the message that the company values their growth and development.

This unique cultural cocktail is a potent elixir for attracting top talent. Graduates from prestigious universities flock to Goldman Sachs, eager to learn from some of the brightest minds in the industry and to be part of a culture that values ambition, hard work, and continuous improvement.

The Goldman Sachs example underscores several key takeaways for leaders:

- **Invest in mentorship and sponsorship programs.**
- **Prioritize continuous learning and development.**
- **Promote a culture of feedback and open communication.**
- **Balance challenge with support.**

By implementing these strategies, leaders can create a culture that not only attracts and retains top talent but also drives innovation, engagement, and long-term success.

Leadership Styles And Their Cultural Impact

Leaders are the cultural architects of their companies, the masterminds behind the scenes crafting the vibe that makes employees either dread Mondays or eagerly leap out of bed. The leadership style they choose isn't just a personal preference —it's a powerful lever that can shift the entire cultural landscape. Much like choosing the soundtrack for a movie: a thriller needs suspenseful music, a comedy needs upbeat tunes, and your company needs the right leadership style to create the culture you want.

Leadership styles aren't one-size-fits-all. It's a spectrum, a kaleidoscope of approaches, each with its own strengths and potential impact on culture. Some leaders blaze a trail with grand visions, while others nurture their teams with a gentle touch. The key is to understand these different styles and harness their power to create a culture that sparks growth, innovation, and a whole lot of "hell yeah!" from your employees.

Transformational Leadership: The Spark That Ignites Change

Transformational leaders are like the charismatic rock stars of the leadership world. They don't just manage; they inspire. They paint a vivid picture of the future, one that's so compelling, so exciting, it gets everyone on board and rowing in the same direction.

These leaders aren't afraid to shake things up. They challenge the status quo, encouraging their teams to push boundaries, experiment, and think outside the box. They set audacious goals, not just for the company, but for each individual, believing that everyone has the potential to achieve greatness.

The result? A culture buzzing with innovation, where

employees are constantly seeking new and better ways to do things. It's a culture of continuous improvement, where change isn't feared but embraced as an opportunity for growth. In this environment, employees feel empowered to take risks, try new things, and learn from their mistakes – all essential ingredients for a company that's ready to take on the world.

Servant Leadership: The Glue That Binds Teams Together

If transformational leaders are the rock stars, then servant leaders are the unsung heroes. They turn the traditional leadership pyramid upside down, putting the needs of their team members front and center. They're not interested in power for power's sake; they're driven by a desire to serve, empower, and uplift those around them.

Servant leaders listen attentively to their team's ideas, concerns, and aspirations. They roll up their sleeves and get their hands dirty, removing obstacles and providing the support and resources their team needs to thrive. They're coaches, mentors, and cheerleaders, celebrating successes and offering guidance during challenges.

This approach creates a culture of trust, collaboration, and mutual respect. Employees feel valued, heard, and appreciated, which fuels their motivation and commitment. It's a culture where teamwork isn't just a buzzword; it's a way of life. And when people feel like they're part of something bigger than themselves, they're more likely to go above and beyond to achieve shared goals.

Take Bain & Company, for example. This global management consulting firm is known for its servant leadership philosophy, which prioritizes the needs of clients and employees alike. This approach has cultivated a supportive and collaborative culture that consistently ranks Bain among the top workplaces in the world.

Authentic Leadership: The Compass That Guides with Integrity

Authentic leaders are the real deal. They lead with transparency, honesty, and a healthy dose of vulnerability. They're not afraid to admit their mistakes, ask for help, or show their human side. In fact, it's this very authenticity that makes them so effective.

When leaders are genuine and transparent, it creates a culture of openness and trust. Employees feel safe to speak their minds, share their ideas, and challenge the status quo. This open communication is the lifeblood of innovation, as it allows for the free flow of ideas and constructive debate.

Furthermore, authentic leaders create a sense of psychological safety within their teams. This means that employees feel comfortable taking risks, making mistakes, and learning from their experiences without fear of judgment or retribution. This psychological safety is essential for encouraging a culture of experimentation and growth.

McKinsey & Company, another leading management consulting firm, places a strong emphasis on open communication and transparency. Leaders at McKinsey encourage a culture of feedback, where employees are encouraged to speak up and share their ideas, even if they contradict the views of senior management. This open dialogue has helped McKinsey maintain its position as a thought leader and innovator in the consulting industry.

Additional Leadership Styles: Expanding the Toolkit

While transformational, servant, and authentic leadership styles are particularly well-suited for supporting growth and risk-taking, other styles can also be effective depending on the context and goals of the organization.

- **Democratic Leadership:** This style involves

seeking input and consensus from team members, and developing a sense of ownership and empowerment.
- **Coaching Leadership:** Coaching leaders focus on developing their team members' skills and capabilities, creating a culture of continuous learning and growth.
- **Affiliative Leadership:** This style prioritizes building strong relationships and creating a harmonious work environment, which can be especially important in times of change or uncertainty.

By understanding the nuances of these different styles and their potential impact on culture, leaders can choose the approaches that best align with their values and the needs of their organization.

Remember, the goal is not to fit into a single leadership mold but to develop a flexible and adaptive approach that can evolve as the company grows and changes. The most effective leaders are those who can seamlessly switch between different styles, depending on the situation and the needs of their team. They are the cultural chameleons, able to adapt and thrive in any environment.

Actionable Tips For Leaders: Nurturing A Growth And Risk-Taking Culture

Leaders are the drummers in the heart of a company's rhythm, setting the beat that everyone else follows. Their actions, words, and decisions echo throughout the halls, shaping the very air employees breathe. But how can leaders transform that rhythm into a vibrant symphony of growth, innovation, and fearless exploration? This section offers a toolkit of actionable strategies to help leaders orchestrate a culture where employees not only feel safe to take risks but are actively encouraged to do so.

Walk the Talk: Leading by Example

Remember the old saying, "Actions speak louder than words"? Well, it's the golden rule of leadership. You can't just talk the talk about your company's values; you've got to walk the walk. Want your employees to be bold risk-takers? Then show them how it's done. Embrace challenges, experiment with new ideas, and don't be afraid to stumble along the way. After all, the most valuable lessons often come from missteps.

McKinsey & Company's leaders don't just sit in ivory towers pontificating about client impact and professional development; they roll up their sleeves and dive into the trenches alongside their teams. They take on the toughest projects, seek out critical feedback, and never stop learning. By living their values every day, they set a powerful example that resonates throughout the organization.

Communicating the Vision: A Culture of Openness and Transparency

Imagine your company culture as a vibrant ecosystem. Communication is the oxygen that keeps it alive and thriving.

Leaders who build open and transparent communication create a space where employees feel safe to speak their minds, share their wildest ideas, and voice concerns without fear of repercussions.

This means utilizing every communication channel at your disposal, from formal meetings and company-wide emails to casual conversations in the break room and lively discussions on internal social platforms. But it's not just about the quantity of communication; it's about the quality. The language leaders use can either fuel a growth mindset or snuff it out. So, ditch the blame game and focus on cultivating a culture of learning, where mistakes are viewed as opportunities for growth and development.

Mentorship and Coaching: Fueling Growth and Development

Mentorship and coaching programs are like rocket fuel for employee development. They provide a structured framework for less experienced employees to learn from seasoned veterans, gaining invaluable insights, guidance, and support along the way.

McKinsey, once again, is a prime example. Their robust mentorship culture ensures that new hires are paired with experienced colleagues who can help them navigate the complexities of the consulting world and accelerate their professional growth. It's like having a personal Sherpa to guide you up the mountain of success.

But mentorship shouldn't be left solely to individual employees. Leaders should actively participate in these programs, both as mentors and mentees. This not only demonstrates their commitment to employee development but also allows them to learn and grow alongside their team members.

Investing in leadership development programs is equally crucial. These programs equip leaders with the cultural competence and awareness they need to shape and maintain a growth-oriented culture effectively. Your company has to give your cultural architects the tools and blueprints they need to build a masterpiece.

Celebrating Cultural Champions: Recognizing and Reinforcing Positive Behaviors

Imagine you're trying to teach a dog a new trick. You reward them with treats and praise when they get it right, reinforcing the desired behavior. The same principle applies to building a positive culture. By regularly recognizing and rewarding employees who exemplify your company's values, you're essentially giving them a cultural treat, reinforcing the behaviors you want to see more of.

This recognition shouldn't be a once-a-year affair during performance reviews. It should be woven into the fabric of your company's day-to-day life. Shout-outs in team meetings, handwritten notes of appreciation, small gifts, or even company-wide celebrations can all be powerful tools for reinforcing positive behaviors.

Don't forget the power of peer-to-peer recognition. When employees feel empowered to acknowledge each other's contributions, it strengthens the sense of community and shared purpose. Plus, it's a lot more fun to get a high-five from a colleague than a pat on the back from the boss.

Creating Cultural Rituals: Building a Sense of Belonging

Cultural rituals are like the inside jokes or traditions that bond a group of friends together. They create a sense of shared identity, belonging, and camaraderie. In the workplace, these rituals can be anything from weekly all-hands meetings where successes are celebrated and challenges are openly discussed, to company-wide retreats focused on team building and innovation.

One particularly creative example is "Failure Fridays," where teams take turns sharing lessons learned from recent setbacks. This ritual not only normalizes the idea that failure is a natural part of the learning process but also encourages open communication and collaboration. It turns stumbling blocks into stepping stones, promoting a resilient culture where employees are not afraid to take risks and try new things.

Leading with Empathy: Building Trust and Safety

Empathy is the secret sauce of effective leadership. Empathetic leaders don't just give orders; they listen. They seek to understand their employees' concerns, fears, and aspirations. They create a safe space where people feel comfortable taking risks, making mistakes, and speaking their minds without fear of judgment or ridicule.

This psychological safety is the fertile ground where trust and innovation take root. When employees trust their leaders, they're more likely to be engaged, motivated, and willing to go the extra mile. They're also more likely to share their creative ideas, knowing that they'll be heard and valued.

Encouraging Feedback: A Culture of Continuous Improvement

A growth-oriented culture is one that constantly seeks to learn and improve. Leaders who encourage feedback create a feedback loop that allows the organization to adapt and evolve in response to changing circumstances.

This means establishing both formal and informal mechanisms for gathering employee input. Regular one-on-one meetings, anonymous surveys, suggestion boxes, and town hall meetings are all valuable tools for tapping into the collective wisdom of your workforce.

But gathering feedback is only half the battle. Leaders must also demonstrate a willingness to act on that feedback, even when it's difficult or uncomfortable. This shows employees that their voices matter and that their contributions are valued. It also creates a sense of ownership and empowerment, as employees see that they have a real stake in shaping the company's future.

The Dark Side of Leadership: A Cautionary Tale

Leaders aren't superheroes. We all make mistakes, and sometimes, those mistakes can have unintended consequences that undermine the very culture we're trying to build. Negative leadership behaviors – like micromanagement, favoritism, unethical conduct, or public criticism – can be toxic, eroding trust, stifling creativity, and driving away top talent faster than you can say "performance review."

Picture this: You're at an industry conference, networking with your peers, when suddenly, the conversation takes a sharp turn. A leader from another company launches into a tirade about an employee's minor, easily fixable mistake. They're indignant, appalled, as they recount the incident in excruciating detail. The room grows silent as you and the other attendees exchange uncomfortable glances.

The awkward silence stretched on, broken only by the leader's increasingly exasperated tone. They seemed oblivious to the room's growing discomfort, their narrative of righteous indignation falling flat against a backdrop of polite disinterest. It was a masterclass in how not to lead, a cringeworthy display of unprofessionalism and a complete lack of self-awareness. This leader, so eager to cast themselves as the hero of their own story, had become the villain in ours.

A true leader wouldn't throw their employee under the bus like that. They'd understand that everyone makes mistakes, especially minor ones. Instead of public shaming, they'd privately address the issue, help the employee learn from the experience, and maybe even turn it into a valuable lesson for the entire team. Because at the end of the day, leadership is about supporting your people, not tearing them down.

Imagine, for a moment, a different scenario. A leader, overwhelmed and frustrated, publicly berates an employee for a small error. This public humiliation not only crushes that individual's spirit but sends a chilling message to everyone else: "It's not safe to make mistakes here." This fear of failure creates a breeding ground for stagnation, where innovation and creativity wither on the vine.

The lesson is clear: Leaders must cultivate self-awareness, practice empathy, and uphold the highest ethical standards. They must focus on building trust, empowering their teams, and nurturing a psychologically safe environment where everyone feels valued and respected. Remember, true leadership isn't about wielding power; it's about empowering others to reach their full potential.

Guiding Cultural Transformation: Your Roadmap To A Thriving Workplace

Every great expedition begins with a map. But before you chart a course towards a thriving workplace culture, it's crucial to understand your starting point. This section guides you through the essential first steps of self-reflection and assessment.

Self-Reflection and Assessment: Where Are We Now?

Every epic journey begins with a single step: knowing where you're starting from. Before you can transform your culture, you need to understand its current state. It's time for a little soul-searching, both for yourself as a leader and for your organization as a whole.

- **Leadership Self-Assessment Tool:**
  - The appendix holds a treasure map to self-discovery: a Leadership Self-Assessment Tool. This isn't your average personality quiz; it's designed to help you, the leader, examine your own behaviors, communication style, and decision-making through the lens of your desired culture. Are you truly walking the talk? Are your actions aligned with your words? Be honest with yourself – this introspection is the first step towards growth, not just for you but for your entire team.
- **Organizational Assessment:**
  - Now, let's zoom out and take a panoramic view of your company's cultural landscape. What are the hidden strengths that can be leveraged? What are the weeds that need to be pulled? Referencing the tools and frameworks we've explored earlier, conduct a thorough assessment of your current culture. Dig

deep and uncover the underlying values, norms, and behaviors that are shaping your workplace. This isn't about pointing fingers; it's about gaining a clear understanding of where you are so you can chart a course towards where you want to be.

Vision and Leadership Alignment: Setting Your Sights on the Summit

Picture this: You're leading a team of adventurers on a quest to climb Mount Everest. Without a clear vision of the summit and a shared commitment to reaching it, your team is likely to wander off course, lose motivation, or worse, give up altogether.

The same principle applies to cultural transformation. A clear, compelling vision for the future is your North Star, your guiding light. It's the rallying cry that unites your team and propels them forward. This vision should articulate the values, behaviors, and norms that will define your new culture – a culture that embraces growth, celebrates risk-taking, and sparks innovation.

But a vision alone isn't enough. It needs the unwavering support and commitment of your entire leadership team. They must not only understand the vision but also actively champion it. They need to be the Sherpas who lead the way, modeling the desired behaviors, communicating the vision with passion and conviction, and holding themselves and others accountable for making it a reality.

The Culture Transformation Roadmap: Your Step-by-Step Guide

1. **Communication is Key:** Open the floodgates of communication! Share the vision for your new culture far and wide, explaining why this change is essential and how it will benefit everyone involved. Utilize every communication channel you have, from

town hall meetings to emails to social media. Create a space for open dialogue where questions are encouraged and concerns are addressed.
2. **Craft a Detailed Action Plan:** It's time to get down to brass tacks. Develop a comprehensive action plan that outlines the specific steps you'll take to reach your cultural summit. This might include implementing new training programs, revamping performance management systems, or even redesigning your physical workspace. Remember, every detail matters.
3. **Implementation with Gusto:** Put your plan into action with a sense of urgency and excitement. Monitor your progress regularly and don't be afraid to adjust your course as needed. Remember, even the best-laid plans can encounter unexpected detours. Celebrate the small wins along the way; they'll keep your team motivated and energized.
4. **Reinforce the New Way:** Cultural change doesn't happen overnight; it requires constant reinforcement. Keep the conversation alive, celebrate successes, recognize those who embody the desired behaviors, and provide ongoing training and development to support the shift. Remember, it's about building new habits, not just checking boxes.
5. **Evaluate and Evolve:** Don't just set it and forget it. Regularly assess the impact of your efforts through surveys, focus groups, or other feedback mechanisms. Use these insights to refine your approach and ensure your culture continues to evolve in a positive direction. After all, the only constant in life (and culture) is change.

Embracing the Journey

Remember, cultural transformation isn't a destination; it's a thrilling adventure with its own twists and turns. It demands continuous attention, adaptation, and a commitment to growth from everyone involved. But for leaders who embrace this journey and invest in building a positive, growth-oriented culture, the rewards are immense. You'll create a legacy that extends far beyond your tenure, shaping a workplace where employees thrive, innovation flourishes, and the organization's future is bright.

Now that you have a roadmap in hand, it's time to dive deeper into the specific strategies and tactics that will bring your vision to life. The following chapters will equip you with the tools and knowledge you need to create a workplace that not only attracts and retains top talent but also unleashes their full potential. Remember, your company's culture is its most valuable asset – invest in it wisely, and it will reward you tenfold.

The Enduring Power Of Culture

In this whirlwind tour of cultural leadership, we've unearthed the incredible power leaders wield in shaping the very essence of their organizations. We've seen how they act as cultural DJs, spinning a mix of values, behaviors, and norms that set the tone for the entire dance floor. We've explored the diverse leadership styles that can ignite innovation, encourage collaboration, and build trust. And we've armed you with a toolkit of actionable strategies to cultivate a workplace where growth and risk-taking aren't just buzzwords, but the lifeblood of your company's success.

But let's not forget: culture isn't a one-hit wonder; it's an evolving masterpiece that demands constant attention. Like a vibrant garden, it needs regular watering, pruning, and a bit of sunshine to truly flourish. As leaders, you are the gardeners of this ecosystem, adapting your approach as your company grows and the world around you changes.

Think of your impact on culture as your personal Sistine Chapel ceiling, a legacy that will long outlast your time at the helm. A positive, growth-oriented culture doesn't just boost the bottom line; it creates a workplace where people feel valued, empowered, and excited to jump out of bed each morning. It's a magnet for top talent who crave more than just a paycheck—they want purpose, growth, and a sense of belonging.

And let's not forget the ripple effect. A thriving culture doesn't just make employees happier; it fuels innovation, resilience, and the kind of adaptability that's essential in today's ever-changing business landscape. It's the secret ingredient that sets companies apart, propelling them to new heights of success.

But as the workplace evolves, so too must our approach to culture. The rise of remote and hybrid work models presents a whole new set of challenges and opportunities. In the next chapter, we'll dive into how to keep your culture vibrant and connected, even when your team is scattered across the globe.

So, leaders, it's time to rise to the challenge. Embrace your role as cultural architects, invest in your people, and build a workplace where innovation flourishes and everyone feels empowered to reach their full potential. Remember, your culture is your greatest asset—a powerful force that can shape the future of your organization and the lives of your employees. It's time to leave your mark, to create a legacy that will inspire generations to come. Your company's culture is your story, and you have the power to make it legendary.

CHAPTER 4: BUILDING A THRIVING CULTURE IN THE REMOTE/HYBRID WORKPLACE

We've all heard the saying, "Culture eats strategy for breakfast." In the previous chapters, we dove deep into how intentionally crafting your company's culture can supercharge your mission, wow your clients, and create a workplace where employees are genuinely happy and engaged. But hold on to your hats, because the game has changed.

The meteoric rise of remote and hybrid work models has thrown a curveball into the world of company culture. Sure, these new ways of working offer tempting perks like flexibility, a wider talent pool, and maybe even a few extra bucks in the company coffers. But let's not kid ourselves – they've also unleashed a whole new beast of challenges.

One of the biggest casualties? Those spontaneous water cooler chats, shared lunches that spark impromptu brainstorming sessions, and those hallway run-ins that somehow magically solve problems. These seemingly trivial moments are the unsung heroes of building trust, rapport, and a sense of belonging. And let's face it, replicating those serendipitous connections in a virtual world is like trying to catch lightning in a bottle.

The truth is, remote and hybrid work can create a breeding ground for miscommunication, misunderstandings, and a whole lot of missed cues. Throw in the fact that we all have different communication styles (more on that later!), and you've got a recipe for friction. Without the chance to really get to know each other, it's easy for judgments to fly and collaboration to fizzle.

Let me tell you a story. During the chaotic days of the pandemic, the company I was with at the time was thrust into the world of remote work. It was a disaster. The existing communication issues got blown out of proportion, and the operational team (yours truly included) was drowning in a deluge of unresolved client requests that were forwarded, but not resolved by the front-line customer service group. Our attempts to fix things? Met with resistance and a whole lot of finger-pointing. It was a classic case of "us versus them," with the company mission taking a backseat to internal squabbles. It was a mess, and it all boiled down to a lack of communication and support in the virtual void.

So, here's the deal: remote work can be a Pandora's box of problems if you're not careful. Morale plummets, productivity tanks, and your company's mission gets lost in the shuffle. Even big names like Elon Musk are sounding the alarm, claiming that remote work stifles innovation and destroys company culture.

But before you throw in the towel and drag everyone back to the office, hear me out. A thriving company culture in a remote/hybrid world isn't about recreating the past; it's about adapting and evolving. It's about finding new and innovative ways to connect, communicate, and build trust, even when we're miles apart.

So, can we replace the magic of the water cooler with a virtual one? Maybe not entirely. But that's where the real adventure begins. By tackling the downsides of remote work head-on and embracing new strategies, we can build cultures that are not only resilient but downright unstoppable.

Navigating The Treacherous Terrain Of Remote/ Hybrid Work

While the shift to remote and hybrid work models has been a godsend for flexibility and work-life balance, let's not sugarcoat it: It's also thrown a wrench in the works of building a kick-ass company culture.

A. The Isolation Blues

Working from home can sometimes feel like solitary confinement. The lack of daily interaction with colleagues can trigger feelings of loneliness, depression, and even anxiety. And guess what? These emotions are productivity killers, zapping motivation and creativity. As a leader, it's your job to be on the lookout for warning signs like withdrawal, disengagement, or sudden changes in work patterns. Remember, a lonely employee is not a happy or productive one.

But it's not just about individual well-being. Remote work also erodes those spontaneous, off-the-cuff conversations that happen naturally in a physical office. Those chats by the coffee machine shared lunches, and hallway run-ins aren't just idle chit-chat – they're the glue that binds teams together, building trust, understanding, and a sense of belonging. When those interactions disappear, misunderstandings breed, trust erodes, and team cohesion crumbles. So how do you fix it? By getting intentional about creating virtual spaces for those water-cooler moments. Think virtual coffee breaks, online team-building games, and dedicated channels for casual conversation.

B. The Communication Conundrum

Communication is the lifeblood of any organization, but it gets a whole lot trickier in a virtual world. Nonverbal cues like facial expressions, body language, and tone of voice, which are crucial for building trust and understanding, get lost in translation. Ever tried to decipher a passive-aggressive email? Yeah, not fun. And that's not all. Asynchronous communication (think emails and text-only messages) can lead to delays, confusion, and frustration.

To top it off, everyone has their own unique communication style, and these differences can become amplified in remote settings. Picture this: an extroverted, fast-talking salesperson trying to communicate with a detail-oriented, introverted engineer. It's a recipe for disaster. The solution? Embrace video calls to add a human touch, set clear expectations for response times, and invest in training to help your team understand and adapt to different communication styles. The idea is to get as close to a virtual water-cooler as you can when remote work is needed.

C. The Blurred Lines of Work-Life Balance

Working from a remote location can be a double-edged sword. On one hand, it's incredibly convenient. On the other hand, it's all too easy for work to bleed into your personal life, leading to burnout, resentment, and a whole lot of pajama-clad Zoom meetings. Setting clear boundaries between work hours and personal time is crucial, as is creating a dedicated workspace that signals to your brain (and your family!) that it's time to focus.

The lack of separation between work and life is a recipe for burnout. Watch out for signs of exhaustion, cynicism, and decreased productivity. And don't forget about disengagement, which can quietly creep in and wreak havoc on your team's morale and performance. To combat this, encourage regular breaks, promote work-life balance, and developing a supportive environment where employees feel comfortable raising concerns.

D. The Trust Factor

Trust is the cornerstone of any successful team, but it's a fragile thing, especially in remote environments. When you can't see your colleagues face-to-face, it's harder to build those bonds of trust that are essential for collaboration, innovation, and problem-solving.

To overcome this challenge, transparency is key. Be open and honest in your communication, deliver on your promises, and celebrate your team's achievements. Encourage a culture of feedback and support, where everyone feels heard and valued. And most importantly, lead by example. Show your team that you trust them, and they'll be more likely to trust you in return.

Seizing The Upside Of Remote/Hybrid Work

While the shift to remote and hybrid work might seem like navigating a minefield of potential cultural pitfalls, it's not all doom and gloom. In fact, these models come with a silver lining – a treasure trove of unique opportunities to not only survive but actually *thrive*.

A. **The Worldwide Talent Hunt**

Ditch the geographic boundaries and unlock a global talent goldmine! Remote work opens the doors to hiring the best and brightest from every corner of the world. This means assembling a dream team with diverse skills, experiences, and perspectives – a potent mix that fuels innovation, sparks creativity, and cracks the toughest problems with a kaleidoscope of solutions. Companies like GitLab, with their 1,300+ strong team hailing from 65+ countries, are living proof that diversity isn't just a buzzword; it's a competitive advantage. But remember, a diverse team is only as good as the inclusive culture that surrounds it. So, invest in cultural sensitivity training, create employee resource groups, and celebrate the beautiful tapestry of your team's backgrounds.

B. **Freedom to Thrive: Flexibility and Autonomy Unleashed**

Who wouldn't love to ditch the soul-sucking commute, trade in fluorescent office lighting for sunshine, and have the freedom to schedule that dentist appointment without a side of guilt? Remote work offers employees the holy grail of work-life balance, flexibility to manage personal commitments, and the autonomy to work wherever and whenever they're most productive. And guess what? Happy employees are motivated employees, and motivated employees deliver results.

But autonomy isn't just about ditching the office. It's about empowering employees to take ownership of their work, make decisions, and unleash their creative genius. When people feel trusted and in control, they're more likely to go above and beyond. Just remember, a little guidance goes a long way. Set clear expectations, provide regular feedback, and encourage collaboration to prevent those autonomous superstars from drifting off into their own isolated orbits.

C. **The Money Saver: Slashing Overhead**

Office space is expensive. Utilities? Expensive. That endless supply of coffee and snacks? You guessed it, expensive. Remote work can slash these costs, freeing up a treasure chest of resources to invest back into your team. Think wellness programs, professional development opportunities, and epic virtual team-building experiences. Not only will your employees thank you, but your bottom line will too. Happy, healthy, and skilled employees are the secret sauce to long-term success.

D. **Innovation Station: Where Creativity Meets Collaboration**

Think remote work means sacrificing collaboration and innovation? Think again. With a plethora of virtual tools at your disposal, real-time collaboration across continents is no longer a pipe dream. Ditch those dreaded email chains and embrace instant messaging platforms with video capabilities. Imagine it: virtual brainstorming sessions where ideas flow freely, team members chiming in from their cozy home offices or sunny balconies.

But remember, technology is just the tool. The real magic happens when you promote a culture that encourages open communication, trust, and the freedom to experiment. A culture where employees feel safe to share their wildest ideas, knowing they'll be heard and supported. That's where innovation truly takes flight.

So, there you have it. Remote and hybrid work may present some hurdles, but they also offer a golden opportunity to build a company culture that is diverse, flexible, innovative, and dare we say, even more awesome than before.

Building Bridges: Strategies For Connection, Communication, And Shared Purpose In The Virtual Frontier

In the Wild West of remote and hybrid work, building a thriving company culture requires a new toolkit and a fresh approach. Let's ditch the outdated playbook and embrace strategies that truly connect, communicate, and ignite a shared sense of purpose among your scattered team.

A. **The Art of Intentional Communication**

Regular check-ins are the lifeblood of remote teams. They are your virtual pulse checks, ensuring everyone's on the same page, feeling supported, and staying connected. But forget boring status updates. Spice things up with a mix of work-related progress, personal check-ins (how's that sourdough starter coming along?), and open-ended conversations that spark real connection. One-on-one video calls are your secret weapon for building trust and rapport, acting as the virtual water cooler where authentic conversations flow freely. Remember, emails and chats are great for sharing information, but they can't replace the human touch of real-time interaction.

Transparency and Active Listening: The Dynamic Duo

Open and honest communication is the bedrock of any healthy relationship, and your company culture is no exception. Leaders, it's time to ditch the corporate jargon and speak from the heart. Share information openly, be honest about challenges, and celebrate victories together. But don't just talk – *listen*. Active listening is the secret sauce that transforms conversations into connections. Be present, ask questions, and show genuine interest in what your team members have to say.

Personality Power-Up: Decoding Communication Styles

Ever feel like you're speaking different languages with your colleagues? That's where understanding personality types comes in. In the upcoming chapters, we'll dive into the DISC model, a powerful tool that reveals how different personalities communicate and collaborate. By understanding these nuances, you can tailor your communication style, bridge those pesky misunderstandings, and transform your team into a well-oiled communication machine. It's like having a universal translator for human behavior!

The Multichannel Mix: Choosing the Right Tool for the Job

Email, chat, video calls, oh my! With so many communication channels available, it's easy to get overwhelmed. Each channel has its strengths and weaknesses. Email is great for formal announcements, but it's not a winner for quick questions or complicated and emotional issues. Have you have received (or sent) one of those email manifestos from someone that is dripping in emotion and could have been easily handled in a brief telephone or video call? Those are relationship killers once someone hits the send button. Instant messaging with video is perfect for real-time collaboration and building rapport, but it can be distracting when you're in deep work mode. The key is to set clear guidelines for when to use each channel, so your team can communicate effectively without getting buried in a digital avalanche.

Leaders: Walk the Talk

Actions speak louder than words, especially when it comes to building a remote culture. Leaders, it's time to step up and be the change you want to see. If you expect open communication and transparency, then be open and transparent yourself. If you want your team to connect and collaborate, then lead by example and participate in virtual events and team-building activities. Remember, your team is watching.

B. Virtual Team Building & Social Events

Ditch the Boring Happy Hours: Spice Up Your Virtual Social Scene

Virtual happy hours are so 2020. It's time to get creative and inject some fun into your team's social calendar. Think virtual cooking classes, book clubs, online escape rooms, or even wellness challenges. The options are endless, and the goal is simple: to create shared experiences that promoting connection and camaraderie, even when you're miles apart. The challenge is that these video calls are limited to two people interacting at a time. Don't go too deep with the group meeting scenarios through video, but keep it in your playbook for what you think it can have a good impact. Sharing best practices is a great way to use group meetings. People can realize they aren't alone in whatever challenge they are facing in the organization. They can build off each other's points and help leaders get clear on where to train their focus.

Variety is the Spice of (Virtual) Life

One size doesn't fit all when it comes to team building. Offer a variety of activities that cater to different interests and personalities. Some team members might be thrilled by a competitive game night, while others might prefer a more relaxed virtual coffee chat. The key is to mix it up and ensure that everyone feels included and engaged.

Empower Your Team: Let Them Take the Reins

Want to guarantee that your team-building activities are a hit? Get your employees involved in the planning process. Not only will this boost engagement, but it also ensures that the activities you choose are truly meaningful and relevant to your team's unique interests and needs.

C. **Shared Rituals and Traditions: The Glue that Binds**

Rituals, even virtual ones, are the secret ingredient for creating a sense of belonging and shared identity. Whether it's a weekly all-hands meeting, a virtual birthday celebration, or a company-wide online game night, these shared experiences create a sense of community and reinforce the bonds that tie your team together. Don't be afraid to get creative and adapt existing traditions to the virtual world. After all, who says you can't have a virtual costume contest or talent show for your next holiday party?

Case Study: The Boston Consulting Group (Bcg) - A Hybrid Model For Cultural Success

The Boston Consulting Group (BCG) serves as a prime example of how to build a strong company culture in a hybrid work environment, proving that geographical dispersion doesn't have to equate to cultural dispersion. BCG achieves this by strategically balancing the flexibility of remote work with the essential in-person interactions that build the foundation of a thriving culture.

BCG's Multifaceted Approach to Culture

- **Strong Values:** BCG establishes a clear set of values—integrity, respect, collaboration, and client impact—that guide every employee's actions and decisions, ensuring a consistent cultural foundation regardless of location.
- **Attracting and Retaining Talent:** By prioritizing recruiting and retaining diverse talent from around the world, BCG ensures a rich tapestry of perspectives, experiences, and ideas that enrich their problem-solving capabilities and encourage a vibrant, inclusive culture.
- **Company Principles:** BCG upholds high standards of ethics and business conduct, creating a culture of trust, accountability, and professionalism that transcends geographical boundaries.
- **Continuous Learning and Development:** Investing in employees' growth through learning programs and development opportunities promote a culture of continuous improvement and knowledge-sharing, even when teams are not physically together.
- **Open Communication:** By encouraging transparent communication and feedback, BCG creates a safe space for employees to share ideas, voice concerns, and collaborate effectively, regardless of their location.

The Hybrid Advantage: Blending Remote and In-Person Interactions

BCG's approach is not solely remote. While employees often work from different locations, the company strategically brings teams together in person on a regular basis. These in-person gatherings serve several crucial purposes:

- **Building Trust and Rapport:** Face-to-face interactions allow for the development of deeper personal connections, trust, and understanding among team members. This is especially important for new employees and teams that haven't had the chance to interact in person before.
- **Promoting Collaboration:** In-person meetings and workshops provide opportunities for brainstorming, problem-solving, and co-creation that are often more difficult to achieve in a virtual environment.
- **Reinforcing Shared Purpose:** Bringing employees together physically reinforces their shared commitment to the company's mission, values, and goals, strengthening the overall culture.

Learning from BCG's Approach:

The Boston Consulting Group's success demonstrates that building a thriving culture in a hybrid work environment is achievable. By strategically combining remote flexibility with intentional in-person interactions, companies can tap into global talent, promote collaboration, and reinforce a shared purpose, ultimately creating a dynamic and adaptable culture that thrives in the modern workplace.

Case Study: Gitlab - Embracing A Remote-First Culture

GitLab, a leading web-based DevOps platform, stands as a shining example of a company that has not only adapted to but thrived in a fully remote environment. They are widely recognized as pioneers in remote work culture, with their innovative practices and commitment to transparency setting a high bar for other organizations.

GitLab's remote-first approach is deeply ingrained in their DNA. It's not just a policy; it's a way of life that permeates every aspect of their operations. Their publicly available handbook, a comprehensive guide to their culture, processes, and communication strategies, is a testament to their commitment to transparency and knowledge sharing.

Key Elements of GitLab's Remote-First Culture:

- **Asynchronous Communication:** GitLab embraces asynchronous communication, allowing employees to work when and where they are most productive. They minimize real-time meetings and rely on written communication, documentation, and collaboration tools to keep everyone aligned.
- **Transparency and Documentation:** Everything at GitLab is documented, from meeting notes to project updates to company-wide decisions. This radical transparency ensures that everyone has access to information and develops a culture of trust and accountability.
- **Intentional Communication:** GitLab emphasizes clear, concise, and respectful communication. They encourage the use of video calls for building rapport and personal connection, while also utilizing written communication

for documentation and knowledge sharing.
- **Strong Values:** GitLab's values, including collaboration, results, efficiency, diversity, inclusion & belonging, iteration, and transparency, guide their actions and decisions, creating a cohesive and aligned culture.
- **Focus on Outcomes:** GitLab prioritizes outcomes over hours worked, empowering employees to manage their own time and work in a way that maximizes their productivity and well-being.
- **Continuous Improvement:** They embrace a culture of continuous improvement, constantly experimenting with new tools, processes, and practices to optimize their remote work environment.

Learning from GitLab's Approach:

GitLab's success demonstrates that a remote-first culture can not only be effective but can also lead to greater innovation, productivity, and employee satisfaction. Their commitment to transparency, documentation, and intentional communication provides a valuable blueprint for other organizations looking to build a thriving remote culture. While not every company may be able to replicate GitLab's fully remote model, there are valuable lessons to be learned from their approach.

By studying GitLab's practices and adapting them to their own unique circumstances, organizations can harness the power of remote work to attract top talent, encourages innovation, and create a culture that empowers employees to do their best work, wherever they may be.

Case Study: Automattic (Wordpress.com) - Thriving On Asynchronous Communication And Autonomy

Automattic, the company behind WordPress.com, has been a champion of remote work since its inception. With employees spread across over 90 countries, they've developed a unique culture that thrives on asynchronous communication and prioritizes employee autonomy.

A Different Approach to Communication:

Unlike many companies that rely on real-time meetings and constant connectivity, Automattic embraces asynchronous communication. This means that employees have the flexibility to work when and where they are most productive, without the pressure of immediate responses or constant interruptions. Instead of synchronous meetings, they rely on written communication, project management tools, and collaborative documents to keep everyone informed and aligned.

Empowering Employees with Autonomy:

Automattic believes in trusting employees to manage their own time and work independently. They provide clear goals and expectations but allow individuals to choose how and when they accomplish their tasks. This autonomy encourages a sense of ownership and responsibility, leading to increased motivation, engagement, and productivity.

Building Community in a Distributed World:

Despite being geographically dispersed, Automattic has created a strong sense of community and belonging among its employees. They achieve this through:

- **Virtual Team Meetups:** Regular virtual meetups allow employees to connect, share ideas, and build relationships.
- **Company-Sponsored Travel:** They offer opportunities for employees to travel and meet their colleagues in person, promoting stronger bonds and a shared sense of purpose.
- **Open Communication Channels:** They have various online channels, such as Slack and internal blogs, where employees can communicate, share knowledge, and ask questions.
- **Shared Values:** Automattic's core values, including "assume positive intent," "communicate as much as possible," and "do the right thing," create a foundation of trust and respect within the company.

Lessons from Automattic's Success:

Automattic's success in building a thriving remote culture challenges traditional notions of what a workplace should look like. Their emphasis on asynchronous communication, autonomy, and intentional community building provides valuable insights for organizations navigating the remote/hybrid landscape. By prioritizing flexibility, trust, and open communication, companies can create a culture that empowers employees to do their best work, regardless of where they are located.

The Path Forward

The future of work is undoubtedly evolving, and remote/hybrid models are here to stay. This shift presents a unique opportunity for companies to redefine what a thriving company culture looks like. As we've explored in this chapter, intentional culture building is even more crucial in this new landscape.

The long-term implications of remote/hybrid work on company culture are significant. We can expect to see:

- **More emphasis on asynchronous communication and output-based evaluation:** The traditional 9-to-5 workday is becoming less relevant, with a greater focus on results and flexibility in how work gets done.
- **Increased need for trust and autonomy among team members:** Remote/hybrid work demands higher levels of trust and autonomy as managers cannot directly supervise employees in the same way.
- **Potential for further blurring of work-life boundaries:** The lines between work and personal life can easily blur in remote settings, requiring proactive strategies to maintain a healthy balance.

Navigating these challenges and harnessing the opportunities of remote/hybrid work requires a deep understanding of individual communication styles and motivations. That's where the DISC personality framework comes in.

The DISC Model as a Cultural Compass

Forget those generic personality quizzes you took in magazines – DISC is the real deal. This powerful tool unlocks the secrets of human behavior, revealing how your team members communicate, what gets them fired up, and how they tackle challenges. Imagine being able to decode the unique motivations and preferences of each person on your team, like having a cheat code for building a high-performing, harmonious workplace.

With DISC, you'll discover the four distinct personality types that make up your team: the decisive and driven Dominants, the enthusiastic and persuasive Influencers, the supportive and collaborative Steadys, and the meticulous and analytical Conscientious individuals. Armed with this knowledge, you can tailor your communication and management style to connect with each person on a deeper level, creating a culture where everyone feels understood, appreciated, and inspired to do their best work.

But the magic of DISC doesn't stop there. By empowering your team with DISC training, you can supercharge their communication and collaboration skills, turning potential conflicts into opportunities for growth and innovation. Picture a workplace where misunderstandings are a thing of the past, and everyone is laser-focused on achieving your company's mission. That's the power of DISC in action.

In the upcoming chapters, we'll take you on a deep dive into the DISC universe, exploring how this versatile tool can be woven into every stage of the employee lifecycle. From attracting top talent and onboarding them seamlessly to maximizing their performance and resolving conflicts like a pro, DISC will be your trusty sidekick, guiding you towards building a thriving, adaptable culture that sets your organization apart.

Call to Action

Don't wait to start implementing the strategies we've discussed in this chapter. Culture building is an ongoing process that requires continuous attention and adaptation. Embrace the challenges of remote/hybrid work as an opportunity to innovate and create a new kind of culture that is tailored to the unique needs of your team and organization.

Transition: Building Your Dream Team with DISC

In Part II of this book, we'll explore how the DISC model can revolutionize your approach to building and managing teams. We'll start by examining how DISC can be used as an X-factor in hiring, helping you identify the right candidates who not only possess the necessary skills but also fit seamlessly into your company culture.

- **Personality: The DISC X-Factor in Hiring:** We'll take a deep dive into the DISC model, explaining how each type contributes to team dynamics and offering examples of roles that typically suit each style. We'll also share a case study of how Pixar leverages a diverse mix of DISC types to fuel its creative success.
- **Skills Assessment: Beyond the DISC Profile:** While personality is important, skills are equally crucial. We'll discuss the importance of assessing both hard and soft skills in hiring and provide guidance on how to use DISC to identify potential strengths and weaknesses in candidates. We'll also look at Google's rigorous skills assessments as a case study.
- **The Interview Reimagined: DISC & Skills in Focus:** We'll show you how to tailor interview questions to elicit DISC-related behaviors and skills, providing sample questions for each type. You'll also learn tips for active listening, rapport-building, and unbiased evaluation, with Warby Parker's interview process as a real-world example.
- **DISC and Conflict Resolution:** We'll explain how different DISC types approach conflict and offer strategies for mediating disagreements effectively. You'll learn how to prevent unresolved conflicts due to communication style clashes, which can erode team morale and productivity.

Creating a Culture of Engagement and Growth

In Part III, we'll shift our focus to creating a culture of engagement and growth. We'll explore how to leverage DISC insights to improve onboarding, recognition and reward programs, performance management, and communication strategies. We'll also share real-world case studies of companies that have successfully implemented DISC-aware practices to create thriving workplace cultures.

By the end of this book, you'll have a comprehensive understanding of how to leverage the DISC model to build a strong, adaptable culture that not only survives but thrives in the dynamic landscape of remote and hybrid work.

CHAPTER 5: PERSONALITY: THE DISC X-FACTOR IN HIRING

Unleash Your Team's Potential With Disc: The Personality Puzzle, Simplified

Forget those complex personality tests that leave you scratching your head. DISC is here to the rescue! It's the friendly, approachable guide to understanding the personalities that make your team tick. No PhD in psychology required!

Why DISC? Because It Just *Clicks*

DISC is like a secret decoder ring for your workplace. Here's what makes it so effective:

- **Simplicity Rules:** Four main personality types? Easy peasy! Dominant, Influential, Steady, and Conscientious – once you get to know them, you'll see them everywhere.
- **Spot-On Descriptions:** Each DISC type has distinct traits and behaviors, making it a breeze to recognize yourself and your colleagues. It's like having a cheat sheet for understanding human interactions!

- **Picture This:** The visual quadrant model makes it even easier to grasp using a personality map, guiding you through the different types and how they connect.
- **Real-World Ready:** DISC isn't just theory. It focuses on how people act *in the workplace*, giving you the tools to improve team building, communication, and even resolve those pesky conflicts.
- **Popular and Packed with Resources:** DISC is widely used, so you'll find tons of helpful guides, workshops, and online communities to dive deeper.

DISC: Your Personality Power Tool

Sure, other assessments like MBTI or Big Five might dig a little deeper, but they can be as confusing as a choose-your-own-adventure novel. DISC cuts through the complexity and gets straight to the good stuff – the actionable insights that make a real difference.

A Word of Caution: The DISC Disclaimer

- **Honesty is Key:** DISC is based on self-assessment. So, encourage everyone to be open and honest for the most accurate results.
- **No Labeling Allowed:** DISC helps us understand tendencies, not stick labels on foreheads. It's about celebrating diversity, not boxing people in.
- **It's a Starting Point:** DISC is a fantastic foundation for self-awareness and improved communication. It's a tool for growth, not a rigid rulebook.

Unleash the Magic of Your Team

When you understand and appreciate the unique strengths of each DISC type, you create a workplace where everyone feels valued and empowered. Improved communication, smoother collaboration, and a high-performing team are just some of the amazing benefits waiting to be unlocked. DISC is your key to transforming your workplace into a vibrant, dynamic, and productive environment where everyone shines.

The Disc Framework: Decoding Workplace Personalities

The DISC model is your key to understanding the diverse personalities that shape your workplace. More than just simple labels, DISC gets into the core motivations and fears that drive individuals, offering a practical framework for enhancing collaboration, communication, and problem-solving. Let's explore each of the four distinct styles:

- **Dominant (D):** These trailblazers thrive on challenge and control. Picture Margaret Thatcher's unwavering leadership or the steely determination of Miranda Priestly from "The Devil Wears Prada." Dominant personalities are driven by results and fear losing control or being taken advantage of.
- **Influential (I):** Energized by social connection and recognition, these individuals are natural-born motivators and persuaders. Think of Oprah Winfrey's inspiring charisma or the infectious enthusiasm of Leslie Knope from "Parks and Recreation." Their biggest fear? Rejection, isolation, and a lack of excitement.
- **Steady (S):** These team players prioritize collaboration and harmony. Envision the genuine empathy of Mr. Rogers or the unwavering loyalty of Samwise Gamgee from "The Lord of the Rings." Steady individuals fear conflict, change, and letting down their colleagues.
- **Conscientious (C):** These detail-oriented thinkers are driven by accuracy and expertise. They value structure and precision, much like the meticulous Bill Gates or the logical Spock from "Star Trek." Their fears center around criticism, being wrong, and chaos.

Quick DISC Self-Assessment

Ready to discover your own DISC style? Take this short quiz to see which type resonates with you most. Remember, there are no right or wrong answers!

For each question, choose the answer that best describes you MOST of the time.

1. When faced with a challenge, I am most likely to:
   o (D) Take charge and find a solution quickly
   o (I) Brainstorm with others and get everyone excited
   o (S) Listen to everyone's ideas and seek consensus
   o (C) Analyze the situation carefully and research options
2. In a team setting, I am most likely to:
   o (D) Be direct and assertive, focusing on results
   o (I) Encourage collaboration and bring a positive attitude
   o (S) Offer support and make sure everyone feels included
   o (C) Pay attention to details and ensure accuracy
3. My communication style is typically:
   o (D) Straightforward and to the point
   o (I) Enthusiastic and expressive
   o (S) Calm and patient
   o (C) Reserved and factual
4. I prefer to work in an environment that is:
   o (D) Fast-paced and results-oriented
   o (I) Energetic and social
   o (S) Supportive and harmonious
   o (C) Structured and organized
5. When making decisions, I am most likely to:
   o (D) Trust my gut instincts and take action
   o (I) Seek input from others and consider different perspectives
   o (S) Weigh all options carefully and consider the impact on others

- (C) Gather all the facts and analyze data before deciding

How to Score Your Quiz

Count how many times you chose each letter:

- Mostly D's: You lean towards the Dominant style.
- Mostly I's: You lean towards the Influential style.
- Mostly S's: You lean towards the Steady style.
- Mostly C's: You lean towards the Conscientious style.

Remember:

Most people are a blend of two or even three styles, with one typically being more dominant. This diversity within individuals is what makes teams dynamic and effective. However, under pressure, a person's dominant style tends to emerge more strongly. Recognizing this interplay of styles is key to understanding team dynamics and encouraging effective communication.

This quiz is just a starting point for self-discovery. For a deeper dive, consider taking a full DISC assessment. But for now, let this be your first step towards unlocking the power of personality in the workplace!

Disc In Action: Where Dream Teams Are Built, Not Born

Understanding individual DISC styles is like having a key to unlock each person's unique potential. But the real magic happens when you combine those keys to open the door to a powerhouse team. DISC isn't just about individual personalities; it's about harnessing the power of diversity to create teams that truly thrive.

Why Diversity Matters: It's Not Just a Buzzword

You need a mix of strengths, perspectives, and superpowers to tackle any challenge that comes your way. The same goes for the workplace. A well-rounded team isn't a group of clones; it's a vibrant mix of DISC styles, each bringing something unique to the table.

- **Dominant (D):** Your go-getters, the ones who drive results and aren't afraid to make tough decisions under pressure.
- **Influential (I):** The social butterflies who build relationships, spread enthusiasm, and can sell ice to Eskimos (metaphorically, of course).
- **Steady (S):** The glue that holds the team together, providing support, harmony, and a calming presence.
- **Conscientious (C):** The detail-oriented detectives, ensuring accuracy, precision, and keeping everyone on track.

By recognizing these unique superpowers, you can strategically assemble a team where each member complements the others, creating a harmonious symphony of strengths.

DISC Synergy: 1 + 1 = 3

When different DISC styles collaborate, the results are often greater than the sum of their parts.

- **D and S: The Dynamic Duo:** A Dominant's decisive nature combined with a Steady's patience creates a powerhouse of well-thought-out decisions and swift action.
- **I and C: The Creative Spark:** An Influential's infectious enthusiasm can ignite a Conscientious person's analytical mind, leading to innovative solutions that wouldn't have emerged otherwise.
- **S and (D or C): The Peacemakers:** A Steady person's diplomatic skills can bridge the gap between a Dominant's assertiveness and a Conscientious person's need for accuracy, preventing conflicts before they arise.

Case Studies: DISC in Action: Where Diverse Teams Thrive

The power of DISC isn't just theoretical; it's a real-world strategy that has been proven to unlock the full potential of teams. Companies across diverse industries have embraced personality diversity as a competitive advantage, using the DISC framework to promotes creativity, innovation, and problem-solving. Let's explore some real-world case studies that showcase how these organizations have harnessed DISC to build high-performing teams and achieve remarkable results.

One such example is **The Container Store**, a retail company renowned for its exceptional customer service. Facing the challenge of consistently delivering top-notch experiences, they turned to DISC to identify the personality traits that would best align with their customer-centric culture.

Case Study: The Container Store's DISC Approach

- **High Influential:** They sought out sales associates who were naturally enthusiastic, engaging, and adept at

building rapport with customers. These individuals could create a welcoming atmosphere and make shopping a genuinely enjoyable experience.
- **High Steady:** For customer service roles, they prioritized individuals with strong empathy and patience. These representatives could calmly handle issues, listen to customer concerns, and find solutions that left everyone satisfied.
- **Mix of Dominant and Conscientious:** In management roles, they looked for a blend of these two styles. Dominant individuals could provide strong leadership and set high standards, while Conscientious individuals ensured operational efficiency and attention to detail.

The Outcome: A Culture of Excellence

By aligning their hiring and training practices with DISC insights, The Container Store has cultivated a workforce that embodies their values. The result? The company is consistently ranked as a top employer and is celebrated for its exceptional customer service and low employee turnover. Their success story demonstrates the power of harnessing DISC to create a team that not only performs well but also genuinely enjoys their work and contributes to a positive company culture.

Case Study: Cisco Systems: Bridging Communication Gaps in a Merging World

The tech giant Cisco faced a common hurdle for rapidly growing companies: integrating diverse teams following mergers and acquisitions. With employees from various backgrounds and cultures coming together, misunderstandings and communication breakdowns were hindering collaboration.

The DISC Solution: A Common Language for Understanding

Cisco turned to DISC training as a unifying tool. By helping employees understand their own communication styles and those of their colleagues, DISC provided a common language for recognizing differences and adapting accordingly.

Specifically, Cisco encouraged:

- **Dominant and Influential** individuals to practice active listening and be mindful of others' feelings, promoting empathy and understanding.
- **Steady and Conscientious** individuals to speak up more assertively and share their ideas, ensuring that all voices were heard and valued.

The Outcome: A More Inclusive and Collaborative Culture

By equipping employees with DISC insights, Cisco was able to create a more inclusive and collaborative environment. This smoother integration of new employees and improved team performance ultimately contributed to the company's continued success in the ever-evolving tech landscape.

Case Study: HubSpot – Empowering Sales Success through DISC

In the competitive world of sales, building a high-performance team is no easy feat. HubSpot, a leading CRM platform, recognized this challenge and turned to DISC to gain a competitive edge.

HubSpot's DISC Strategy

HubSpot's DISC approach focuses on identifying and developing sales representatives who possess the ideal personality traits for success. Through DISC assessments, they discovered that individuals with high Dominant (D) and Influential (I) tendencies tend to thrive in sales roles. These individuals possess the drive, persuasiveness, and relationship-building skills that are crucial for closing deals and exceeding targets.

By understanding the unique strengths of each DISC style, HubSpot was able to tailor their training and development programs to maximize individual potential. They focused on enhancing the natural abilities of their Dominant and Influential sales reps, while also providing them with tools to overcome their potential blind spots.

The Result: A Sales Powerhouse

HubSpot's focus on DISC has yielded remarkable results. By intentionally recruiting and developing individuals with the right personality fit for sales, they have built a high-performing team that consistently surpasses expectations. Their success story demonstrates the power of aligning personality with roles, ultimately creating a sales powerhouse that drives revenue and growth for the company.

These case studies prove that DISC isn't just about understanding personality; it's a strategic tool for building teams that go above and beyond.

Disc And Hiring: The Secret Decoder Ring For Finding Your Dream Team

Hiring isn't just about ticking boxes on a resume. It's about finding the missing puzzle pieces that complete your team's vibrant picture. DISC is your secret decoder ring, revealing the hidden personalities that can supercharge your workforce.

Unlocking the Power of DISC in Hiring

DISC assessments go beyond mere skills and experience, diving deep into the personality traits that truly make a difference. It's like having X-ray vision into a candidate's potential, allowing you to see how they'll interact with colleagues, approach challenges, and ultimately contribute to your company's unique culture.

Identifying Key Traits: Matching Personalities with Positions

DISC helps you pinpoint those magical candidates whose natural tendencies perfectly align with the role you're trying to fill.

- **High Influence (I):** These charismatic communicators thrive in roles that demand persuasive charm and relationship-building. Sales, customer service, or anything that involves captivating an audience – that's their jam.
- **High Dominance (D):** Born leaders, these decisive individuals shine in positions that call for quick thinking, assertiveness, and a thirst for results. Think management, project leadership, or crisis response – where the pressure's on, and they deliver.
- **High Steadiness (S):** These supportive souls excel in collaborative environments where patience, empathy,

and diplomacy reign supreme. Customer service, HR, or administrative roles – they're the calming presence that keeps everything running smoothly.
- **High Conscientiousness (C):** These meticulous masterminds thrive on precision and accuracy. Analytical roles like accounting, engineering, or data analysis – that's where they flex their intellectual muscles.

But wait! Don't get boxed in by these stereotypes. The beauty of DISC is that it's not about pigeonholing people. Remember, everyone's a unique blend, and sometimes the most unexpected combinations create the most brilliant results.

Predicting Job Performance: A Peek into the Future

Research suggests there's a fascinating link between certain DISC styles and job performance. For example, those Dominant (D) folks often make stellar leaders, while the Influential (I) types can be sales superstars. But hold your horses! DISC isn't a crystal ball. It's one valuable tool among many to help you make informed hiring decisions.

Cultural Fit: Where Personalities and Companies Click

Hiring the right skills is great, but imagine a workplace where everyone *vibes*. That's where cultural fit comes in. DISC can help you find those candidates who not only have the right skills but also seamlessly blend with your company's unique personality.

Here's a quick guide:

- **Dominant (D):** Thrives in competitive, fast-paced, results-driven cultures.
- **Influential (I):** Lights up in social, energetic, and collaborative environments.
- **Steady (S):** Feels at home in supportive, harmonious cultures where teamwork is key.
- **Conscientious (C):** Flourishes in structured, organized

settings that value accuracy and expertise.

By understanding how DISC styles interact with your company culture, you can refine your recruitment strategy, tailor onboarding experiences, boost engagement, and ultimately reduce turnover.

Beyond the Stereotypes

Don't limit your search to the "typical" DISC profiles for a given position. By looking beyond stereotypes and recognizing the diverse strengths individuals bring to the table, you can unlock a wealth of untapped potential and build teams that excel in unexpected ways.

Traditional vs. Untapped Potential

DISC Type	Common Roles	Untapped Potential
Dominant (D)	Leadership, Sales, Management	Crisis Management, Customer Advocacy
Influential (I)	Sales, Marketing, Public Relations	Project Management, Team Building
Steady (S)	Customer Service, HR, Administrative Support	Creative Direction, Mediation
Conscientious (C)	Accounting, Engineering, Data Analysis	Training & Development, Quality Assurance

To evaluate fit, consider the following:

- **Core Strengths:** Identify the essential personality traits for the role (e.g., decisiveness for a leader, empathy for customer service) and assess if the candidate possesses them, regardless of their primary DISC style.
- **Motivations:** Understand what drives the candidate – are they seeking autonomy, collaboration, stability, or recognition? Ensure their motivations align with the role and company culture.

Success Stories from Unexpected Places

Let's look at some examples of individuals who thrived in roles that might not traditionally align with their DISC style:

- **The Steady Creative Director (Sarah):** Sarah's collaborative approach and empathy encourages a creative and innovative team environment.
- **The Conscientious Sales Star (David):** David's meticulousness and analytical skills led to exceptional sales performance through thorough preparation and building client trust.
- **The Dominant Project Manager (Mark):** Mark's decisiveness and drive for results ensured projects were completed on time and under budget, even in the face of complex challenges.
- **The Influential Customer Service Representative (Emily):** Emily's enthusiasm and ability to connect with people transformed the customer service team, boosting satisfaction scores and employee morale.

DISC: More Than a Strengths Finder – Your Early Warning System

DISC isn't just about celebrating strengths; it's also your secret weapon for spotting potential pitfalls *before* they become problems. The evaluation alerts you to potential challenges that could arise based on a candidate's unique DISC style.

Red Flags on the Radar

For instance, your high-flying Dominant (D) superstar might struggle in a role that requires meticulous attention to detail or lots of collaboration. And that analytical Conscientious (C) whiz might not be the best fit for a fast-paced, ever-changing environment.

By recognizing these potential red flags early on, you can be proactive:

- **Tailor the Role:** Maybe a slight tweak in responsibilities could play to the candidate's strengths.

- **Provide Training:** A little coaching could go a long way in helping them develop the skills they need to succeed.
- **Set Realistic Expectations:** Being upfront about potential challenges allows everyone to prepare and adapt.

By addressing these issues head-on, you're not just preventing problems; you're nurturing a culture of growth and continuous improvement.

DISC: Your Conflict Resolution Guru

Remember, different DISC styles have different approaches to conflict. Understanding these tendencies is like having a secret decoder ring for workplace disagreements. Dominant types might charge in headfirst, while Steady types might seek compromise and harmony. Armed with DISC knowledge, you can navigate these differences like a pro, turning potential conflicts into opportunities for growth.

But that's a topic for an upcoming chapter later in the book...

Key Takeaways: Embrace the Unexpected (and the Perfectly Predictable)

The beauty of DISC lies in its ability to reveal the unexpected. It challenges us to look beyond stereotypes and recognize the diverse strengths within our teams. It reminds us that:

- **Personality Isn't One-Size-Fits-All:** The best teams are a symphony of different styles, each contributing unique talents.
- **Self-Awareness is Empowering:** Understanding your DISC style unlocks hidden potential and opens doors to new possibilities.
- **Diversity is a Superpower:** When we embrace and leverage the strengths of each DISC type, we create a more creative, adaptable, and high-performing workforce.

By thoughtfully incorporating DISC into your hiring and

development strategies, you'll be well on your way to building a team that not only excels in their roles but also thrives in a culture of collaboration, understanding, and mutual respect.

Beyond Skills And Experience: Ignite Your Team's Passion

Sure, skills and experience are the price of admission. But to build a truly exceptional team, you need to go beyond the resume and tap into something deeper: **intrinsic motivation**. It's the secret sauce that transforms employees from clock-punchers to passionate contributors.

A. The Power of Intrinsic Motivation: The Fuel for High Performance

A car needs gas to run, right? Well, employees need intrinsic motivation to truly go the distance. This is the fire that burns within, fueled by their deepest desires, values, and aspirations. It's what makes them jump out of bed in the morning, eager to tackle challenges and make a meaningful difference.

When your team is intrinsically motivated, amazing things happen:

- **Engagement Explodes:** They're not just working for a paycheck; they're on a mission, and they're all in.
- **Productivity Soars:** Fueled by passion, they consistently go above and beyond, exceeding expectations and driving innovation.
- **Loyalty Takes Root:** They're not job-hopping; they're invested in your company's success and want to be part of the journey for the long haul.

B. Crafting a Brand That Beckons: DISC and Employer Branding

Your employer brand is your company's siren song – the message that draws in the right talent. So, crank up the volume and tailor your tune to each DISC style:

- **Dominant (D):** Lead with opportunities for leadership, high-impact projects, and a fast track to career advancement.
- **Influential (I):** Showcase your positive and collaborative culture, spotlight opportunities for recognition, and sprinkle in some fun and social events.
- **Steady (S):** Highlight your stable work environment, emphasize teamwork and support, and don't forget to mention work-life balance!
- **Conscientious (C):** Lay out clear career paths, opportunities for mastery, and a structured work environment that values accuracy and expertise.

By speaking directly to the heart of what motivates each DISC type, you'll attract candidates who are not only qualified but also excited about joining your team.

C. DISC and Employee Engagement: Fueling the Fire

The journey doesn't end with the hire! DISC is your secret weapon for keeping that motivational fire burning bright:

- **Tailored Recognition & Rewards:** Don't just give everyone a generic pat on the back. A High D craves public recognition, while a High S might prefer a heartfelt thank-you note.
- **DISC-Friendly Culture:** Create an environment where everyone feels valued and understood. Encourage open communication, embrace different perspectives, and cultivate a culture of continuous learning and development.

D. The Perfect Match

Ultimately, recruitment isn't just about filling vacancies; it's about finding the perfect match – a symphony of skills, personalities, and aspirations that create a harmonious and high-performing team. By understanding the "why" behind your candidates and employees, you'll build a workplace where everyone feels empowered to contribute their best work and achieve their fullest potential.

The journey doesn't end here! In the next chapter, we'll explore how you can use DISC to enhance communication, navigate conflict, and unleash the collective brilliance of your team. Stay tuned for more DISC-powered insights!

Putting Disc To Work: Your Hiring Toolkit, Upgraded

So, you've got the lowdown on DISC – awesome! But how do you *actually* use this personality powerhouse in your hiring process? Buckle up, because we're about to level up your recruitment game.

A. Choosing Your DISC Weapon: The Assessment Arsenal

The market's overflowing with DISC assessments, each promising to be the holy grail of hiring. But hold your horses! Before you pick one, channel your inner Sherlock Holmes and investigate:

- **Reliability:** Does this assessment deliver consistent results? You don't want a flaky tool that changes its mind every time someone takes it.
- **Validity:** Does it actually measure what it claims to measure (those awesome DISC styles)? Don't be fooled by a flashy package; make sure it's the real deal.
- **Relevance:** Is it tailored to the workplace and the specific roles you're hiring for? A generic personality test won't cut it; you need one that speaks your company's language.
- **Ease of Use:** Can your hiring team easily administer and interpret the results? And will candidates actually enjoy taking it (because no one likes a tedious test)?
- **Cost:** Let's be real, budgets matter. Weigh the costs and benefits to find the perfect assessment that doesn't break the bank.

Remember, choosing the right DISC assessment is like picking the perfect sidekick. It should complement your skills and make your job a whole lot easier.

B. The DISC Advantage: Your Hiring Dream Team

DISC isn't a solo act; it's part of a superhero team of hiring tools. Combine DISC insights with your trusty sidekicks:

- **Structured Interviews:** These are your deep dives into a candidate's past. Ask behavioral questions that uncover how they've flexed their DISC muscles in real-life scenarios. Get them talking about how they've tackled challenges, led teams, or persuaded clients.
- **Reference Checks:** It's time for a little detective work! Ask references targeted questions about the candidate's DISC style and how they play with others. You want to know if they've been a team player in the past.

But wait, there's more! Don't forget these powerful additions to your hiring arsenal:

- **Skills Assessments:** These tests give you the hard proof of a candidate's abilities. Do they have the technical know-how to save the day?
- **Trial Periods or Projects:** Let candidates show off their skills in a real-world setting. You'll get a glimpse of how they'll perform when the pressure's on.

By combining DISC with these trusty sidekicks, you'll have a 360-degree view of your candidates, making it easier to spot your next superhero hire.

C. Maximizing DISC's Impact: Beyond the Hiring Process

Congrats, you've successfully integrated DISC into your hiring process! But the journey doesn't end there. To truly maximize the impact of this powerful tool, consider these additional steps:

1. **Train Your Team:** DISC assessments aren't fortune cookies; they require skilled interpretation. Ensure your hiring managers and HR team are well-versed in DISC theory and application to avoid

misinterpretations or biases.
2. **Share the Insights:** Don't keep the DISC results a secret! Sharing them with candidates builds transparency and opens a dialogue about their strengths, potential challenges, and how they can best contribute to your team.
3. **Personalize Development:** Use DISC insights to create tailor-made onboarding, training, and development plans for your new hires. This shows you care about their individual growth and sets them up for success.
4. **Stay Ethical:** Always use DISC responsibly and ethically. Be transparent about how results will be used and avoid discriminating against any personality type.
5. **Keep It Fresh:** The workplace is constantly evolving, and so should your use of DISC. Regularly review and update your assessment practices to ensure they remain relevant and effective.

By embracing these practices, you'll turn DISC into a powerful catalyst for growth – not just for your new hires, but for your entire organization.

Disc - Your Secret Weapon For Building A Dream Team (And More!)

Congratulations, DISC master! You've now got a powerful tool in your leadership toolkit. But this is just the beginning of your journey to creating a workplace where personalities align, teams thrive, and productivity soars.

A. Recap: DISC, Your Hiring Hero

Remember, DISC isn't just about filling positions; it's about finding the *right* people. Those who not only have the skills, but the drive, the passion, and the personality to truly thrive in your company culture. By understanding their motivations, you're not just hiring employees, you're assembling a dream team – one where everyone feels valued, understood, and empowered to bring their best selves to work.

B. The Adventure Continues: Level Up Your DISC Expertise

This chapter has been your DISC crash course, but there's a whole world of knowledge waiting to be explored! Ready to dive deeper? Here are a few quests to embark on:

- **Hit the Books (or the Internet):** Uncover even more DISC secrets with in-depth resources – from insightful books and articles to engaging online courses.
- **Become a DISC Guru:** Consider getting certified in DISC! It's the ultimate power-up for HR professionals and managers, giving you the expertise to transform your workplace.
- **Know Thyself:** Keep exploring your own DISC style. The more you understand yourself, the better you'll understand others. It's a win-win for your communication and leadership skills!

C. DISC: Not Just for Hiring (But We'll Get to That...)

While we've focused on hiring, DISC is a multi-purpose tool with endless possibilities. It can be your trusty sidekick for ongoing team development, conflict resolution, and even boosting employee engagement.

But before we unveil those secrets, we need to make sure your dream team has the right skills to match their stellar personalities. So, get ready to embark on the next phase of our adventure...

D. The Journey Continues: Skills Assessment Awaits

In the next chapter, we'll tackle another crucial piece of the puzzle: **Skills Assessment: Beyond the DISC Profile.** While DISC illuminates the *who*, it's equally important to assess the *what* – the unique skills and knowledge each individual brings to the table. We'll explore the difference between hard and soft skills, dive into essential skill sets for various roles, and give you the lowdown on choosing the right assessments to build a team that's both talented *and* compatible.

CHAPTER 6: SKILLS ASSESSMENT: BEYOND THE DISC PROFILE

Introduction

Remember those earlier chapters where we waxed poetic about the power of a strong company culture? How it acts like a magnet for top-tier talent, a turbocharger for innovation, and a superglue that holds teams together? You bet – that thriving culture is your golden ticket to success.

But let's be real, culture isn't something you can just "set and forget" like your morning coffee maker. It's a living, breathing entity that needs constant care and feeding to adapt and thrive amidst the ever-shifting sands of the business world.

Enter the unsung hero of culture building: skills assessment. Sure, personality tests like DISC or MBTI are great for getting to know your employees on a personal level, but skills assessments take it a step further. They reveal the raw horsepower of your workforce – the actual competencies and capabilities that fuel productivity and growth.

Personality is knowing someone's favorite color, while skills are like understanding their ability to build a house. Both are important, but one is far more actionable when it comes to achieving results.

Skills assessments aren't just a personal development tool; they're a secret weapon for shaping your company's very essence. By getting a crystal-clear picture of the skills that reside within your teams, you can pinpoint hidden strengths, expose potential weaknesses, and make laser-focused decisions about who to hire, who to promote, and how to tailor training programs for maximum impact. The result? A culture of continuous learning and growth that propels your organization to new heights.

Cracking The Skills Code: Hard Skills Vs. Soft Skills – Why Both Matter Now More Than Ever

Let's talk about skills, the building blocks of any successful career. But not just *any* skills – we're diving into the dynamic duo that shapes the modern workforce: hard skills and soft skills. In this chapter, we're going to unravel the mystery behind these terms and show you why mastering both is the key to unlocking your full potential and future-proofing your career.

A. Skills Decoded: What's Hard, What's Soft, and Why You Need Both

Hard skills are the "know-how" – the concrete, measurable abilities your employees gain through education, training, or experience. These are the programming languages they've mastered, the financial analysis expertise they bring, or the project management methodologies they've perfected. These are the skills that shine on a resume and often serve as the initial criteria for evaluating a candidate's qualifications.

But let's not underestimate the power of soft skills – the "know-who." These are the interpersonal skills, the emotional intelligence, the ability to build rapport, influence others, and navigate complex workplace dynamics. Soft skills might not be as easily quantifiable, but they are the secret sauce that transforms a competent employee into a true asset to your organization.

The reality is, you need both hard and soft skills in your workforce. Hard skills provide the technical foundation for getting the job done, but soft skills are the X-factor that elevates performance, fosters collaboration, and drives innovation.

B. The Perfect Pairing: How Hard and Soft Skills Work Together

Imagine your star programmer can't communicate their elegant code solutions to the team, or your financial analyst struggles to explain complex concepts to clients. A brilliant mind without the ability to connect and collaborate is like a sports car with no steering wheel – impressive on paper, but ultimately ineffective.

That's because in today's workplace, hard skills are only half the equation. While technical expertise is undoubtedly the foundation for any role, soft skills are the X-factor that truly differentiates top performers. These interpersonal and cognitive abilities are the glue that holds teams together, the catalyst for innovation, and the driving force behind customer satisfaction.

Hard skills may get a candidate in the door, but soft skills determine how far they'll climb within your organization. They're the secret sauce behind stronger team dynamics, smoother collaborations, happier clients, and a workforce that's more engaged, creative, and resilient.

C. The Robot Revolution: Why Soft Skills Are Your Ace in the Hole

The rise of automation and AI is undeniable, but don't panic – the robots aren't here to take over the entire workforce. They're simply taking over the repetitive, mundane tasks, leaving ample space for your human talent to shine. This is where soft skills become your organization's secret weapon.

As AI and automation streamline routine work, the demand for uniquely human skills is soaring. Communication, creativity, empathy, adaptability – these are the qualities that machines simply can't replicate. And studies show that these soft skills aren't just a bonus anymore; they're the dealbreakers that set high-performing teams apart.

Look at the healthcare industry, for example. While medical professionals need their hard-earned clinical expertise, their ability to connect with patients on a human level, build trust, and explain complex information is just as critical for providing quality care.

Or consider the tech sector. Even the most brilliant coders won't get far without the ability to collaborate effectively, translate technical jargon for non-technical stakeholders, and adapt to rapidly evolving technologies.

And let's not forget the rise of remote and hybrid work. In these virtual environments, soft skills like communication, time management, and self-motivation have become non-negotiable.

The message is clear: soft skills are the key to unlocking your organization's full potential in the age of automation. By investing in the development of these skills, you're not just preparing your workforce for the future – you're giving your organization a competitive edge that no machine can match.

Comprehensive List Of Essential Skills

The business world is a whirlwind of change. Technology is advancing at breakneck speed, economic trends are shifting constantly, and the way we work is being redefined every day. To stay ahead of the game and lead your organization into a thriving future, you need a workforce that's not just adaptable, but ahead of the curve.

This chapter guides you through the essential skills that are the bedrock of every successful industry and role. But we're not stopping there. We're going beyond the basics to reveal the cutting-edge, emerging skills that are shaping the very future of work itself.

These are the skills that will empower your employees to tackle complex challenges, spark innovation, and lead your organization into a new era of growth and impact. By understanding and investing in these skills, you're not just building a team – you're building a powerhouse of talent that's ready for anything the future throws your way.

Whether you're looking to attract top-tier talent, upskill your existing team, or simply stay ahead of the curve, this comprehensive guide to essential and emerging skills will equip you with the knowledge you need to navigate the exciting and ever-evolving landscape of the modern workplace.

A. Categorization

Skills by Industry:

Each industry has its own unique set of essential skills, encompassing both technical expertise (hard skills) and interpersonal abilities (soft skills). Understanding these industry-specific requirements is crucial for individuals seeking to enter or advance within a particular field, as well as for organizations looking to build effective teams. Let's investigate the diverse skill sets demanded by some prominent industries:

- **Technology:**
  - **Hard Skills:** Programming languages (Python, Java, C++), cloud computing, cybersecurity, data analysis, software development, systems administration
  - **Soft Skills:** Problem-solving, adaptability, collaboration, communication, critical thinking
- **Healthcare:**
  - **Hard Skills:** Medical terminology, patient care, pharmacology, diagnostic procedures, electronic health records (EHR) systems
  - **Soft Skills:** Empathy, communication, teamwork, attention to detail, stress management
- **Finance:**
  - **Hard Skills:** Accounting, financial modeling, risk assessment, investment analysis, regulatory compliance
  - **Soft Skills:** Analytical thinking, decision-making, negotiation, communication
- **Real Estate:**
  - **Hard Skills:** Property valuation, market analysis, real estate law, negotiation, property management software
  - **Soft Skills:** Communication, negotiation, interpersonal skills, salesmanship, problem-solving

By Role: Skills for Professional Success

Sure, every industry has its own flavor of expertise. But what about the specific roles that make your organization tick? Whether it's the visionary leadership, the persuasive sales team, the creative marketing gurus, or the customer service champions, each role requires a unique blend of skills to truly shine.

Let's break down the essential hard and soft skills that fuel success in these critical positions. This is your playbook for understanding the diverse skill sets that will elevate your team's performance and drive your organization forward.

- **Leadership:**
  - **Hard Skills:** Strategic planning, budgeting, performance management, decision-making
  - **Soft Skills:** Communication, emotional intelligence, delegation, conflict resolution, vision
- **Sales:**
  - **Hard Skills:** Product knowledge, sales techniques, CRM software, negotiation, closing
  - **Soft Skills:** Persuasion, active listening, relationship building, resilience
- **Marketing:**
  - **Hard Skills:** Content creation, SEO, social media marketing, data analysis, campaign management
  - **Soft Skills:** Creativity, communication, storytelling, adaptability
- **Customer Service:**
  - **Hard Skills:** Product knowledge, CRM software, problem-solving
  - **Soft Skills:** Empathy, active listening, patience, communication

B. Emerging Skills: Navigating the Future of Work

The workplace is a whirlwind of innovation and disruption. Cutting-edge technologies, shifting economic tides, and evolving employee expectations are rewriting the rules of the game faster than ever before. To not only survive but lead in this dynamic landscape, your organization needs a workforce that's more than just adaptable – it needs to be *ahead* of the curve.

Welcome to the future of work. In this section, we'll uncover the emerging skills that are reshaping industries and redefining what it means to be a high-performing professional. These aren't your run-of-the-mill competencies; these are the game-changers that will empower your team to solve complex problems, ignite innovation, and drive your organization to new heights.

By understanding and investing in these in-demand skills, you'll transform your workforce into a powerhouse of talent that's ready to tackle any challenge, seize any opportunity, and lead your organization into a brighter tomorrow.

- **Artificial Intelligence (AI) and Machine Learning:** Understanding how these technologies work and how they can be applied to automate tasks, analyze data, and make predictions is becoming essential in various fields.
- **Data Science and Analytics:** The ability to collect, analyze, and interpret large datasets to gain insights and inform decision-making is in high demand across industries.
- **User Experience (UX) Design:** Creating intuitive and user-friendly interfaces for digital products and services is crucial for attracting and retaining customers.
- **Cloud Computing:** As more businesses move their operations to the cloud, the demand for professionals who can manage and maintain cloud infrastructure is growing.
- **Blockchain:** Understanding the fundamentals of blockchain technology and its potential applications in areas like finance, supply chain management, and healthcare is becoming increasingly valuable.
- **Internet of Things (IoT):** The ability to develop and manage connected devices and systems is in demand as the IoT continues to expand.
- **Cybersecurity:** With the growing threat of cyberattacks,

the need for professionals who can protect sensitive data and systems is more critical than ever.
- **Digital Marketing and Social Media:** The ability to leverage digital channels to reach and engage with customers is essential for businesses of all sizes.
- **Creativity and Innovation:** The ability to generate new ideas and approaches is increasingly valuable in a rapidly changing world.
- **Critical Thinking and Problem-Solving:** These skills are essential for tackling complex challenges and finding innovative solutions.
- **Emotional Intelligence:** Understanding and managing your own emotions, as well as empathizing with others, is crucial for building strong relationships and navigating workplace dynamics.
- **Adaptability and Flexibility:** The ability to learn quickly, embrace change, and thrive in ambiguity is essential in today's fast-paced business environment.

Mastering Skills Assessments: Your Blueprint For Unlocking Workforce Potential

Get ready to level up your talent management game! Skills assessments aren't just a box to check off during the hiring process – they will help your organization build a powerhouse team that can conquer any challenge. These are a diagnostic tool, revealing the hidden strengths and untapped potential within your workforce.

A. Choosing the Right Tool for the Job

Imagine trying to fix a leaky faucet with a hammer. It just doesn't work, right? The same principle applies to skills assessments – you need the right tool for the job. Lucky for you, there's a whole toolbox of assessments out there, each with its unique strengths.

1. Tests: Knowledge and Cognitive Powerhouses

When it comes to measuring raw knowledge, comprehension, or cognitive abilities, tests are your trusty sidekick. These assessments can take various forms, from quick multiple-choice quizzes to in-depth essays, and can be administered online or in person. Tests are a great fit for assessing technical knowledge (e.g., coding skills, financial regulations), language proficiency, or general aptitude. They're also useful for evaluating critical thinking, problem-solving, and decision-making skills in a standardized format.

What They're Good For:

- Objective measurement of knowledge and cognitive abilities
- Easy to administer and score
- Cost-effective for large-scale assessments

What They're Not So Good For:

- Limited in assessing practical skills and real-world application
- May not capture a candidate's creativity or ability to think outside the box
- Can be prone to test anxiety and may not accurately reflect performance in a work environment

2. Simulations: Experience the Real Deal

If you want to see how candidates handle real-world challenges, simulations are your ticket to a front-row seat. These assessments put candidates in the driver's seat of realistic scenarios, allowing you to observe their practical skills, problem-solving abilities, and decision-making prowess in action.

When to Use Them: Simulations are ideal for assessing skills that require hands-on experience and interaction with others. They're particularly effective for roles like sales, customer service, project management, and leadership, where the ability to navigate complex situations and interact with stakeholders is crucial.

What They're Good For:

- Assessing practical skills in a realistic context
- Evaluating problem-solving, decision-making, and interpersonal skills
- Providing a more engaging and interactive assessment experience

What They're Not So Good For:

- Can be more time-consuming and expensive to develop and administer
- May require specialized equipment or technology
- Results can be more subjective and difficult to

standardize

3. Work Samples: Show, Don't Tell

Want to cut through the fluff and see what a candidate can *really* do? Work samples are your answer. By reviewing past projects, portfolios, or code samples, you get a direct glimpse into a candidate's technical skills, creativity, and ability to deliver tangible results.

When to Use Them: Work samples are best suited for assessing skills that involve creating tangible outputs. They're particularly relevant for roles like software development, marketing, design, and writing, where a portfolio of past work can demonstrate a candidate's experience and capabilities.

What They're Good For:

- Directly assessing technical skills and ability to produce results
- Evaluating creativity and problem-solving in real-world projects
- Providing a more comprehensive picture of a candidate's experience and expertise

What They're Not So Good For:

- Can be time-consuming to review and evaluate
- May not be feasible for entry-level positions where candidates lack extensive experience
- Results can be subjective and may not be representative of future performance in a different context

4. Behavioral Assessments: Decoding Personality and Motivation

Curious about what makes your employees tick? Behavioral assessments can offer valuable insights into personality traits, motivations, and work style preferences. These assessments typically involve questionnaires, surveys, or interviews designed to uncover patterns of behavior and thinking.

When to Use Them: Behavioral assessments are useful for understanding how individuals are likely to interact with others, approach challenges, and handle stress. They can be helpful in identifying potential cultural fit issues, predicting job performance, and understanding how different personalities can complement each other on a team.

What They're Good For:

- Understanding personality traits, motivations, and work style preferences
- Predicting potential job performance and cultural fit
- Identifying potential strengths and weaknesses in interpersonal interactions

What They're Not So Good For:

- Results can be influenced by self-presentation bias
- Should not be used as the sole basis for hiring or promotion decisions
- May not capture the full complexity of an individual's personality and behavior

5. 360-Degree Feedback: The Panoramic View

Want a well-rounded perspective on an employee's performance? 360-degree feedback provides just that. By gathering feedback from multiple sources – peers, managers, and subordinates – you gain a holistic view of an individual's strengths, weaknesses, and overall impact on the team.

When to Use It: 360-degree feedback is particularly useful for assessing leadership, communication, and teamwork skills. It can also be used to identify areas for development and create targeted improvement plans.

What It's Good For:

- Providing a comprehensive view of an employee's

performance and impact
- Identifying blind spots and areas for development
- Encouraging open communication and feedback within the team

What It's Not So Good For:

- Can be time-consuming and resource-intensive to administer
- Results can be influenced by personal biases and relationships
- May not be appropriate for all roles or organizational cultures

The key is to choose the right assessment for the skills you're looking to measure. Hard skills often lend themselves to tests or work samples, while soft skills might be better captured through simulations or behavioral assessments. And for those all-important leadership roles, a combination of approaches might be the winning formula.

B. Validity and Reliability: The Gold Standard of Assessment

Let's be honest, a faulty assessment is about as useful as a chocolate teapot. That's why validity and reliability are the gold standard when it comes to choosing the right tools.

- **Validity:** The compass that ensures your assessment is pointing you in the right direction. A valid assessment actually measures what it claims to measure – no more, no less.
- **Reliability:** This is all about consistency. A reliable assessment will produce similar results for the same candidate over time and across different evaluators. It's like a trusty measuring tape that always gives you the same measurement.

So, how do you find assessments that meet these standards? Look for evidence from reputable sources like research studies, independent reviews, and professional organizations. Don't just take the provider's word for it – do your homework to ensure you're investing in tools that will actually deliver results.

C. Fairness and Bias: Leveling the Playing Field

Even the best-intentioned assessments can sometimes harbor hidden biases that disadvantage certain groups. It's like a race where not everyone starts at the same starting line.

- **Cultural Bias:** Assessments might unintentionally favor individuals from certain backgrounds due to language or cultural references.
- **Gender Bias:** Subtle biases can sneak into assessments, giving an unfair advantage to one gender over another.
- **Cognitive Bias:** Evaluators themselves might have unconscious biases that cloud their judgment.

To ensure a level playing field, choose assessments that are designed to minimize cultural bias, train your evaluators to recognize and overcome their own biases, and use multiple assessment methods to get a well-rounded picture of each candidate. Remember, fairness isn't just about ethics – it's about finding the best talent for your organization.

D. Beyond Hiring: Skills Assessments for Continuous Growth

Think skills assessments are only for hiring? Think again! These versatile tools are like Swiss Army knives, offering a range of benefits beyond the initial recruitment process.

- **Employee Development:** Identify individual strengths and weaknesses to create personalized training programs that help employees reach their full potential.
- **Performance Management:** Set clear expectations, provide targeted feedback, and identify high-potential employees who are ready for the next level.
- **Succession Planning:** Pinpoint future leaders based on

their skills and potential, ensuring a smooth transition when key positions become vacant.

By embracing skills assessments as an ongoing part of your talent management strategy, you're not just building a team – you're creating a culture of continuous learning and growth. And that's the kind of environment where top talent thrives, innovation flourishes, and your organization can achieve its boldest ambitions.

Inside The Playbook: How Top Companies Ace The Cultural Fit Game

Want to build a team that's more than just a group of employees, but a tribe of passionate, driven individuals who are all rowing in the same direction? It's not magic, it's about nailing cultural fit. Let's peek behind the curtain at three industry giants – Nvidia, Nike, and Blackrock – and see how they've cracked the code to create cultures that breed success.

Nvidia: Where "One Team, One Dream" Fuels Tech Domination

This global tech titan isn't just about mind-blowing graphics and AI; it's about encouraging a work environment that's as cutting-edge as their products. Their "One Team, One Dream" mantra isn't just a slogan – it's the lifeblood of their collaborative, high-performance culture.

- **Values-Based Hiring:** Nvidia isn't just looking for tech wizards; they want innovators, passionate problem solvers, and team players who are all-in on the company's mission. Their hiring process is a deep dive into a candidate's values, ensuring they're not just a skills match, but a cultural one too.
- **Promoting Collaboration:** At Nvidia, it's not about lone wolves, it's about the pack. They actively seek out individuals who thrive on collaboration, knowing that diverse perspectives and skillsets are the fuel for groundbreaking innovation.
- **Holistic Interviews:** Technical skills are a given, but Nvidia goes beyond the resume. Their interviews probe past experiences, revealing a candidate's work style, problem-solving approach, and alignment with Nvidia's values. They even have "Fit Check" interviews, where

potential teammates get to weigh in on the cultural vibe.

The result? A team of top-notch talent who are all-in on pushing the boundaries of technology, united by a shared passion and a hunger for innovation.

Nike: Where the "Just Do It" Spirit Reigns Supreme

Nike's not just about selling sneakers and sportswear; they're selling a lifestyle, a mindset. And that mindset is all about pushing limits, embracing challenges, and never settling for anything less than greatness.

- **Passion for Sport and Fitness:** Nike's not your typical 9-to-5 gig. They're looking for people who live and breathe sport and fitness – individuals who are genuinely stoked about helping athletes of all levels reach their peak potential.
- **Diversity as a Superpower:** Nike knows that a diverse team is a creative team. They actively seek out individuals from all walks of life, believing that a wide range of perspectives leads to better ideas and a more inclusive brand.
- **Unleashing the "Just Do It" Spirit:** Nike's behavioral interviews are designed to uncover stories of resilience, teamwork, and the unwavering drive to succeed. They want to know if you've got that "Just Do It" fire in your belly.
- **The "Nike Fit":** It's not just about being a good athlete; it's about embodying Nike's values. "Nike Fit" interviews gauge a candidate's alignment with the company's unique culture, ensuring a perfect match for both sides.

The payoff? A team that's as diverse as it is driven, united by a shared passion for sport and a relentless pursuit of excellence. It's this cultural synergy that keeps Nike at the top of its game, year after year.

BlackRock: A Culture of Performance and Purpose

The world's largest asset management firm isn't just about numbers; it's about people. BlackRock's culture is a blend of high performance, unwavering integrity, and a deep commitment to making a positive impact on the world.

- **Values at the Core:** BlackRock's core values aren't just buzzwords; they're the foundation of everything they do. Fiduciary duty, passion for performance, and a dedication to creating a better financial future are non-negotiable.
- **Intellectual Curiosity as a Must-Have:** In the fast-paced financial world, continuous learning is the only way to stay ahead. BlackRock seeks out individuals with an insatiable thirst for knowledge and a passion for exploring new ideas.
- **Rigorous Assessment of Skills and Fit:** BlackRock's interviews are a multi-faceted assessment. They probe past experiences to gauge cultural alignment, present real-world business scenarios to test problem-solving skills, and even offer informal "coffee chats" with employees for a firsthand look at the company culture.

The result? A team of sharp minds and big hearts, driven by a shared purpose and a commitment to excellence. It's this unique cultural blend that propels BlackRock's success and makes it a leader in the global financial landscape.

These case studies showcase the diverse approaches companies take to weave cultural fit into their hiring DNA. While the specifics may vary, the common thread is clear: a strong cultural fit is more than just a perk – it's the secret ingredient that unlocks extraordinary results.

Empowering Your Workforce: Strategies For Skills Assessment And Future-Readiness

Beyond simply assessing current skills, forward-thinking organizations must proactively address potential gaps and anticipate the evolving needs of the modern workplace. This section equips you with the tools and strategies to not only bridge existing gaps but also prepare your workforce for the challenges and opportunities that lie ahead.

A. Skills Gap Analysis: Sharpening Your Competitive Edge

Skills gap analysis is a health check for your organization's talent. It's a way to identify the difference between the skills your team currently possesses and the skills they *need* to conquer your business goals.

Several factors can contribute to these gaps:

- **Technological Whirlwind:** It's no secret that technology is moving at warp speed. What was cutting-edge yesterday might be obsolete tomorrow. New tech often demands new skills, leaving your team scrambling to catch up.
- **Industry Evolution:** Your industry isn't standing still either. Regulations change, customer expectations shift, and competitors are always breathing down your neck. Staying ahead requires a workforce that can adapt to new demands and seize emerging opportunities.
- **The Customer is Always Right (And They're Changing):** Customer preferences are a moving target. The rise of digital channels, for example, has created a demand for online customer service whizzes, social media marketing gurus, and data analysis experts.
- **Internal Shuffle:** Promotions and restructuring can shake things up. Suddenly, employees might find

themselves in roles that require skills they haven't yet mastered.

Understanding the root causes of skills gaps is your first step towards crafting a winning strategy. It's time to take a closer look at your team and ask yourself: What skills are we missing? Where are our strengths and weaknesses?

Assessing Your Current Team:

Here are some tried-and-true methods for getting a handle on your workforce's skills:

- **Employee Surveys & Self-Assessments:** Ask your employees directly! They often have valuable insights into their own strengths and areas for growth.
- **Performance Reviews & Feedback:** Regular performance evaluations are a goldmine of information. They can highlight areas where employees are excelling and where they might need a little extra support.
- **360-Degree Feedback:** This multi-perspective approach gathers feedback from peers, managers, and subordinates, giving you a comprehensive view of an employee's skills and potential.
- **Benchmarking:** Compare your team's skills against industry standards and job descriptions. Are you meeting the mark, or is there room for improvement?
- **Learning Management System (LMS) Data:** If you're using an LMS, dive into the data. It can reveal valuable insights into employee learning progress and pinpoint areas where additional training is needed.

Addressing Skills Gaps: Tailor-Made Solutions for a Stronger Team

Once you've identified the gaps, it's time to bridge them. But remember, a cookie-cutter approach won't cut it. Every employee is unique, with their own learning styles and preferences. By tailoring your development strategies to individual needs, you'll maximize engagement, accelerate learning, and build a team that's truly unstoppable.

Here are some proven strategies to close those skills gaps:

- **Targeted Training & Development:** Invest in programs that address your team's specific needs. Think online courses, workshops, conferences, or even personalized coaching.
- **Mentoring & Coaching:** Pair less experienced employees with seasoned pros who can share their wisdom and expertise.
- **Job Rotations & Cross-Training:** Give employees a chance to explore different roles and expand their skill sets.
- **Hiring for Specific Skills:** If the gaps are significant, consider bringing in fresh talent with the expertise you need.
- **Upskilling & Reskilling:** Empower your existing employees to learn new skills or update their existing ones through training, workshops, or online courses.

Remember, skills development isn't a one-and-done deal. It's an ongoing process that requires continuous assessment, adaptation, and investment. By making it a priority, you'll create a workforce that's not only equipped to meet today's challenges but also prepared to thrive in the ever-evolving world of work.

B. Future of Skills: Your Guide to Staying Ahead of the Curve

The workplace is a whirlwind of innovation and disruption. Cutting-edge technologies, shifting economic tides, and evolving employee expectations are rewriting the rules of the game faster than ever before. To not only survive but lead in this dynamic landscape, your organization needs a workforce that's more than just adaptable – it needs to be *ahead* of the curve.

Welcome to the future of work. In this section, we'll uncover the emerging skills that are reshaping industries and redefining what it means to be a high-performing professional. These aren't your run-of-the-mill competencies; these are the game-changers that will empower your team to solve complex problems, ignite innovation, and drive your organization to new heights.

By understanding and investing in these in-demand skills, you'll transform your workforce into a powerhouse of talent that's ready to tackle any challenge, seize any opportunity, and lead your organization into a brighter tomorrow.

The Skills Odyssey: Charting A Course For The Future

In this whirlwind adventure through the skills landscape, we've unearthed a treasure trove of insights that will empower your organization to conquer the ever-changing world of work. We've cracked the code on the dynamic duo of hard and soft skills, revealing their symbiotic relationship and the importance of cultivating both for a well-rounded, unstoppable team.

We've also journeyed into the heart of the evolving workplace, where automation, digital transformation, and remote work are reshaping the very definition of success. This thrilling expedition has revealed the emerging skills that are becoming the new currency of the modern workplace – skills like data wizardry, cybersecurity mastery, and digital marketing magic that will unlock a future of limitless possibilities.

To illustrate the power of these concepts in action, we looked at how companies like Nvidia, Nike, and BlackRock prioritize cultural fit in their hiring processes. Each company's unique approach reflects its values and the type of talent it seeks to attract and retain.

Nvidia, with its "One Team, One Dream" mentality, builds a collaborative culture where innovation and passion thrive. **Nike**, with its "Just Do It" spirit, seeks individuals who embody a passion for sports, diversity, and a relentless pursuit of excellence. **BlackRock**, with its culture of performance and purpose, prioritizes individuals who share their commitment to client service, continuous learning, and making a positive impact.

These examples demonstrate that cultural fit is not a one-size-fits-all concept. It's about finding the right match between an individual's values and aspirations and the unique culture of an organization.

But it doesn't stop there. We've explored the power of skills assessments – your secret weapon for understanding your workforce's capabilities, uncovering hidden talents, and making strategic decisions that fuel growth and innovation. And we've examined the art of assessing cultural fit, discovering how companies like Nvidia, Nike, and BlackRock create vibrant cultures that attract and retain top talent.

Remember, this is just the beginning of your skills odyssey. Armed with this newfound knowledge, it's time to embark on your own adventure. Craft a tailored skills assessment strategy that aligns with your organization's unique goals. Embrace a culture of continuous learning, where your team is empowered to grow, adapt, and conquer new horizons.

By investing in your people's skills, you're not just building a team; you're forging a powerhouse of talent that's ready to face any challenge, seize any opportunity, and propel your organization towards a future of limitless potential.

And now, the next chapter awaits: "The Interview Reimagined: DISC & Skills in Focus." Get ready to discover how to transform the interview process into a dynamic tool for assessing not only skills but also that elusive "it" factor – cultural fit. It's time to take your talent strategy to the next level and build a team that's not just good, but unstoppable.

CHAPTER 7: THE INTERVIEW REIMAGINED: DISC AS YOUR COMPASS FOR CULTURAL FIT

Disc: Hire More Superstars

Traditional job interviews are like looking at a map – they give you a basic overview, but they don't always reveal the hidden treasures or potential pitfalls that lie beneath the surface. To truly understand what makes a candidate tick, you need a tool that goes beyond the standard Q&A. Enter DISC – your X-ray vision into the heart of a candidate's motivations, behaviors, and potential for success within your company.

The Limitations of Traditional Interviews: The Tip of the Iceberg

Sure, traditional interviews can be helpful. They give you a glimpse into a candidate's skills, experience, and qualifications. But let's be honest, they often feel like a stilted conversation where everyone's putting on their best face. It's like trying to judge a fish by its ability to climb a tree.

The reality is, traditional interviews often fall short in several key areas:

- **Surface-Level Insights:** We can't judge a book by its cover, and the same goes for candidates. Questions about past achievements rarely uncover the deeper "why" behind their actions and choices.
- **Limited Predictive Power:** Just because someone excelled at their last job doesn't mean they'll automatically thrive in yours. A mismatch in values and work styles can derail even the most talented individuals.
- **Subjectivity and Bias:** Even the most seasoned interviewers have unconscious biases that can cloud their judgment.
- **The "Interview Persona":** Let's face it, most candidates are putting on a show. It's natural to emphasize strengths and downplay weaknesses, but this can mask potential red flags that could derail their success in your company.

DISC: Your Crystal Ball for Candidate Potential

DISC is the key to cracking the code of human behavior in the workplace. It's like having a crystal ball that reveals each candidate's unique drivers, allowing you to tailor your approach and make more informed hiring decisions.

With DISC, you'll discover:

- **The "Why" Behind the "What":** DISC uncovers the core motivators that drive each candidate's actions and decisions. You'll learn whether they're fueled by challenges (D), recognition (I), collaboration (S), or precision (C).
- **A Glimpse into the Future:** By understanding a candidate's DISC style, you can anticipate how they'll likely behave in your workplace. This allows you to predict if they'll thrive in your company's unique

environment and make proactive decisions to ensure their success.
- **Questions That Spark Authentic Responses:** Armed with DISC knowledge, you can tailor your interview questions to resonate with each candidate's individual style. This unlocks deeper insights and reveals their true potential within your organization.

Aligning DISC with Company Culture: The Secret Sauce

Hiring for cultural fit isn't just about finding someone who seems nice and friendly. It's a strategic imperative that can make or break your company's success. DISC acts as your compass, guiding you toward candidates whose values, communication styles, and work preferences align with your unique culture.

When you hire for cultural fit, you're not just filling a position; you're building a team of individuals who are:

- **Motivated:** They're driven by the same things that drive your company's success.
- **Productive:** They thrive in your work environment, leading to higher output and better results.
- **Committed:** They're loyal to your company's mission and values, reducing turnover and creating a more stable workforce.

DISC Beyond the Interview: A Tool for Growth

But DISC isn't just a hiring tool; it's a catalyst for growth. By understanding and leveraging DISC throughout the employee lifecycle, you can:

- **Personalize Onboarding and Development:** Create tailored experiences that help new hires quickly ramp up and feel valued.
- **Build Stronger Teams:** Encourage understanding and appreciation for diverse work styles, leading to improved

collaboration and communication.
- **Empower Leaders:** Equip managers with the insights they need to inspire and motivate employees with different personalities and preferences.

In short, DISC is a versatile tool that can transform your organization from the inside out. It's not just about hiring the right people; it's about creating a workplace where everyone feels valued, understood, and empowered to reach their full potential.

Understanding Disc In The Hiring Process: A Comprehensive Guide

Building on the foundational knowledge of the four DISC styles from previous chapters, we now go deeper into how these distinct personalities manifest in the workplace. Each style brings a unique set of strengths and challenges to the table, influencing interactions, work styles, and overall team dynamics. Recognizing these nuances is crucial for crafting effective interview questions and building high-performing teams.

Refresher on the Four DISC Styles: Tailoring Your Approach

Let's revisit the key characteristics, motivations, strengths, and potential challenges of each DISC style:

- **Dominant (D):**
    - **Key Traits:** Direct, decisive, results-oriented, competitive, risk-taking.
    - **Motivations:** Challenges, authority, control, tangible outcomes.
    - **Strengths:** Leadership, problem-solving, initiative, efficiency.
    - **Challenges:** Impatience, insensitivity, overly demanding, can overlook details.
- **Influential (I):**
    - **Key Traits:** Outgoing, enthusiastic, optimistic, persuasive, people-oriented.
    - **Motivations:** Recognition, social interaction, positive relationships, making a good impression.
    - **Strengths:** Building rapport, inspiring others, communication, collaboration, networking.
    - **Challenges:** Overly optimistic, impulsive, conflict-avoidant, may struggle with follow-through.

- **Steady (S):**
  - **Key Traits:** Patient, supportive, team-oriented, good listener, reliable, calm under pressure.
  - **Motivations:** Stability, security, harmony, helping others, making a genuine difference.
  - **Strengths:** Building trust, loyalty, teamwork, conflict resolution, creating a positive atmosphere.
  - **Challenges:** Resistant to change, indecisive, may avoid confrontation, difficulty with prioritization.
- **Conscientious (C):**
  - **Key Traits:** Analytical, detail-oriented, accurate, systematic, quality-focused.
  - **Motivations:** Mastery, expertise, accuracy, quality, following procedures.
  - **Strengths:** Critical thinking, problem-solving, attention to detail, data analysis, quality assurance.
  - **Challenges:** Perfectionism, overly critical, can get bogged down in details, may be seen as aloof.

Navigating Dynamics, Maximizing Strengths, and Promoting Collaboration

Understanding how these styles interact is key to building successful teams. Each style's strengths and challenges can complement or clash with others, influencing communication, collaboration, and overall productivity.

- **Strengths and Challenges:**
  - The D's drive can be balanced by the S's patience.
  - The I's enthusiasm can be tempered by the C's analytical approach.
  - The S's supportiveness can encourage the C's collaboration.
- **Communication Styles:** Recognizing different communication preferences is vital.
  - Direct communication from a D may be perceived as harsh by an S.

- o The I's expressive style may overwhelm a C who prefers concise facts.
- **Collaboration Strategies:** By understanding each other's styles, teams can leverage their differences for greater success.
  - o A D and I can combine their drive and enthusiasm for ambitious goals.
  - o An S and C can create a harmonious and high-performing team by blending support with expertise.

The key is to appreciate the value that each DISC style brings to the table and create an environment where everyone feels empowered to contribute their unique strengths. By doing so, you'll build a diverse and dynamic workforce that excels in both individual and collaborative achievements.

Communication Styles: The Key to Effective Collaboration

Understanding the communication preferences of each DISC style is crucial for building rapport, preventing misunderstandings, and encouraging collaboration.

- **Dominant (D):** Prefer direct, concise communication focused on results. They value efficiency and may come across as assertive or blunt.
- **Influential (I):** Communicate with enthusiasm and expressiveness, often focusing on building relationships and creating a positive atmosphere.
- **Steady (S):** Value open communication and active listening. They are patient and empathetic, seeking to understand others' perspectives.
- **Conscientious (C):** Prefer logical, data-driven communication. They are precise and may come across as reserved or formal.

Collaboration Strategies: Leveraging Differences for Success

While DISC styles can sometimes clash, they also offer

complementary strengths that, when harnessed effectively, can lead to exceptional team performance.

- **D-I:** The D style's drive and I style's enthusiasm can be a powerful combination for achieving ambitious goals.
- **D-S:** Balancing the D style's directness with the S style's supportive nature creates a productive and respectful environment.
- **D-C:** The D style's initiative combined with the C style's analytical skills can tackle complex challenges with precision and efficiency.
- **I-S:** The I style's persuasiveness and the S style's ability to build consensus create a collaborative and harmonious team dynamic.
- **I-C:** Balancing the I style's optimism with the C style's attention to detail ensures thoroughness and accuracy in project execution.
- **S-C:** The S style's support and the C style's expertise create a harmonious and high-performing team where everyone feels valued and contributes their best work.

By understanding these dynamics, you can promote an environment where diverse DISC styles not only coexist but also thrive, leveraging their unique strengths to achieve shared goals.

Pre-Screening Power:

Imagine this: You're drowning in a sea of resumes, each one boasting impressive qualifications. How do you quickly identify the hidden gems—the candidates who not only have the skills but also the right attitude and drive to succeed in your unique work environment?

DISC assessments can be your life raft. By administering these assessments early in the hiring process, you can quickly sift through the applicants and zero in on those whose DISC styles align perfectly with the role and your company's vibe.

This targeted approach saves you valuable time and resources, ensuring you're only interviewing the cream of the crop.

Post-Interview Clarity:

Even after a stellar interview, questions can linger. Did the candidate's enthusiastic answers reflect their true self, or were they just putting on a show? How will their personality mesh with the existing team?

DISC assessments provide that extra layer of insight, allowing you to analyze interview responses through a more objective lens. By comparing their assessment results with their interview performance, you gain a deeper understanding of their motivations, communication style, and how they'll likely fit into your company culture.

Team Building and Beyond:

But the power of DISC doesn't end with the hiring decision. By incorporating DISC assessments into onboarding, training, and team-building initiatives, you create a culture of understanding and appreciation for diverse personalities. This leads to smoother communication, enhanced collaboration, and a more cohesive, high-performing team.

Choosing the Right DISC Assessment: A Strategic Decision

Just like a superhero wouldn't settle for a flimsy cape, you shouldn't settle for just any DISC assessment. There are many options out there, each with its own strengths and weaknesses.

Popular choices like Everything DiSC and Extended DISC are well-respected in the field, but it's important to explore all your options. Consider your specific needs and budget, as well as the assessment's ease of use and interpretation resources.

You wouldn't use a hammer to fix a leaky faucet, right? Similarly, you want a DISC assessment that aligns with your specific hiring goals and organizational needs.

Remember, the right DISC assessment can be a game-changer, transforming your hiring process and propelling your team to new heights. So, take the time to research, compare, and choose wisely. It's an investment that will pay off in spades as you build a workforce that not only excels in their roles but also thrives in your company's unique environment.

- **Alignment with Organizational Needs:** Does the assessment offer features and reports that cater to your specific hiring goals, such as team dynamics analysis or leadership development insights?
- **Cost-Effectiveness:** Assessments vary in price, so weigh the investment against the potential return on investment (ROI) in terms of improved hiring decisions and team performance.
- **Usability:** Opt for an assessment that is user-friendly for both administrators and test-takers. If your team lacks extensive DISC experience, prioritize a model with intuitive interfaces and clear instructions.
- **Interpretation Resources:** A comprehensive assessment package should include detailed reports, training materials, and access to certified professionals who can help you decipher the results and apply them effectively.

Partnering with a DISC Guru: Your Shortcut to Hiring Success

Certified DISC professionals have navigated the ins and outs of this powerful tool, and their expertise can be invaluable as you embark on your own DISC journey. They'll help you steer clear of common pitfalls, unlock hidden insights, and ensure you're getting the most out of your investment.

With a DISC pro by your side, you can rest assured that assessments are administered and interpreted accurately. They'll help you decode the results, translating those seemingly complex graphs and charts into actionable insights that you can directly apply to your hiring decisions.

But their expertise goes beyond just interpretation. DISC professionals can also help you develop customized strategies for leveraging DISC insights throughout your entire talent management process. They'll show you how to create job descriptions that attract the right DISC styles, design interview questions that get to the heart of a candidate's motivations, and even tailor onboarding and training programs to ensure new hires thrive.

Choosing a DISC assessment without expert guidance is like trying to navigate a new city without a map. You might eventually find your way, but it's a lot easier (and less stressful) with a knowledgeable guide by your side.

Remember, selecting the right DISC assessment is a strategic decision that can have a lasting impact on your organization. By partnering with a certified DISC professional, you're not just making a smart investment; you're unlocking the full potential of DISC to build a thriving workplace culture where everyone feels valued, understood, and empowered to succeed.

So, before you dive headfirst into the world of DISC, consider enlisting the help of a seasoned expert. They'll be your trusted advisor, ensuring you make the most of this powerful tool and achieve your hiring goals with confidence.

Pre-Interview Disc Assessments: Your Hiring Process Crystal Ball

Imagine having a glimpse into a candidate's potential before they even step foot in the interview room. Pre-interview DISC assessments offer just that – a powerful tool to peek behind the curtain of resumes and cover letters, revealing the unique blend of traits that make each candidate tick.

The Power of Pre-Interview Assessments: A Head Start on Hiring Success

DISC assessments give you a sneak peek into a candidate's behavioral tendencies, allowing you to tailor your approach and make more informed decisions right from the start.

By administering DISC assessments early in the process, you unlock a treasure trove of information:

- **Strengths Spotlight:** Discover each candidate's unique superpowers – the areas where they'll naturally shine and excel in your organization.
- **Challenge Radar:** Pinpoint potential areas where a candidate might need extra support or development, ensuring you can proactively address any potential roadblocks.
- **Interviewing Cheat Sheet:** Armed with these insights, you can craft laser-focused interview questions that dive deep into the candidate's motivations, work style, and how they'll mesh with your team.

No more generic questions and canned responses – this is your chance to have a truly meaningful conversation that goes beyond the bullet points on a resume.

The Upside of Assessments: A Hiring Manager's Dream

Let's be real, the hiring process can be a time-suck. Sifting through countless resumes, scheduling interviews, and playing phone tag with references – it's enough to make anyone's head spin. But pre-interview DISC assessments can be a hiring manager's dream, offering a host of benefits:

- **Efficiency Boost:** Quickly identify candidates whose DISC styles align with the role and your company culture, saving you precious time and resources.
- **Targeted Interviewing:** No more fishing in the dark! Assessments arm you with the knowledge you need to ask relevant, pointed questions that reveal a candidate's true potential.
- **Unmasking Hidden Talents:** Discover the unique qualities and motivations that might not be apparent on a resume, giving you a more holistic view of each candidate.

A Word of Caution: The DISC Assessment Reality Check

While DISC assessments are undeniably powerful, they're not a magic bullet. It's important to be aware of their limitations and use them responsibly:

- **Bias Alert:** Interpreting assessment results can be tricky. We all have our own biases, and it's easy to project them onto the data. Remember, DISC is just one piece of the puzzle.
- **Honesty is the Best Policy:** Assessments rely on honest self-reflection, and let's face it, not everyone is brutally honest with themselves. Take the results with a grain of salt and use them as a starting point for further exploration.
- **Candidate Experience Matters:** Nobody likes jumping through hoops. Adding an extra step to the application process might deter some candidates, so communicate the value of the assessment and be mindful of their time.

Best Practices for a Smooth Assessment Journey

To get the most out of DISC assessments and ensure a positive candidate experience, follow these golden rules:

- **Be Transparent:** Openly communicate the purpose of the assessment, how the results will be used, and who will have access to them. This builds trust and sets clear expectations.
- **Assessments are a Sidekick, Not the Superhero:** Use assessments as a valuable tool to inform your interview process, not as the sole decision-maker. Combine them with in-depth interviews and reference checks for a well-rounded view of each candidate.
- **Call in the Experts:** When in doubt, consult a certified DISC professional. Their expertise ensures accurate interpretation of the results and helps you avoid common pitfalls.

By following these best practices, you can seamlessly integrate DISC assessments into your hiring process, transforming them into a powerful tool for identifying the perfect candidates who will not only excel in their roles but also contribute to your company's unique culture and long-term success.

Crafting Disc-Focused Interview Questions: Your Cheat Code For Unlocking Hidden Potential

So, you've got a handle on the four DISC styles and how they play out in the workplace. Now, it's time to turn that knowledge into a hiring superpower! By crafting interview questions that speak directly to each DISC style, you'll unlock a whole new level of understanding about your candidates – their motivations, their behaviors, and their untapped potential.

Forget those tired, generic interview questions that everyone has heard a million times. It's time to dig deeper, get creative, and uncover the real person behind the polished resume. We're talking about questions that reveal a candidate's core values, communication style, problem-solving prowess, and most importantly, whether they'll be a cultural rockstar at your company.

You're not just interviewing for a job, you're auditioning for a team member. And just like any good director, you need to find the perfect actor for each role. That's where DISC-focused interview questions come in. They're your cheat code for finding the hidden gems in your candidate pool, the ones who will not only excel in their roles but also elevate your entire team.

In this section, we'll give you the inside scoop on tailoring questions for each DISC style, dish out some juicy sample questions (both behavioral and situational), and share the secrets of gauging cultural fit like a pro. Whether you're hunting for a decisive leader, a persuasive influencer, a collaborative team player, or a detail-obsessed analyst, we've got you covered.

Behavioral Questions:

Focus on past experiences that demonstrate the candidate's skills and how they align with the DISC type.

- **Dominant (D):**
  - Describe a time when you had to make a quick decision under pressure. What was the situation, and how did you handle it?
  - Share an example of a time when you took charge of a challenging project and led it to success.
  - Tell me about a time when you faced resistance from others. How did you overcome it and achieve your objectives?
  - How do you typically handle setbacks or obstacles?
  - Describe your approach to delegation and empowering others.
  - What strategies do you use to stay motivated and focused on achieving goals?
  - Share an example of a time when you had to adapt to a rapidly changing situation.
  - How do you prioritize tasks and manage your time effectively?
  - Tell me about a time when you had to negotiate a difficult situation to achieve a positive outcome.
  - Describe a time when you had to take a calculated risk to achieve a significant result.

- **Influential (I):**
  - How do you build rapport and establish trust with new people?
  - Share an example of a time when you successfully persuaded others to see your point of view.
  - Tell me about a time when you had to collaborate with a difficult colleague or team member.
  - How do you approach building relationships with clients or customers?
  - Describe a time when you used your

communication skills to resolve a conflict or misunderstanding.
- What strategies do you use to stay motivated and energized in a team environment?
- Share an example of a time when you presented an idea or proposal to a group.
- How do you handle receiving feedback, both positive and constructive?
- Tell me about a time when you had to adapt your communication style to effectively communicate with someone from a different background or culture.
- Describe your approach to networking and building professional relationships.

- **Steady (S):**
  - Tell me about a time when you helped a team overcome a conflict or disagreement.
  - Share an example of how you've successfully collaborated with a diverse team to achieve a common goal.
  - How do you typically approach building consensus within a team?
  - Describe a time when you provided support to a colleague or team member who was struggling.
  - What strategies do you use to stay calm and composed under pressure?
  - Tell me about a time when you had to adapt to a change in your work environment or responsibilities.
  - How do you prioritize the needs of others while still meeting your own deadlines and goals?
  - Share an example of a time when you went above and beyond to help a customer or client.
  - Describe your approach to building trust and rapport with colleagues.

- How do you ensure that everyone on a team feels heard and valued?

- **Conscientious (C):**
  - Share an example of a project where you had to pay close attention to detail and ensure accuracy.
  - Tell me about a time when you had to analyze a complex problem and develop a solution.
  - Describe a time when you had to gather and interpret data to inform a decision.
  - How do you approach setting and achieving goals?
  - What strategies do you use to stay organized and efficient in your work?
  - Share an example of a time when you identified a potential risk or issue and took proactive steps to address it.
  - How do you handle receiving feedback on your work, especially constructive criticism?
  - Tell me about a time when you had to learn a new skill or technology quickly.
  - Describe your approach to research and information gathering.
  - How do you ensure that your work meets high standards of quality and accuracy?

Situational Questions: Putting Your Candidates to the Test (Hypothetically, of Course!)

While behavioral questions give you a glimpse into a candidate's past experiences, situational questions are your crystal ball for predicting their future performance. These questions aren't about theoretical knowledge; they're about real-world decision-making. How would they handle a tight deadline? What would they do if a project went off the rails? By gauging their responses, you'll get a front-row seat to their problem-solving skills, decision-making process, and ability to adapt on the fly – all crucial ingredients for success in your organization.

So, buckle up and get ready to put your candidates to the test! The following situational questions are designed to simulate a variety of challenges they might encounter in the role, from leading a team through a crisis to resolving a conflict with a disgruntled customer.

1. If you were leading a project that was falling behind schedule, how would you approach the situation?
2. Imagine you're working with a colleague who has a very different communication style from yours. How would you navigate that relationship?
3. How would you handle a situation where a customer or client was unhappy with your work?
4. If you were asked to take on a new project outside of your area of expertise, how would you approach it?
5. Describe a time when you had to deal with a difficult customer or client. How did you handle the situation?
6. If you were given a tight deadline and a limited budget, how would you prioritize your tasks and resources?
7. Imagine you're working on a team project, and there's a disagreement about the best approach. How would you help the team reach a consensus?
8. How do you handle a situation where you made a mistake?
9. What steps would you take to build trust with a new team?
10. If you were asked to present your work to a group of senior leaders, how would you prepare and deliver your presentation?

Cultural Fit Questions:

Skills and experience are important, sure, but let's face it: they're not the whole story. To truly thrive in a role, a candidate needs to vibe with your company's unique personality. That's where cultural fit questions come in.

These questions go beyond the "what" of a candidate's past accomplishments and dive into the "how" and "why" of their work style, values, and interpersonal mojo. They're designed to uncover whether a candidate will not only excel in the role but also genuinely enjoy coming to work every day.

Much like dating – you might be attracted to someone's looks or resume (the equivalent of skills and experience), but it's their personality and shared values that determine if there's a real spark (or a cultural fit).

By incorporating DISC-informed cultural fit questions into your interview, you'll get a sneak peek into how a candidate operates in the real world. Do they thrive in a collaborative environment? Are they driven by competition? Do they prioritize harmony and relationships?

With these insights, you can confidently determine whether a candidate is not just a good fit for the job, but a great fit for your company's unique culture. And that's the key to building a happy, productive, and long-lasting team.

1. Describe a time when you experienced a strong sense of cultural fit in a previous workplace. What made it a good fit?
2. Our company values are [list your values]. Can you share an example from your own experience where you demonstrated one or more of these values?
3. How would you describe your ideal work environment and company culture?
4. What are some of the most important things you look for in a company culture?
5. How do you think your personal values align with our company's values?
6. Can you tell me about a time when you faced a

conflict with a colleague or manager? How did you handle it?
7. What are your thoughts on collaboration and teamwork? How do you typically approach working with others?
8. Describe a time when you took the initiative to solve a problem or improve a process. What was your approach?
9. How do you handle feedback? Can you share an example of a time when you received constructive criticism and how you responded?
10. What questions do you have for me about our company culture?

Interpreting Disc Assessments And Using Results Effectively

Understanding DISC assessments isn't just about labeling people with four letters; it's about unlocking the secrets of their unique personalities and how they'll shine in your workplace. DISC, when properly used, reveals hidden motivations, strengths, and potential challenges that a resume alone can't capture.

Understanding DISC Profiles: Beyond the Surface

DISC isn't about putting people in boxes; it's about appreciating the rich tapestry of human behavior. Each style exists on a spectrum, with individuals expressing different levels of intensity for each factor. While someone might have a dominant "D" style, they also possess traces of the other three, creating a unique blend of traits.

It's like those cool DNA tests that reveal your ancestry – you might be mostly Irish, but you also have a dash of Italian and a sprinkle of Scandinavian. DISC works the same way, uncovering the complex mix of personality traits that make each candidate one-of-a-kind.

Decoding a DISC graph is a bit like reading a treasure map. The dot placements, shading, and other visual cues reveal clues about the dominance of each style. Once you know how to interpret these graphs, you can quickly identify a candidate's primary and secondary styles, giving you a better understanding of their overall behavior and how they might approach their work.

But remember, no single DISC style is the "best." Each style brings unique strengths to the table, and a diverse team with a variety of styles can be a recipe for success. Just as a gourmet meal is made up of different ingredients, a high-performing team needs a diverse mix of personalities to truly excel.

Finally, it's important to be aware that different DISC assessment models exist, each with its own terminology and reporting style. They are different dialects of the same language – the core message is the same, but the way it's expressed might vary slightly.

Analyzing Interview Responses Through a DISC Lens: Decoding the Hidden Message

Now that you've mastered the DISC lingo, it's time to put it into practice. When you're interviewing a candidate, pay close attention to their words, tone of voice, and body language. Are they speaking with the directness and confidence of a High D, or the enthusiasm and charm of a High I? Do they emphasize collaboration and teamwork like a High S, or focus on details and accuracy like a High C?

By connecting their interview responses to their DISC profile, you can unlock a deeper understanding of their motivations, communication style, and potential fit within your team. You'll be able to anticipate how they'll approach their work, interact with colleagues, and respond to challenges.

Applying DISC Insights to Hiring Decisions: The Path to a Dream Team

Now comes the fun part: using your DISC knowledge to build a dream team that's perfectly aligned with your company's unique culture.

You want a mix of powers and personalities that complement each other, not clash. DISC helps you identify candidates whose natural tendencies and work preferences harmonize with your company's vibe, creating a team that's more than the sum of its parts.

But DISC isn't just about cultural fit; it's also about predicting job performance. While it's not a foolproof method, DISC can offer valuable clues about a candidate's likely strengths and weaknesses in a particular role. This allows you to proactively address potential challenges and tailor their onboarding and development plans to maximize their potential.

Practical Tips for Integrating DISC Assessments: Your Roadmap to Success

Incorporating DISC assessments into your hiring process is easier than you might think. With a bit of forethought and clear communication, this powerful tool can seamlessly integrate into your existing workflow, providing valuable insights that enhance your decision-making.

Timing is Key: Consider the optimal time to introduce the assessment. If you have a large pool of applicants, using DISC early on can be a helpful screening tool, allowing you to focus on those whose styles best align with the role. Alternatively, introducing the assessment before final interviews allows you to tailor your questions based on the candidate's DISC profile, leading to more meaningful conversations.

Transparency Builds Trust: Be upfront and honest with candidates about the assessment's purpose. Explain how the results will be used and who will have access to them. This transparency not only builds trust but also sets clear expectations, ensuring candidates feel respected and valued throughout the process.

Ethical Use is Non-Negotiable: DISC assessments should never be used to discriminate against any candidate. Respect their privacy by keeping results confidential and only sharing them with those directly involved in the hiring process. Focus on how a candidate's unique DISC style can contribute to their success in the role and within your organization.

By following these simple yet powerful tips, you can smoothly integrate DISC assessments into your hiring process. This strategic move will not only streamline your efforts but also empower you to make more informed decisions, ultimately leading to a more engaged, productive, and culturally aligned workforce.

The Art Of The Disc-Informed Interview: Mastering The Human Connection

Active Listening and Rapport Building: Your Interviewing Superpowers

Let's be honest, interviews can be nerve-wracking for both the interviewer and the candidate. But here's the secret: the best interviews feel more like engaging conversations than interrogations. And the key to unlocking those conversations? Active listening and rapport building – your interviewing superpowers.

Active listening is more than just nodding along while someone speaks. It's about truly tuning in, understanding the message beyond the words, and making the candidate feel heard and valued. This creates a positive connection, encouraging them to open up and reveal their true potential.

So, how do you activate your superpowers? It's a mix of subtle cues and intentional actions:

- **Be a Non-Verbal Ninja:** Make eye contact, nod to show you're following along, and use open body language to convey approachability. These small gestures can make a big difference in putting the candidate at ease.
- **Speak the Language of Affirmation:** Sprinkle in phrases like "I see" or "Tell me more" to show you're actively engaged in the conversation. Paraphrase what you've heard to confirm your understanding, and ask open-ended questions that invite the candidate to elaborate.
- **Tailor Your Style:** Just like you wouldn't wear a tuxedo to a beach party, you shouldn't use the same communication style with every candidate. Adapt your approach based on their DISC style:
    - **D:** Get straight to the point, focus on the challenge,

and let them take the lead.
- **I:** Be enthusiastic, share personal anecdotes, and let them shine in the spotlight.
- **S:** Create a relaxed atmosphere, listen patiently, and offer reassurance.
- **C:** Be well-prepared, provide detailed information, and allow them time to process and analyze.

Virtual Vibes: In the era of remote work, mastering virtual rapport is essential. Ensure a strong internet connection, good lighting, and minimal background noise. Since non-verbal cues can be harder to read on screen, be extra mindful of your own body language and facial expressions. And don't be afraid to get creative! Use interactive elements like screen sharing or virtual whiteboards to keep the conversation engaging.

Unbiased Evaluation: The Fair Play Rulebook

DISC can be an invaluable tool, but it's important to remember that it's just one piece of the puzzle. To make truly fair and objective hiring decisions, you need to follow the fair play rulebook:

- **Know Thyself:** Be aware of your own DISC style and how it might unconsciously influence your perceptions. We all have biases, but recognizing them is the first step towards overcoming them.
- **Structure for Success:** Use standardized interview questions and a clear scoring rubric to reduce subjectivity and ensure consistency across candidates.
- **Two Heads are Better Than One (or More):** Incorporate multiple interviewers with diverse DISC styles to get a 360-degree view of each candidate. This helps to uncover strengths and weaknesses that a single interviewer might miss.
- **Data Doesn't Tell the Whole Story:** While DISC assessments provide valuable insights, don't let them be the sole decider. Consider the entire interview experience,

references, and the candidate's overall potential.

Leveraging DISC for Deeper Insights: The Detective Work Begins

With DISC as your detective's magnifying glass, you can analyze interview responses and uncover a deeper understanding of each candidate's potential for success.

- **Read Between the Lines:** Pay attention to how candidates communicate. Are they direct and assertive (D), enthusiastic and expressive (I), calm and patient (S), or reserved and analytical (C)? Their communication style can reveal a lot about how they'll interact with colleagues and clients.
- **Crack the Problem-Solving Code:** Observe how they approach hypothetical scenarios. Do they take charge and make quick decisions (D), brainstorm creative solutions (I), seek consensus (S), or carefully analyze all the data before acting (C)? This gives you a glimpse into their decision-making process and how they'll handle challenges on the job.
- **Flexibility is Key:** Explore how they react to change and uncertainty. Are they adaptable and open to new ideas, or do they prefer a predictable routine? This will tell you how well they'll navigate the ever-changing landscape of your workplace.

Post-Interview Disc Debrief: Cracking The Code For The Perfect Fit

The interview is over, but your work isn't done yet. Now it's time to gather your detective team (aka your fellow interviewers) and put on your Sherlock Holmes hats. The post-interview DISC debrief is where the real magic happens, where you transform those raw interview impressions and assessment results into a crystal-clear picture of each candidate's potential.

The Debriefing Huddle: More Than Just Water Cooler Gossip

This isn't your average water cooler chat. The post-interview debrief is a strategic session where you and your fellow interviewers, ideally representing a mix of DISC styles, come together to share observations, dissect responses, and ultimately, crack the code of each candidate's potential fit.

It's like piecing together a puzzle: each interviewer brings a unique perspective, and by combining your collective wisdom, you can create a more complete picture than any one person could alone. So, gather your notes, queue up those interview recordings, and get ready to dive deep into the data.

Analyzing Responses Through a DISC Lens: The X-Ray Goggles

By analyzing each candidate's responses through a DISC lens, you'll uncover hidden patterns and insights that go beyond the surface.

Were they direct and to-the-point (D)? Bubbly and enthusiastic (I)? Thoughtful and patient (S)? Or perhaps meticulous and detail-oriented (C)? By recognizing these communication styles and comparing them to their assessment results, you'll gain a deeper understanding of their motivations, strengths, and potential challenges.

Evaluating Cultural Fit: The Matchmaker's Toolkit

Now for the ultimate compatibility test: evaluating cultural fit. This is where DISC really shines. By comparing the candidate's profile to the dominant DISC styles in your company and the specific team they'd be joining, you can assess whether their values, work style, and communication preferences are in harmony with your culture. It's like finding that perfect puzzle piece that not only fits the job description but also completes the beautiful picture of your team.

Remember, a mismatch can lead to frustration, disengagement, and even turnover. But a good match can ignite a spark of passion and productivity that benefits both the employee and the organization.

Making Informed Hiring Decisions: The Final Verdict

After all this analysis and discussion, it's time to make the call. Remember, DISC is just one tool in your toolbox. Weigh the insights gained from DISC alongside other factors, like skills, experience, and references. Discuss the candidate's potential strengths and challenges, and how their DISC style might impact their performance and interactions with colleagues.

This collaborative process ensures you're making the most informed decision possible. It's not just about filling a vacancy; it's about finding the right person who will not only excel in the role but also contribute to your company's vibrant culture and long-term success.

Crafting Your Dream Team: The Art Of Candidate Personas

Forget vague job descriptions and hit-or-miss recruitment tactics. It's time to take a page out of the marketing playbook and create candidate personas – detailed profiles of your ideal hires that go beyond skills and experience.

The Power of Personas: Your Hiring Crystal Ball

Just like marketers create customer personas to understand their target audience, you can craft candidate personas to unlock the secrets of your ideal hires. By identifying their personality traits, motivations, and even their favorite coffee shops (okay, maybe not that last one), you gain a deeper understanding of who they are, what drives them, and what they're looking for in a workplace.

With this insider knowledge, you can:

- **Write Job Descriptions That Sizzle:** Forget boring, generic postings. Use your personas to craft descriptions that speak directly to your ideal candidates, showcasing your company's unique culture and the exciting challenges that await them.
- **Find Your People, Faster:** No more wasting time on unqualified applicants. By tailoring your outreach messages and sourcing strategies to your target personas, you'll attract the right people right off the bat.
- **Make Smarter Hiring Decisions:** Say goodbye to gut feelings and guesswork. With a clear picture of your ideal candidate, you can make confident, data-driven decisions that lead to long-term success.

Interviewing Hiring Managers: The Inside Scoop on Superstar Employees

Your first stop on this persona-building adventure? The hiring managers who work day in and day out with your current superstars. They're the ones who know firsthand what it takes to excel in each role.

So, grab a coffee (or a virtual one) and have a chat with your hiring managers. Ask them about:

- **The A-Team:** Who are the top performers in this role, and what makes them so awesome?
- **Secret Ingredients:** What specific skills, behaviors, or personality traits set these superstars apart?
- **Origin Stories:** Where did they come from? What's their educational background, previous experience, and career path?
- **Inner Drive:** What motivates them? What challenges do they face, and how do they overcome them?

The more you learn about your current rockstars, the clearer your ideal candidate persona will become. So, don't be afraid to ask those probing questions and dig deep. The insights you gain will be invaluable as you embark on your quest to build the ultimate dream team.

Ask open-ended questions that encourage them to elaborate on their observations:

- Who are your top performers in this role?
- What sets them apart from others? What do they do differently?
- What are their backgrounds? Where did they work previously? What kind of education do they have?
- What motivates them and what challenges do they face?
- What personality traits make them successful?
- What are their career goals and aspirations?

Probe deeper by asking about specific instances where a top performer exceeded expectations, the common characteristics of successful hires, and the biggest challenges in filling this type of position.

Interviewing Top Performers: Getting Firsthand Insights

To truly understand what makes a top performer tick, there's no substitute for speaking with them directly. Their firsthand insights can reveal invaluable information about their motivations, preferences, and career paths.

Engage in open-ended conversations, asking questions like:

- How did you discover this job opportunity?
- What attracted you to our company and this specific role?
- What aspects of your work do you find most and least enjoyable?
- What are your career goals and aspirations?
- How do you stay up-to-date with industry trends and developments?

Encourage them to describe their ideal work environment and company culture, and seek their advice for someone considering this career path.

Interviewing Internal Customers: Understanding the Role's Impact

Gaining feedback from those who interact with the role, whether they are colleagues, managers, or clients, can provide a broader perspective on the position's requirements and challenges.

Ask questions like:

- How does this role impact your work and team?
- What are the most important qualities you look for in someone in this role?
- What challenges have you faced in working with people in this position?
- What are your expectations of someone in this role?

Be sure to select internal customers who have regular and

meaningful interactions with the target position.

From Data to Dream Hire: Creating Your Candidate Personas

You've done the legwork: interviewed your rockstar employees, picked the brains of your hiring managers, and gathered insights from the people who interact with the role on a daily basis. Now, it's time to turn that mountain of data into something truly magical: your ideal candidate personas.

This is your "Frankenstein moment," but instead of creating a monster, you're assembling the perfect employee – a composite sketch of the ideal skills, experience, motivations, and personality traits that will make them a superstar in your organization.

Building the Perfect Specimen:

Start by sifting through your interview notes and data, looking for patterns and common threads. What traits do your top performers share? What motivates them? What are their communication styles? Combine these qualitative insights with any quantitative data you've collected, like performance reviews or turnover rates, to create a well-rounded picture of your ideal candidate.

Next, it's time to bring your persona to life! Give them a name, a backstory, and even a photo if you're feeling creative. The more detailed and relatable your persona, the more effective it will be in guiding your hiring decisions.

Putting Your Personas to Work:

Your candidate personas are more than just pretty pictures on a wall. They're powerful tools that can revolutionize your recruitment efforts:

- **Job Descriptions That Woo:** Ditch the generic language and craft job descriptions that speak directly to your ideal candidates, showcasing the unique aspects of your

company culture and the exciting challenges that await them.
- **Targeted Talent Search:** Forget casting a wide net and hoping for the best. Use your personas to pinpoint exactly where your ideal candidates are hanging out online, tailoring your outreach messages to resonate with their specific interests and career goals.
- **Hiring with Confidence:** Say goodbye to gut feelings and hello to data-driven decisions. Your personas will act as a filter, helping you quickly identify the candidates who are the best fit for your team and your company's overall goals.

Keeping Your Personas Fresh:

Remember, your ideal candidate personas aren't set in stone. As your company evolves, so too should your personas. Regularly revisit and update them based on feedback from new hires, changes in your industry, or shifts in your company culture.

By investing the time and effort to create and maintain accurate candidate personas, you're not just making your hiring process easier; you're setting your organization up for long-term success. You'll attract top talent who are genuinely excited about your company, leading to higher engagement, productivity, and overall happiness in the workplace.

The Pitfalls Of Over-Assessment: Avoiding The Data Dumps And Finding The Right Fit

In the quest for the perfect hire, it's easy to get caught up in a whirlwind of assessments. After all, more data must mean better decisions, right? Not so fast! Bombarding candidates with an endless stream of tests and evaluations can backfire, creating confusion, frustration, and ultimately, driving away top talent.

The "Too Much Data" Problem: When Information Overload Leads to Decision Burnout

Too much information, too fast, can leave you feeling overwhelmed and unable to make sense of it all. The same goes for hiring managers who are drowning in assessment data. Instead of gaining clarity, they can experience "analysis paralysis," second-guessing themselves and delaying crucial decisions.

Remember, the goal is to gain *insightful* data, not just amass a mountain of numbers. Each assessment should serve a specific purpose, shedding light on a particular aspect of the candidate's potential. Avoid generic assessments that don't provide actionable information and focus on those that directly measure the skills, knowledge, and personality traits that are essential for success in the role.

The Candidate Experience: A Delicate Dance of Respect and Efficiency

Let's face it, nobody enjoys jumping through hoops. A lengthy and tedious assessment process can leave candidates feeling frustrated and undervalued. In today's competitive talent market, top performers have plenty of options, and they won't hesitate to walk away from a company that doesn't value their time.

Strive for a streamlined and respectful assessment process. Clearly communicate the purpose of each assessment, provide a realistic timeline, and offer regular updates to keep candidates engaged. Remember, you're not just evaluating them; they're also evaluating you.

Analysis Paralysis: The Perils of Overthinking

Ironically, too much data can be as unhelpful as too little. When faced with an overwhelming amount of information, it's easy to overthink and second-guess your instincts. This analysis paralysis can lead to missed opportunities, as you might overlook a talented candidate who doesn't fit perfectly into a pre-defined mold.

Don't let the numbers overshadow your human judgment. Assessments are valuable tools, but they shouldn't replace your intuition and experience as a hiring manager. Remember, hiring is ultimately about finding the right *person*, not just the right data points.

Finding the Sweet Spot: A Balanced Approach

The key to effective assessment is striking the right balance between data and intuition. Prioritize quality over quantity, choosing assessments that directly measure the most critical factors for success in the role. Streamline the process to respect candidates' time and combine assessment results with other valuable information, such as interviews, references, and work samples.

Don't be afraid to think outside the box. Explore alternative assessments like trial projects or work simulations that allow candidates to showcase their skills in a real-world context. And most importantly, engage in meaningful conversations with candidates to uncover their motivations, values, and aspirations beyond what any assessment can reveal.

By taking a holistic approach, you'll not only make better hiring decisions but also create a positive candidate experience that strengthens your employer brand and attracts top talent. Remember, the goal is to find the right fit, not just the perfect score.

Disc As Your Hiring Compass – Navigating Toward A Thriving Workforce

As we've explored throughout this chapter, DISC offers a powerful framework for transforming your hiring process. By moving beyond traditional methods and embracing DISC, you gain a deeper understanding of candidates' motivations, behaviors, and potential for success within your organization.

DISC empowers you to:

- **Uncover Hidden Potential:** Go beyond surface-level qualifications to reveal a candidate's true drivers and how they are likely to perform in your unique workplace.
- **Assess Cultural Fit:** Identify individuals whose values, work styles, and communication preferences align with your company's culture, ensuring a harmonious and productive environment.
- **Tailor Interviewing and Onboarding:** Craft targeted questions and personalized onboarding experiences that resonate with each candidate's individual style, setting them up for success from day one.
- **Reduce Bias and Subjectivity:** Implement structured interviews and DISC assessments to mitigate unconscious biases and ensure fairness in your hiring decisions.
- **Build Stronger Teams:** Promote understanding and appreciation for diverse DISC styles, leading to improved communication, collaboration, and conflict resolution within your teams.
- **Increase Employee Engagement and Retention:** Create a more engaged and loyal workforce by hiring individuals who not only possess the right skills but also feel valued, understood, and empowered to contribute their unique talents.

Building a Dream Team: It's Not Just About Skills, It's About Vibe

Throughout this book, we've hammered home the idea that company culture isn't some magical phenomenon that just *happens*. It's a living, breathing entity that you actively create, nurture, and shape. And the people you bring on board? They're either fuel for the fire, igniting your culture and making it burn brighter, or they're a wet blanket, dampening the flames and leaving you with a lukewarm mess.

Hiring isn't just about filling seats; it's about finding the missing puzzle pieces that complete the picture of your ideal team. The wrong fit can be a disaster, even if they have all the right qualifications on paper. It's like trying to force a square peg into a round hole – it's just not going to work.

That's where DISC comes in, your trusty guide through the wild world of personalities and workplace dynamics. But DISC isn't just a one-trick pony. To truly unleash its power, you need a holistic hiring strategy that puts culture at the center of every decision.

It all starts with getting crystal clear on your ideal candidate. Sure, skills and experience are important, but they're just the tip of the iceberg. You need to dig deeper, uncovering their motivations, their communication style, their values – basically, the secret sauce that makes them tick.

You wouldn't swipe right on someone just because they have a good job and a nice smile, would you? You'd want to know more about their personality, their interests, their sense of humor. The same goes for hiring. You need to find that perfect match – someone who not only has the skills to get the job done but also vibes with your company culture.

And that's where the real magic happens. When you align your hiring strategy with your company culture, you're not just building a team, you're creating a community. A group of individuals who share the same values, work together seamlessly, and genuinely enjoy coming to work each day. That's the recipe for a thriving, high-performing, and downright fun workplace.

Crafting Your Ideal Candidate Persona

To achieve this understanding, create detailed candidate personas that go beyond simple job descriptions. These personas should encompass:

- **DISC Profiles:** What DISC styles thrive in your company culture and the specific role?
- **Skills and Experience:** What are the essential technical and soft skills required for success?
- **Cultural Fit Considerations:** What values, work styles, and communication preferences align with your organization?

By painting a comprehensive picture of your ideal candidate, you lay the groundwork for a targeted and effective hiring process.

Aligning Every Step of the Process

Once you have defined your ideal candidate personas, it's time to align every step of your hiring process with these profiles:

- **Job Descriptions:** Craft descriptions that resonate with your target candidates by using language, tone, and keywords that speak to their motivations and values.
- **Sourcing Strategies:** Utilize the information in your personas to identify the platforms and communities where your ideal candidates are most likely to be found.
- **Interviewing:** Develop DISC-informed interview questions that assess not only skills and experience but also cultural fit and alignment with the role's requirements.

- **Onboarding:** Create personalized onboarding experiences that welcome new hires and cater to their individual needs and preferences, ensuring they feel valued and supported from day one.
- **Ongoing Development:** Implement targeted training and development programs that align with each employee's DISC style, encouraging their growth and maximizing their potential within your organization.

The Path to Continuous Improvement: Your Ever-Evolving Hiring Compass

Building a hiring process that perfectly aligns with your company culture isn't a destination—it's an exciting journey of continuous growth and evolution. Just as your company adapts to new challenges and opportunities, so too should your approach to attracting and retaining top talent.

Your hiring process needs regular check-ups, tune-ups, and the occasional makeover to ensure it's always performing at its best. By actively seeking feedback from new hires, analyzing data, and staying attuned to the ever-changing needs of your organization, you can fine-tune your process to perfection.

This dynamic and intentional approach to hiring will pay off in spades. You'll build a workforce that's not just a collection of skilled individuals but a team of passionate, engaged employees who are deeply aligned with your company's values and goals. And that, my friend, is the secret sauce for a truly thriving organization.

More Than a Hiring Tool

But hold on, we're not done yet! DISC is like that gift that keeps on giving, offering a treasure trove of benefits that extend far beyond the initial hiring process. DISC as a Swiss Army knife for your organization. It's not just about picking the right people; it's about empowering them to thrive. In the next chapter, we'll dive deeper into how DISC can be leveraged to supercharge your leadership development, build stronger teams, and even resolve conflicts like a pro. Get ready to discover how DISC can transform your workplace into a powerhouse of collaboration, innovation, and unstoppable success.

Level Up Your Leadership: DISC empowers leaders to become maestros of motivation. By understanding the different personalities on their team, they can tailor their approach to inspire each individual, creating a symphony of productivity and engagement.

Build a Dream Team: Forget boring team-building exercises. DISC helps you create a team that's more than just a collection of individuals – it's a powerhouse of diverse talents working together in harmony. Through DISC-based workshops and activities, you can turn conflict into collaboration and unlock your team's full potential.

Turn Conflict into Collaboration: Let's face it, conflict is part of life, even in the workplace. But with DISC, you can transform those clashes into opportunities for growth and understanding. By recognizing how different DISC styles approach conflict, you can defuse tense situations, find common ground, and turn disagreements into creative solutions.

Unleash Individual Potential: Imagine a workplace where everyone is self-aware, confident in their strengths, and actively working on their weaknesses. DISC makes this a reality by empowering individuals to understand their own unique style and how it impacts their interactions with others. This leads to stronger relationships, improved communication, and a more fulfilling work experience.

Embrace Diversity, Amplify Success: The beauty of DISC is that it celebrates diversity. By recognizing and valuing the unique contributions of each DISC style, you create a dynamic, innovative, and resilient workforce. It's like having a team of superheroes, each with their own special powers, working together to save the day (or, in this case, achieve your company's goals).

DISC is more than just a tool – it's a mindset, a philosophy, a way of life. By embracing DISC, you're not just building a team; you're cultivating a culture of growth, collaboration, and mutual respect. And that's the kind of environment where everyone can thrive.

But DISC's transformative power doesn't stop there. In the next chapter, we'll take a deep dive into how DISC can be help your organization resolve conflicts and turning disagreements into opportunities for growth and understanding. Get ready to discover how DISC can empower your team to navigate even the most challenging situations with grace, empathy, and a dash of humor.

Case Studies: Disc In Action

Case Study 1: Warby Parker: Seeing Eye to Eye on Cultural Fit

Warby Parker, the disruptive eyewear retailer, has a reputation for its strong company culture, characterized by creativity, collaboration, and a customer-centric approach. To ensure new hires embody these values, Warby Parker incorporates DISC assessments into its interview process.

- **Pre-Interview Assessments:** Candidates complete a DISC assessment before their first interview, providing hiring managers with insights into their communication style, motivations, and potential fit with the company's culture.
- **Targeted Interviewing:** Interviewers use DISC profiles to tailor their questions, focusing on areas that align with the candidate's strengths and potential challenges. This allows for more meaningful conversations and a deeper understanding of how the candidate might contribute to the team.
- **Cultural Fit Emphasis:** Warby Parker places a strong emphasis on cultural fit, seeking candidates who not only possess the necessary skills but also share the company's values and passion for customer service. DISC helps identify individuals who are likely to thrive in the company's collaborative and innovative environment.

Positive Outcomes:

- **Reduced Turnover:** By hiring for cultural fit, Warby Parker has seen a significant reduction in employee turnover, saving the company time and resources in recruitment and onboarding.
- **Increased Engagement:** Employees who feel a strong sense of alignment with the company culture are more likely to be engaged, motivated, and productive.

- **Stronger Teams:** The diversity of DISC styles within teams builds a collaborative and innovative work environment.

Lessons Learned:

- **Transparency is Key:** Warby Parker is transparent about its use of DISC assessments, explaining their purpose and value to candidates upfront.
- **DISC is Just One Tool:** While DISC is an important factor in hiring decisions, it's not the sole determinant. Warby Parker considers a variety of factors, including skills, experience, and references.
- **Ongoing Learning:** The company invests in ongoing training for its hiring managers and HR team to ensure they are using DISC effectively and ethically.

Case Study 2: American Express: Creating a High-Performing Sales Team

American Express, a global financial services company, has leveraged DISC assessments to build a high-performing sales team.

- **Candidate Profiling:** Before interviews, American Express asks candidates to complete a DISC assessment. This helps recruiters and hiring managers identify individuals who possess the key traits associated with successful salespeople, such as persuasiveness (High I), drive (High D), and relationship-building skills (High I).
- **Targeted Interview Questions:** Interviewers tailor their questions based on the candidate's DISC profile. For example, a High D candidate might be asked about their experience with taking initiative and overcoming challenges, while a High I candidate might be asked about their approach to building rapport and influencing others.
- **Onboarding and Training:** New hires receive DISC-based

training to help them understand their own strengths and weaknesses and how to leverage those to excel in their roles. This personalized approach accelerates their ramp-up time and increases their chances of success.

Positive Outcomes:

- **Increased Sales Performance:** American Express has seen a significant improvement in sales performance since implementing DISC assessments in its hiring process.
- **Reduced Turnover:** By hiring candidates who are a good fit for the sales role and the company culture, American Express has reduced turnover within its sales team.

Lessons Learned:

- **Matching DISC Styles to Roles:** It's important to consider the specific demands of the role when interpreting DISC assessments.
- **Tailored Development:** Personalized onboarding and training based on DISC profiles can maximize employee performance and engagement.
- **Data-Driven Decisions:** Tracking the impact of DISC assessments on hiring outcomes allows for continuous improvement of the hiring process.

Case Study: Target: Hitting the Bullseye with DISC-Powered Hiring

Target, a leading retail giant renowned for its customer-centric approach, understands the critical role that employee personalities play in delivering exceptional service and thriving in a fast-paced environment. To ensure the right fit, Target is believed to utilize DISC assessments in its hiring process.

DISC-Driven Hiring at Target

- **Identifying Customer Service Stars:** Recognizing that

different DISC styles excel in various aspects of customer service, Target utilizes DISC to identify candidates who possess the ideal blend of traits for interacting with customers. High I individuals, known for their warmth and enthusiasm, are often drawn to roles requiring strong interpersonal skills. High S individuals, with their patience and supportive nature, are well-suited for roles demanding empathy and conflict resolution.

- **Thriving in a Fast-Paced Environment:** The retail industry is characterized by its fast pace and ever-changing demands. Target leverages DISC to identify candidates who can adapt quickly and remain calm under pressure. High D individuals, known for their decisiveness and action-oriented approach, often excel in fast-paced settings. Meanwhile, High C individuals, with their meticulous attention to detail and ability to follow procedures, can ensure accuracy and efficiency even under tight deadlines.
- **Building Cohesive Teams:** Target recognizes that a diverse team with a variety of DISC styles can lead to enhanced creativity, problem-solving, and overall performance. By strategically placing individuals with complementary styles together, the company encourages collaboration and minimizes potential conflicts. For instance, pairing a High D's initiative with a High C's analytical skills can lead to a well-balanced and effective team.

Positive Outcomes

- **Enhanced Customer Experience:** By hiring employees who possess the DISC styles best suited for customer service, Target has elevated its customer experience. Customers report feeling heard, valued, and well-served by knowledgeable and friendly staff.
- **Increased Employee Engagement:** Employees who feel like their natural talents and work styles are appreciated

and utilized are more likely to be engaged in their roles. This translates to higher job satisfaction, increased productivity, and reduced turnover.
- **Efficient Operations:** Identifying individuals who thrive in fast-paced environments has allowed Target to maintain smooth operations even during peak seasons and unexpected challenges. Employees are equipped to handle high volumes of customers and tasks efficiently, ensuring a positive shopping experience for all.

Lessons Learned

- **Tailored Assessments:** Target recognizes that different roles require different DISC profiles. By tailoring assessments to the specific requirements of each position, the company can identify the most suitable candidates.
- **Holistic Approach:** DISC is not used in isolation. Target combines assessment results with interviews and other evaluation methods to gain a comprehensive understanding of each candidate.
- **Ongoing Training and Development:** The company invests in training for hiring managers and employees to ensure they understand how to interpret and apply DISC insights effectively.

By integrating DISC assessments into its hiring and talent management practices, Target has cultivated a workforce that is both customer-centric and adaptable. This strategic approach has not only enhanced the company's reputation for exceptional service but also created a work environment where employees feel valued and empowered to succeed.

CHAPTER 8: DISC AND CONFLICT RESOLUTION: BUILDING BRIDGES IN A DIVERSE WORKPLACE

Decoding The Drama Of Workplace Clashes

Picture this: Jenna, the project manager, meticulously color-coded and armed with a spreadsheet for every contingency, sits across from John, the charismatic sales executive, practically bouncing in his chair with his next big idea. Their weekly meeting is less a collaboration and more a clash of the titans. Jenna insists on sticking to "the plan," while John's eyes glaze over at the mere mention of Gantt charts. It's a scene from a workplace sitcom, and if it feels familiar, you're not alone.

These personality clashes aren't just a source of office gossip; they're a real drain on productivity. Research shows unresolved conflict can slash your team's effectiveness by a whopping 25%! But imagine if you could decipher the secret code behind these clashes, understand what makes each person tick, and transform tension into teamwork.

That's where DISC comes in. It will help navigate the diverse personalities that shape your workplace. By understanding the four primary personality types – Dominance (D), Influence (I), Steadiness (S), and Conscientiousness (C) – you'll unlock the key to resolving conflict and building a more harmonious, productive team.

DISC: Your Personality Cheat Sheet

Think of DISC as a cheat sheet for understanding your colleagues. Remember:

- **Ds** are your go-getters, driven by results and ready to take charge.
- **Is** are the social butterflies, energizing the team with their enthusiasm and optimism.
- **Ss** are the glue that holds everything together, valuing collaboration and stability above all else.
- **Cs** are the detail-oriented analysts, ensuring accuracy and quality in every task.

While everyone is a unique blend of these styles, recognizing the dominant traits in your team members is like having a superpower. You'll be able to anticipate potential friction points, tailor your communication to resonate with each individual, and ultimately create a workplace where everyone feels understood and valued.

Conflict: The Spark That Ignites (or Burns) Your Team

Conflict is an inevitable part of any workplace where different personalities collide. It's like the friction that can spark a fire or burn everything down. Differences in perspectives, values, and working styles will create some heat. But here's the secret: conflict, when managed well, can be a powerful fuel for innovation and growth. It forces us to challenge assumptions, think outside the box, and find solutions we wouldn't have discovered otherwise.

The Leader's Role: The Evolution from Referee to Coach

Traditionally, leaders might have seen themselves as referees, stepping in to resolve disputes and declare a winner. But in today's world, effective leaders are more like coaches, guiding their teams through conflict towards a shared victory. They create a safe space for open dialogue, help team members understand each other's perspectives, and support a collaborative environment where everyone feels empowered to contribute.

This new approach requires a different skill set. We call it "DISC fluency." Leaders who are fluent in DISC can quickly decode the communication styles at play in a conflict and adapt their coaching strategies accordingly. It's like having a multilingual translator in your pocket, helping you bridge the gap between different personality types.

Imagine a workplace where conflict isn't feared, but welcomed as an opportunity for growth. A place where diverse personalities don't just coexist, but collaborate and thrive. In this chapter, we'll show you how DISC can make that vision a reality. You'll learn how to decipher the underlying motivations behind conflict, develop targeted mediation strategies, and build a team where everyone feels heard, understood, and valued.

Understanding Conflict Through The Disc Lens

The key to untangling workplace conflict often lies hidden within the personalities involved. The DISC model, your trusty personality compass, can help you decipher how people approach disagreements, paving the way for smoother resolutions.

In-Depth Analysis of Conflict Styles: Your DISC Decoder Ring

Each DISC style brings a unique flavor to the conflict table, influenced by their core desires and deepest fears:

Dominance (D): The Fearless Leaders

- **In the Ring:** Assertive, decisive, and not afraid to take charge. They'll cut to the chase and push for quick results.
- **Their Kryptonite:** Losing control, inefficiency, or being taken advantage of.
- **Clash of the Titans:** You'll see sparks fly when a D clashes with an S over decision-making speed (D wants it now, S needs more time) or with a C over the big picture versus the nitty-gritty details (D sees the forest, C sees the trees).
- **Real-World Rumble:** Imagine a Dominant support manager clashing with a Steady salesperson over how quickly to resolve customer issues. The D wants immediate action, while the S prioritizes nurturing long-term relationships.

Influence (I): The Social Butterflies

- **In the Ring:** Enthusiastic, persuasive, and always looking for the bright side. They love to collaborate and keep the energy high.
- **Their Kryptonite:** Rejection, disapproval, or being left out of the loop.
- **Clash of the Titans:** Watch out for fireworks when

an I clashes with a C over data versus gut feelings (I trusts their instincts, C wants cold hard facts) or with an S over the pace of change (I craves excitement, S prefers stability).
- **Real-World Rumble:** Picture an Influential support rep butting heads with a Conscientious operations manager over rigid processes. The I wants flexibility to meet unique customer needs, while the C values sticking to established procedures.

Steadiness (S): The Harmonizers

- **In the Ring:** Calm, supportive, and always ready to lend an ear. They're the team players who value harmony above all else.
- **Their Kryptonite:** Sudden change, confrontation, or hurting anyone's feelings.
- **Clash of the Titans:** Things can get tense when an S faces off against a D who's pushing too hard or a C who seems overly critical.
- **Real-World Rumble:** Envision a Steady support agent struggling to communicate a tough decision to a customer due to pressure from a Dominant sales manager who prioritizes speed over empathy.

Conscientiousness (C): The Meticulous Masters

- **In the Ring:** Analytical, detail-oriented, and laser-focused on quality and accuracy. They're your problem-solvers and fact-checkers.
- **Their Kryptonite:** Criticism, making mistakes, or being unprepared.
- **Clash of the Titans:** Expect friction when a C clashes with a D over impulsiveness or an I over a lack of attention to detail.
- **Real-World Rumble:** Picture a Conscientious support specialist frustrated with an Influential salesperson who consistently overlooks important details in customer

interactions, potentially jeopardizing accuracy and compliance.

Advanced Mediation Strategies: Your DISC Conflict Resolution Toolbox

Understanding these styles is like getting a backstage pass to the drama unfolding in your workplace. But knowledge alone isn't enough. You need the right tools to navigate the complex world of personality clashes. That's where our advanced mediation strategies come in. We'll provide you with step-by-step guides for each DISC pairing, teaching you how to tailor your communication, build trust, and find solutions that work for everyone involved.

You'll learn how to:

- **Decode:** Identify the underlying motivations behind each person's behavior in conflict.
- **Diffuse:** Use tailored communication strategies to de-escalate tensions and build rapport.
- **Direct:** Guide the conversation toward collaborative solutions that satisfy everyone's needs.

Remember, active listening and empathy are your most powerful tools. When you truly understand where someone is coming from, you're halfway to finding a resolution that works for everyone. So, let's dive deeper into the world of DISC and discover how it can transform your approach to conflict resolution.

Case Study: The "I" And The "C" – From Misunderstanding To Mutual Respect

Scenario: A creative agency experienced tension between a Creative Director (an "I") and a Data Analyst (a "C"). The Creative Director, brimming with innovative ideas, often presented concepts that lacked concrete data or a clear implementation plan. The Data Analyst, valuing accuracy and evidence-based decision-making, was frustrated by the perceived lack of structure and rigor. This clash hindered the team's ability to execute effective campaigns.

DISC-Driven Solution: Recognizing the escalating conflict, the agency's CEO (trained in DISC) intervened. The CEO held separate meetings with each individual, listening to their concerns and validating their perspectives. The Creative Director expressed a need for freedom and recognition, while the Data Analyst sought clarity and structure.

The CEO then brought the two together for a facilitated discussion, emphasizing the importance of both creativity and data in achieving campaign success. They established a new process where the Creative Director would present their ideas along with initial data points and a proposed implementation plan. The Data Analyst would then provide feedback and additional analysis to refine the campaign. This collaborative approach leveraged the strengths of both individuals, leading to more effective and impactful campaigns.

Lessons Learned:
- Effective communication requires understanding and adapting to different DISC styles.
- A structured approach can help bridge the gap between "big picture" thinkers and detail-oriented individuals.
- Collaboration between different DISC styles can lead to innovative solutions that neither could achieve alone.

Proactive Conflict Prevention With Disc: Building A Culture Of Collaboration

In the workplace, understanding isn't just about knowing *what* tasks to complete, but also *how* individuals prefer to work together. This is the difference between knowing the lyrics to a song and understanding the rhythm that makes people want to dance. DISC offers you the chance to not only learn the lyrics but to become the DJ, creating a harmonious workplace playlist where everyone feels like they belong on the dance floor.

Understanding and Leveraging DISC Profiles: Your Conflict Crystal Ball

Each DISC style comes with its own unique dance moves - strengths that can also be potential trip-ups when they collide with other styles. For instance, the assertive, direct Dominant (D) might step on the toes of the Steady (S) who craves harmony. The enthusiastic, social Influencer (I) may spin circles around the detail-oriented Conscientious (C) type, who prefers a more methodical two-step.

By understanding these natural tendencies, you gain a crystal ball into potential conflict hotspots. You'll know when a D and a C might butt heads over decision-making speed (D wants a quick waltz, C wants a slow foxtrot) or when an I might overwhelm an S with their boundless energy (I wants a conga line, S prefers a gentle sway).

Learning to analyze your team's DISC profiles is the shortcut for workplace harmony. It lets you spot potential friction points *before* they turn into full-blown dance battles, giving you the chance to choreograph a smoother, more collaborative routine.

Customizing Communication & Collaboration: Finding Your Team's Rhythm

DISC isn't just about predicting clashes; it's about finding the right rhythm for each interaction. It gives you a roadmap for tailoring your communication and collaboration strategies so everyone feels heard and valued.

- **With Dominants (D):** Cut to the chase, focus on results, and let them lead.
- **With Influencers (I):** Amp up the energy, brainstorm ideas together, and give them the spotlight.
- **With Steadiness (S):** Offer support, patience, and a collaborative environment where everyone feels included.
- **With Conscientious (C):** Provide detailed data, present logical arguments, and allow plenty of time for careful consideration.

By adapting your project management style, meeting formats, and feedback delivery to suit different DISC types, you create a playlist that everyone can groove to. This might mean more structure for the Cs, more brainstorming for the Is, and crystal-clear expectations for the Ds and Ss. The result? A more inclusive, productive, and dare we say, *fun* work environment.

Building a DISC-Aware Culture: Creating a Harmonious Dance Floor

A workplace that truly embraces DISC is like a well-choreographed dance performance. Everyone knows their steps, respects each other's style, and moves in sync toward a common goal.

Open Communication & Mutual Understanding:

Imagine a dance floor where everyone feels safe to express themselves, even if their moves are a little different. That's the kind of open communication a DISC-aware culture promotes. It's a place where employees feel comfortable sharing their opinions, even if they disagree with the majority. Leaders play a vital role in creating this safe space, facilitating conversations that respect diverse viewpoints and encourage active listening. By using DISC language as a neutral way to discuss communication styles, teams can avoid judgment and focus on understanding each other's unique rhythms.

Valuing Diversity:

A DISC-aware culture doesn't just tolerate differences; it celebrates them. It recognizes that a diverse team, with a mix of Ds, Is, Ss, and Cs, is like a symphony orchestra, capable of producing a richer, more complex sound than any one instrument alone. When a team embraces their diverse styles, they can harness the full power of their collective talents, leading to more creative solutions, better decision-making, and a more resilient team overall.

Team-Building with DISC: Learning the Choreography Together

DISC-Based Workshops & Activities:

Investing in DISC-based team-building activities is like giving your team a crash course in choreography. These workshops and activities can include personality assessments, role-playing scenarios, and interactive games that help team members:

- **Discover their own DISC styles:** Understand their strengths, challenges, and how they contribute to the team.
- **Learn the steps of others:** Develop empathy and appreciation for different communication styles.
- **Practice dancing together:** Hone their collaboration skills through fun and engaging exercises.

By participating in these activities, team members learn to appreciate each other's unique dance moves, leading to a more harmonious and productive workplace.

Ongoing DISC Integration:

Building a DISC-aware culture is an ongoing process, like refining a dance routine. Encourage regular team check-ins and discussions using DISC as a framework. Integrate DISC into performance reviews and feedback sessions, giving employees a deeper understanding of how their style impacts their work and interactions with others. And most importantly, promote continuous learning about DISC, so your team can continue to evolve and adapt, just like the most captivating dance performances.

Case Study: The "D" And The "S" – From Impasse To Innovation

Scenario: A high-tech company faced a deadlock between the Head of Product Development (a "D") and the Lead Engineer (an "S"). The Head of Product Development, driven by a need for speed and market dominance, wanted to launch a new product quickly. However, the Lead Engineer, valuing thoroughness and quality, insisted on more extensive testing and refinement. This conflict was causing delays and frustration within the team.

DISC-Driven Solution: A consultant, trained in DISC, was brought in to mediate. After individual interviews and observing team interactions, the consultant identified the root cause: a clash between the Dominant's desire for quick results and the Steady's need for security and stability.

The consultant then facilitated a series of meetings where both parties were encouraged to express their concerns and motivations. Using DISC language, the consultant helped the Head of Product Development understand the Lead Engineer's concerns about potential risks and quality issues. Conversely, the Lead Engineer was helped to see the potential benefits of a faster launch.

The result was a compromise. The Head of Product Development agreed to a slightly extended testing phase, while the Lead Engineer committed to streamlining certain processes to accelerate the timeline. This solution not only resolved the immediate conflict but also builds a greater understanding and appreciation of each other's strengths.

Lessons Learned:

- Recognizing the underlying motivations behind each DISC style is crucial for effective conflict resolution.
- Using DISC language can create a neutral and objective framework for discussing differences.
- Finding common ground and compromising are often essential for resolving conflicts between different DISC styles.

The Leader's Role: Choreographing Harmony In The Workplace Ballet

In the intricate ballet of workplace personalities, clashes are inevitable. But as a leader, you're not just a spectator; you're the choreographer, guiding your dancers through missteps and transforming potential disasters into graceful performances. Your DISC knowledge helps you navigate the delicate interplay of different styles and create a harmonious workplace ensemble.

From Referee to Maestro: Redefining the Leader's Role

First things first: ditch the referee whistle and pick up the conductor's baton. Your primary role isn't to judge who's right or wrong in a conflict, but to orchestrate a symphony of understanding and collaboration. This means shifting your focus from assigning blame to facilitating open dialogue, promoting empathy, and guiding your team towards win-win solutions.

You're not just resolving a dispute; you're building a stronger, more resilient team. To do that, you need to be a neutral conductor, not a biased judge. This means keeping your personal opinions in check, basing your decisions on facts and a deep understanding of each person's DISC style.

Creating a safe space for open communication is like setting the stage for a successful performance. Your team needs to know they can express their concerns without fear of judgment or reprisal. By building trust and actively listening to each dancer's unique rhythm, you'll create a harmonious environment where everyone feels heard and valued.

But to truly master this art form, you need to become fluent in DISC – your backstage pass to understanding the motivations and communication styles of each performer. This knowledge allows you to adapt your leadership style to connect with every member of your team, building rapport and de-escalating tensions before they turn into a full-blown drama.

A DISC-Powered Playbook for Conflict Resolution: Your Four-Act Masterpiece

Think of conflict resolution as a four-act play, and you, the leader, are the director:

Act 1: Gather Intel – Listen, Observe, Analyze

Before the curtain rises, you need to understand the characters and their motivations. Conduct private conversations with each person involved, actively listening to their concerns and needs. Observe how they interact with others, noticing patterns of communication and conflict. If available, gather data from other sources to gain a 360-degree view of the situation.

Act 2: Unmask the Villain – Identify the Root Cause

Every conflict has an underlying cause, a hidden villain lurking in the shadows. Is it a simple miscommunication? Clashing DISC styles? Competing goals? Lack of resources? Or something more toxic, like bullying or harassment? By uncovering the root cause, you can tailor your resolution strategy to address the specific issues at hand.

Act 3: The Grand Resolution – Facilitate Collaboration

It's time for the characters to take center stage and work together to find a solution. As the director, you'll facilitate this process, creating a safe space for open dialogue, encouraging active listening, and helping the parties identify shared goals and common ground. You might also need to provide training and support to equip your team with the skills they need to collaborate effectively.

Act 4: The Encore – Follow Up, Celebrate, and Improve

Conflict resolution isn't a one-and-done performance; it's an ongoing process. Regularly check in with your team to ensure the solution is working and that the conflict hasn't reappeared in a different form. Celebrate successes and acknowledge positive behaviors to reinforce a collaborative culture. And don't forget to use the conflict as a learning experience, continuously refining your team's processes, communication, and overall dynamics.

Curtain Call: Your Leadership Legacy

By embracing your role as a facilitator and adopting this DISC-powered approach, you can transform conflict from a dreaded drama into a standing ovation. You'll create a workplace where diverse personalities not only coexist but shine, where every dancer feels valued, heard, and empowered to contribute their unique talents to the performance.

Avoiding The Drama: Common Missteps And How To Sidestep Them

Mastering the art of DISC-driven conflict resolution isn't just about knowing the right moves; it's also about avoiding the wrong ones. Even the most well-intentioned leaders can stumble, making missteps that turn a minor disagreement into a full-blown workplace soap opera.

But fear not! By understanding these common pitfalls, you can become a conflict resolution ninja, gracefully dodging drama and guiding your team towards harmony.

- **The "Judge Judy" Trap:** Resist the urge to jump to conclusions or take sides when a conflict first arises. Remember, you're the mediator, not the judge. Gather information from all parties involved, listen without judgment, and base your decisions on facts, not gossip or gut feelings.
- **The "One-Size-Fits-All" Fiasco:** Treating all conflicts the same is like trying to fit a square peg into a round hole. Different DISC styles require different approaches. A direct confrontation might work with a Dominant (D) type, but it could send a Steady (S) type into hiding. Tailor your communication and mediation strategies to the unique personalities involved.
- **The "Ostrich Strategy":** Burying your head in the sand won't make conflict disappear. In fact, it usually makes it worse. Be proactive, address issues early on, and create a safe space for open dialogue. Remember, unresolved conflict is like a ticking time bomb, waiting to explode.
- **The "Problem-Focused Tunnel Vision":** Don't forget that behind every conflict are real people with real feelings. Focusing solely on the problem can make individuals feel like their concerns are being ignored. Take the time to

understand each person's perspective, build empathy, and create a more positive and collaborative environment.
- **The "One-and-Done" Myth:** Conflict resolution isn't a quick fix; it's an ongoing process. Regularly check in with your team to ensure the solution is working and that old wounds aren't festering. Celebrate successes and acknowledge positive behaviors to reinforce a culture of collaboration. And remember, conflict is a learning opportunity—use it to continuously improve your team's communication and processes.
- **The "Toxic Tolerance" Trap:** If you encounter toxic behavior, such as bullying, harassment, or chronic disrespect, don't sweep it under the rug. Take swift and decisive action to address it. Turning a blind eye can have devastating consequences for your team's morale and productivity.

Your Path to DISC-Powered Leadership

By sidestepping these common pitfalls, you'll transform yourself into a conflict resolution guru, capable of turning even the most challenging disagreements into opportunities for growth. Remember, conflict is not a sign of failure; it's a natural part of any dynamic workplace. By embracing DISC as your guide, you can empower your team to navigate conflict constructively, building a more harmonious, productive, and fulfilling work environment.

Ready to take your leadership to the next level? Let's dive deeper into the world of DISC and discover how it can transform your approach to conflict resolution, team building, and overall organizational success.

Case Study: Building Bridges Between Support And Sales

Scenario: A software company experienced ongoing friction between their support and sales teams. Support agents, primarily "S" types, felt overwhelmed by unrealistic customer expectations set by the "D" and "I" sales representatives. The sales team, in turn, felt that support was too slow to respond to customer issues, potentially jeopardizing deals.

DISC-Driven Solution: The company initiated a DISC-based team-building workshop. Team members learned about the different DISC styles and their typical behaviors in conflict situations. They participated in role-playing exercises that simulated challenging customer interactions, practicing how to communicate effectively with different personality types.

Following the workshop, the company implemented several changes:

- **Clearer Communication:** The sales team committed to setting realistic customer expectations and communicating any potential issues to the support team proactively.
- **Streamlined Processes:** The support team established a tiered system for prioritizing customer requests, ensuring that urgent issues were addressed promptly.
- **Regular Check-Ins:** Both teams agreed to hold regular meetings to discuss challenges, share feedback, and celebrate successes.

Lessons Learned:

- DISC-based team-building activities can build mutual understanding and improve communication between different departments.

- Establishing clear processes and communication channels can help reduce friction and prevent conflicts from escalating.
- Regular check-ins and open communication are essential for maintaining positive working relationships between teams.

Redesigning Your Workplace: A Disc-Powered Blueprint For Harmony

Think of your company's structure as the architectural blueprint that shapes how your employees interact, communicate, and collaborate. If this blueprint isn't designed with different personality types in mind, it can lead to friction, frustration, and even full-blown meltdowns. That's why evaluating and adapting your organizational structure through a DISC lens is crucial for creating a workplace where everyone can thrive.

Personality Assessment and Analysis

Imagine having a clear understanding of your team's personalities, understanding their strengths, weaknesses, and how they tick. That's the power of personality assessments like DISC or MBTI. By conducting these assessments at both the individual and team levels, you can paint a vivid picture of the dominant DISC styles within your organization and how they're distributed across departments and roles.

Once you have this data in hand, it's time to play detective. Analyze the results to identify patterns and trends. Are certain personality types clustered in specific areas? Are there potential mismatches between certain styles and their roles?

Don't stop there! Gather feedback directly from your employees through surveys or focus groups. Ask them how well they feel the current structure supports their needs, their preferred communication styles, decision-making processes, and the resources available to them. This firsthand intel will be invaluable in guiding your structural changes.

**Evaluating Organizational Structure:
A DISC-Guided Makeover**

Now that you have a deep understanding of your team's personality landscape, it's time to give your organizational structure a DISC-informed makeover.

- **Hierarchy vs. Flat Structure:** Is your company a rigid pyramid or a collaborative village? Consider how your structure impacts different DISC styles. A strict hierarchy might feel stifling to independent-minded Ds and Is, while a loose, flat structure could leave Ss and Cs craving more direction and clarity. Find the sweet spot that empowers all personalities.
- **Team Structure:** Are your teams set up for success? Some folks, like Is and Ds, thrive in large, dynamic groups where they can bounce ideas off each other and take charge. Others, like Ss and Cs, might prefer smaller, more intimate teams where they can build deeper relationships and focus on meticulous work. Design teams that cater to these different needs.
- **Decision-Making Processes:** Are decisions made by a select few, or does everyone have a voice? Ensure your decision-making processes are inclusive and consider the perspectives of all DISC styles. For instance, balance data-driven analysis (a C's dream) with brainstorming sessions (an I's paradise) to arrive at well-rounded decisions.
- **Support Systems and Resources:** Think of your organization as a buffet of support options. Do you offer diverse communication channels (email, instant messaging, face-to-face meetings) to cater to different preferences? What about training programs to help employees understand and work effectively with different personality types? Mentoring and coaching can be a lifeline for those needing extra support navigating your company culture's complexities. And don't forget about flexible work arrangements—they can be a game-changer for employees who thrive in different environments or have unique needs.

The Perils of Silos: A Cautionary Tale

To illustrate the importance of a DISC-informed approach, let's consider a hypothetical company where operational staff (mainly Ds and Is) are solely responsible for client relationships, while a separate customer service team (mostly Ss) handles initial inquiries but passes complex issues to the operational staff. This creates a communication bottleneck and an uneven distribution of workload.

The result? Operational staff are overwhelmed, unable to take time off without facing a mountain of work upon return. This leads to burnout, resentment, and a revolving door of employees. In desperation, they start redirecting inquiries back to customer service, sparking conflict. Leadership's response? A threat of termination, further fueling the flames.

This scenario highlights several critical leadership failures:

- **Ignoring the Root Cause:** The company's leaders fail to address the underlying structural issues, resorting to threats instead of solutions.
- **Disregarding DISC Differences:** They overlook the unique needs and motivations of each DISC style, exacerbating the conflict.
- **One-Size-Fits-All Approach:** Leadership's heavy-handed response demonstrates a lack of understanding that different individuals and teams require different approaches to communication and collaboration.

A DISC-Powered Solution: Building Bridges, Not Walls

A more effective approach would involve:

- **Analyzing DISC Profiles:** Understanding the dominant styles within each team to tailor communication and collaboration strategies.
- **Re-evaluating Workload Distribution:** Redistribute

responsibilities based on individual strengths and preferences.
- **Enhancing Communication:** Implement clear communication channels between teams to ensure everyone has the information and support they need.
- **Empowering Teams:** Give autonomy to those who thrive on it (Ds and Is), while offering clear guidance and support to those who need it (Ss and Cs).
- **Building a Collaborative Culture:** Promote an environment where everyone feels heard and valued, regardless of their DISC style.

By applying DISC insights, this company could transform a toxic situation into a positive, productive, and sustainable work environment.

Epilogue: Turning Workplace Clashes Into Standing Ovations

Conflict, like a sudden storm cloud on a sunny day, often gets a bad rap in the workplace. But what if we told you that these storms aren't just inevitable, they're *essential*? Without a little friction, pearls wouldn't exist, and diamonds wouldn't shine. Conflict, when channeled correctly, can be the crucible that forges innovation, deepens understanding, and propels your team to new heights.

DISC is your trusty weather vane, helping you predict those storms, navigate their turbulence, and even harness their energy for good. It's not about labeling your team members, but about truly understanding the unique melody each person brings to the workplace symphony.

As a leader, you have the power to create a workplace where every instrument—every personality—is not only heard but celebrated. By embracing the diversity of DISC styles, you're not just doing the right thing; you're unlocking a treasure trove of creativity, problem-solving prowess, and untapped potential.

So, the next time conflict rears its head, don't cower in fear. Step into the storm, armed with your DISC knowledge. Transform those clashes into collaborative breakthroughs, turning frowns into high-fives and tense standoffs into standing ovations. Remember, a workplace where diverse personalities thrive isn't just a happy accident—it's a masterpiece of leadership, crafted with intention, understanding, and the power of DISC.

Now that you've mastered the art of navigating conflict with DISC, let's turn our attention to another critical phase in the employee lifecycle: onboarding.

Just as a conductor carefully orchestrates the entry of each instrument into a symphony, so too must a leader orchestrate the smooth integration of new team members. This is where DISC can once again shine, offering valuable insights into how to tailor onboarding experiences to individual styles, foster connection, and set the stage for long-term success.

In the next chapter, we'll explore how DISC can revolutionize your onboarding process, creating a more welcoming and supportive environment for new hires, regardless of their personality type. Get ready to discover how a DISC-aware approach can turn those first few weeks on the job from a nerve-wracking experience into a harmonious introduction to your company culture.

CHAPTER 9: ONBOARDING AND INTEGRATION: SETTING THE DISC STAGE FOR SUCCESS

Setting The Stage With Disc

Starting a new job? It's a whirlwind of emotions – a mix of excitement, anticipation, and maybe even a touch of anxiety. There's a mountain of information to absorb, a sea of new faces to remember, and a whole new culture to navigate. It's no wonder that onboarding, while crucial, can often feel like a baptism by fire for both employees and organizations.

The traditional one-size-fits-all onboarding approach often misses the mark, leaving new hires feeling lost, overwhelmed, or even disconnected. But what if we could crack the code to onboarding success? What if there was a way to make every new hire feel seen, understood, and empowered from day one?

Enter DISC: a game-changer for onboarding – a tool that unlocks the secrets to understanding how each individual prefers to communicate, learn, and collaborate. By embracing DISC-aware onboarding, you're not just handing out employee handbooks; you're crafting a personalized adventure tailored to each new hire's unique style.

Imagine this: a "Dominant" personality diving headfirst into a challenging project with clear goals and the freedom to take charge. An "Influential" type thriving in a collaborative brainstorming session, buzzing with ideas and camaraderie. A "Steady" individual finding their place on a team, supported by clear expectations and a predictable routine. And a "Conscientious" person diving deep into the details, analyzing information, and becoming the go-to expert in their field.

This isn't just a pipe dream – it's the power of DISC in action. By tailoring communication, task assignments, and team dynamics to each DISC style, we can unlock a level of engagement, productivity, and collaboration that was previously unimaginable.

But the benefits don't stop there. DISC-aware onboarding isn't just about the first few weeks; it's about laying the foundation for a thriving, long-term employee-employer relationship. When people feel understood and supported, they're more likely to become passionate advocates for your company, driving innovation, and boosting your bottom line.

So, are you ready to revolutionize your onboarding process? Buckle up as we dive into the world of DISC, exploring how to tailor your approach to each style, sharing inspiring success stories, and giving you the tools to create an onboarding experience that truly sets the stage for success.

Cracking The Disc Code For Onboarding & Team Success

Communication – it's the lifeblood of any team, but it's not always easy to get it right. The truth is, we're not all wired the same way. Some of us are direct and to the point, while others prefer a more collaborative approach. Some thrive on brainstorming and big ideas, while others prefer to carefully analyze every detail. This is where DISC comes in – a secret weapon for decoding communication styles and creating a more harmonious workplace.

DISC is a personality compass, pointing you in the right direction for effective communication with each new hire. Let's break it down:

- **Dominant (D) – The Trailblazers:** These folks are all about action. They're decisive, results-oriented, and love a challenge. To communicate with them effectively, be direct, get to the point, and focus on the big picture. Don't get bogged down in details; they want to know the what and why, not necessarily the how.
- **Influential (I) – The Enthusiasts:** These social butterflies thrive on interaction and positive energy. Engage them in conversations, share stories, and show appreciation for their ideas. Keep things upbeat, and don't be afraid to let their enthusiasm ignite the team.
- **Steady (S) – The Team Players:** Collaboration and harmony are their jam. Communicate in a calm, supportive manner, emphasizing teamwork and cooperation. Be transparent about changes and reassure them during transitions – they value stability and predictability.
- **Conscientious (C) – The Analysts:** These detail-oriented folks crave accuracy and precision. Provide them with

comprehensive information, data-driven insights, and time to analyze. Acknowledge their expertise and avoid pushing them into hasty decisions.

By fine-tuning your communication style to match each DISC profile, you'll create a more positive, productive, and inclusive onboarding experience.

But DISC isn't just about communication. It's also a powerful tool for assigning tasks that play to each individual's strengths. Imagine your new "D" hire leading a high-stakes project with a tight deadline, while your "I" hire rallies the troops and generates creative solutions. Meanwhile, your "S" hire ensures everyone feels heard and supported, and your "C" hire meticulously analyzes data to guide the team's decisions. By leveraging DISC insights, you'll optimize task allocation, boost engagement, and watch your new hires flourish.

But wait, there's more! DISC can even help prevent conflicts before they start. By understanding the potential communication breakdowns and clashes that can arise between different styles, you can proactively address issues and cultivate a more harmonious work environment. Encourage open communication, create a safe space for dialogue, and watch as your team transforms into a well-oiled machine, humming with collaboration and mutual respect.

With DISC as your guide, you can unlock the full potential of your team, one personality at a time. So, ditch the one-size-fits-all approach and embark on a personalized onboarding adventure where everyone feels seen, heard, and valued.

Crafting The Perfect Onboarding Experience: A Disc-Style Guide

Understanding the unique preferences of each DISC style is your secret weapon for creating an onboarding experience that truly resonates with new hires. Let's dive into how to tailor your approach and unlock the full potential of your team, one personality at a time:

Dominant (D) Onboarding: Unleashing the Go-Getters

Dominant personalities are all about action, results, and making things happen. To get them firing on all cylinders, your onboarding should be like a high-octane fuel injection.

- **Give Them the Big Picture:** Skip the fluff and get straight to the point. Present a clear, concise roadmap outlining their role, responsibilities, and the key metrics that define success.
- **Empower Early and Often:** Dominant types are born leaders, so don't hold them back. Give them meaningful projects early on, allowing them to take the reins and showcase their decision-making prowess.
- **Show Them the Numbers:** Feedback is their fuel. Provide regular, data-driven insights into their performance, highlighting their wins and the tangible impact they've made.
- **Keep it Snappy:** Skip the lengthy orientations and administrative tasks. Instead, focus on hands-on learning, skill-building workshops, and opportunities to dive into real projects where they can shine.

Influential (I) Onboarding: Igniting the Spark

Influential personalities are like human sunshine – they thrive on positive interactions, collaboration, and a good dose of recognition. Your onboarding should be a warm welcome party.

- **Roll Out the Red Carpet:** Create a buzz from day one with a personalized welcome message and introductions to key team members. Make them feel like the guest of honor at their own onboarding celebration.
- **Make Connections Happen:** Fuel their social butterfly nature with team lunches, coffee chats, and social events. The sooner they forge bonds with colleagues, the sooner they'll feel at home.
- **Unleash Their Creativity:** Invite them to brainstorm sessions and group projects early on, where their ideas can take flight and their infectious enthusiasm can inspire others.
- **Show Them the Horizon:** Paint a picture of their future at the company, highlighting growth opportunities, mentorship programs, and exciting career paths that align with their passions.
- **Cheer Them On:** Influential types love recognition. Celebrate their wins, big and small, with verbal praise, shout-outs, or even a fun team ritual.

Steady (S) Onboarding: Building the Foundation

Steady personalities value stability, teamwork, and a sense of belonging. Your onboarding should be a sturdy bridge that guides them smoothly into their new role.

- **Create a Clear Roadmap:** Provide a detailed onboarding plan that outlines each step of the journey, including timelines, milestones, and expectations. This predictability will set their minds at ease.
- **Buddy Up:** Pair them with a supportive mentor or colleague who can answer questions, offer guidance, and help them navigate the company culture.
- **Teamwork Makes the Dream Work:** Integrate them into team projects early on, giving them a chance to contribute

to shared goals and build camaraderie.
- **Keep it Consistent:** Establish a predictable onboarding schedule with regular check-ins, creating a sense of stability and routine.
- **Show Your Commitment:** Highlight your company's commitment to its people through employee testimonials, company values, and initiatives that support work-life balance and well-being.

Conscientious (C) Onboarding: Nurturing the Experts

Conscientious personalities thrive on accuracy, expertise, and a deep understanding of their role. Your onboarding should be a knowledge buffet, providing them with the tools they need to excel.

- **Information Overload (in a good way):** Give them access to detailed manuals, training documents, and even subject matter experts who can answer their burning questions.
- **Let Them Set the Pace:** Allow for self-paced learning, giving them the flexibility to digest information at their own speed and seek clarification as needed.
- **Celebrate Their Expertise:** Emphasize the importance of their role in maintaining accuracy and quality. Create opportunities for them to showcase their knowledge and provide valuable insights.
- **Sharpen Their Skills:** Offer training sessions, workshops, or online courses to help them deepen their expertise and stay on the cutting edge of their field.
- **Set the Bar High (and Clearly):** Clearly define quality standards and performance metrics, providing regular feedback on their progress and recognizing their meticulous attention to detail.

By tailoring your onboarding approach to each DISC style, you'll not only accelerate your new hires' learning curves but also create a more engaged, productive, and harmonious work environment.

Examples Of Successful Disc-Aware Onboarding Programs

Case Study: Skybound Dynamics – A Tech Startup's DISC-Driven Turnaround

Challenge: Skybound Dynamics, a fast-growing tech startup, was experiencing alarmingly high turnover rates, particularly among new hires within the first six months. Exit interviews revealed that new employees often felt overwhelmed, isolated, and unsure of their roles within the company. The lack of a structured onboarding process and personalized support contributed to a sense of disconnect and dissatisfaction.

Solution: Recognizing the need for a change, Skybound Dynamics decided to revamp its onboarding program with a DISC-based approach.

1. **DISC Assessments:** All new hires completed a DISC assessment before their start date, providing insights into their individual communication styles, preferences, and motivators.
2. **Personalized Onboarding Plans:** The company developed tailored onboarding plans based on each new hire's DISC profile. These plans included:
   - **Dominant (D):** Challenging projects with quick wins and opportunities for leadership.
   - **Influential (I):** Team-building activities, social events, and frequent positive feedback.
   - **Steady (S):** Structured training schedules, clearly defined roles, and supportive mentorship.
   - **Conscientious (C):** Detailed documentation, access to resources, and opportunities for skill development.
3. **DISC-Informed Management Training:** Managers

received training on DISC to better understand their team members' communication styles and adapt their leadership approaches accordingly.

Impact:

Within a year of implementing the DISC-based onboarding program, Skybound Dynamics saw a significant decrease in turnover rates. New hires reported feeling more engaged, valued, and connected to the company culture. The personalized onboarding plans helped them quickly integrate into their teams and contribute to the company's success. Managers also reported improved communication and collaboration within their teams, leading to increased productivity and overall performance.

Key Takeaways:

- **DISC assessments can be a valuable tool** for understanding the unique needs and preferences of new hires.
- **Personalized onboarding plans** based on DISC profiles can significantly improve employee engagement and retention.
- **Training managers in DISC** empowers them to lead and communicate more effectively with their teams.
- A DISC-aware onboarding program is an investment in both the individual and the organization, leading to long-term benefits in terms of employee satisfaction, productivity, and overall company success.

Case Study: Global Financial Services Firm - Transforming Team Integration with DISC

Challenge:

At a leading global financial services firm, the onboarding process had become a significant pain point. Despite a rigorous selection process that attracted top talent, new hires struggled to integrate into existing teams. The firm's diverse workforce, spanning multiple continents and cultures, resulted in a wide range of personalities and working styles. This diversity, while a strength in many ways, often led to communication breakdowns, misunderstandings, and conflicts, hindering team cohesion and productivity.

Solution:

Recognizing the need for a more personalized and effective onboarding approach, the firm decided to leverage the power of DISC. The initiative involved the following key steps:

1. **DISC Assessment for All:** All employees, both new hires and existing team members, underwent a DISC assessment to identify their individual behavioral styles.
2. **DISC-Integrated Onboarding:** DISC profiles were integrated into the onboarding process for new hires.
    - Each new hire received a personalized onboarding plan based on their DISC profile, outlining specific strategies for communication, collaboration, and conflict resolution.
    - New hires were paired with mentors who had complementary DISC styles to facilitate smooth integration and offer tailored guidance.
3. **Team DISC Workshops:** Teams participated in DISC workshops to learn about the different styles, understand their collective strengths and weaknesses, and develop strategies for effective communication and collaboration.
4. **DISC-Informed Communication Guidelines:** Teams developed communication guidelines that took into account the diverse DISC styles within the team. These guidelines promoted respectful and effective communication, helping to prevent

misunderstandings and conflicts.
5. **Ongoing DISC Training and Coaching:** Managers received ongoing training and coaching in DISC to help them understand their team dynamics, tailor their leadership styles, and effectively address any DISC-related challenges that arose.

Impact:

The implementation of DISC-based onboarding and team integration strategies had a transformative impact on the firm:

- **Improved Team Cohesion:** Teams reported significantly improved cohesion and collaboration, with members feeling more understood and appreciated.
- **Reduced Conflict:** Misunderstandings and conflicts decreased as team members learned to communicate and collaborate more effectively across DISC styles.
- **Enhanced New Hire Engagement:** New hires expressed higher levels of satisfaction and engagement, feeling more welcomed and supported during their onboarding journey.
- **Increased Productivity:** Teams reported increased productivity, as they were able to leverage their diverse strengths and work together more effectively.

Key Takeaways:

This case study demonstrates the power of DISC in transforming team integration within a diverse and complex organization. By understanding and leveraging individual behavioral styles, organizations can create a more inclusive and collaborative work environment where everyone can thrive.

The financial services firm's success underscores the importance of:

- **Personalization:** Tailoring onboarding experiences to individual DISC styles.
- **Education:** Providing DISC training to both new hires and existing team members.
- **Collaboration:** Creating a culture of open communication and collaboration that embraces diversity.
- **Ongoing Support:** Providing ongoing coaching and support to managers to help them effectively navigate DISC dynamics.

Case Study: Sunshine Valley Hospital - Transforming Onboarding with DISC

The Challenge:

Sunshine Valley Hospital, a renowned healthcare institution, faced challenges with its generic onboarding program. New hires, ranging from nurses and physicians to administrative staff, often felt overwhelmed by the one-size-fits-all approach. This led to frustration, disengagement, and even turnover in the early stages of employment. Recognizing the need for a more personalized approach, the hospital sought a solution that would cater to the unique needs and preferences of its diverse workforce.

The Solution: DISC-Driven Onboarding

Sunshine Valley Hospital partnered with a DISC consultant to revamp its onboarding program. The new approach centered on understanding and leveraging the DISC profiles of new hires to create a tailored and engaging experience. The key elements of the DISC-driven onboarding program included:

1. **DISC Assessment and Profiling:** All new hires completed a DISC assessment to determine their primary and secondary behavioral styles. This

information was used to create personalized onboarding plans and match new hires with mentors who had complementary DISC styles.
2. **Customized Onboarding Plans:** Each new hire received a personalized onboarding plan that considered their DISC profile, role, and learning preferences. For example, a "D" style nurse received a fast-paced orientation with clear expectations and opportunities for independent decision-making, while a "C" style administrator was given ample time to review detailed manuals and procedures.
3. **DISC-Specific Training Modules:** The hospital developed training modules that addressed the communication, conflict resolution, and stress management styles of each DISC type. For instance, "I" style employees attended sessions on active listening and building rapport, while "S" style employees learned techniques for managing change and maintaining a collaborative environment.
4. **Mentoring and Support Groups:** New hires were paired with mentors who had complementary DISC styles, encouraging understanding and facilitating knowledge transfer. Additionally, the hospital introduced DISC-based support groups where new hires could connect with colleagues with similar styles, share experiences, and learn from each other.
5. **Inclusive Onboarding Environment:** The hospital created an inclusive onboarding environment that celebrated individual differences. New hires were encouraged to embrace their unique DISC styles and leverage them to contribute to the hospital's success.

The Impact:

The DISC-driven onboarding program at Sunshine Valley Hospital yielded remarkable results:

- **Increased New Hire Satisfaction and Engagement:** New hires reported feeling more valued, understood, and supported during their onboarding experience.
- **Reduced Turnover Rates:** Turnover rates among new hires decreased significantly within the first year of implementing the program.
- **Improved Communication and Collaboration:** The program supported a more positive and collaborative work environment, with team members better understanding and appreciating each other's communication styles.
- **Enhanced Patient Care Outcomes:** The improved communication and collaboration among staff directly translated into better patient care outcomes, as teams worked more effectively together to provide the highest quality of care.

Conclusion:

By embracing DISC as a tool for personalization, Sunshine Valley Hospital transformed its onboarding process from a generic experience into a tailored journey that empowered new hires to thrive. The hospital's commitment to understanding and celebrating individual differences not only improved the onboarding experience but also developed a more inclusive and collaborative workplace culture, ultimately benefiting both employees and patients alike.

Real-World Results In Talent Development

The impact of DISC doesn't stop at onboarding. Imagine a workplace where everyone speaks the same language of personality, where teams are built on mutual understanding, and leaders effortlessly connect with their diverse employees. This isn't just a dream; it's a reality for companies that have woven DISC into the very fabric of their culture.

Unleashing the Power of DISC: Beyond Onboarding

Incorporating DISC into your organization doesn't have to be an all-or-nothing approach. Here are a few additional strategies to consider:

- **DISC-Based Training:** Offer workshops or training sessions to help employees understand their own DISC styles, learn about the styles of their colleagues, and develop strategies for effective communication and collaboration.
- **Personalized Onboarding Plans:** Tailor onboarding plans to each new hire's DISC profile, ensuring that they receive the information and support they need in a way that resonates with them.
- **DISC-Informed Mentoring:** Assign mentors with complementary DISC styles to new hires to build mutual understanding and facilitate a smooth transition into the company culture.
- **Feedback Loop:** Encourage new hires to provide feedback on their onboarding experience, including how DISC was incorporated. Use this feedback to continually refine and improve your onboarding program.

Leading companies across industries have discovered the transformative power of DISC, using it to fuel everything from sales growth to innovative breakthroughs. Let's take a closer look at how some of these companies are leveraging DISC to achieve remarkable results.

Real-World Examples of DISC Integration: Leading Companies Putting DISC into Practice

Many leading companies have harnessed the power of DISC to enhance various aspects of their operations, from sales and customer service to leadership development and talent acquisition. Let's explore how some of these companies have put DISC to work, reaping significant benefits for both their employees and their bottom line.

Salesforce: Boosting Sales and Leadership with DISC

Salesforce, the global CRM powerhouse, has seamlessly woven DISC assessments into its sales training and leadership development programs. By helping sales representatives understand their communication styles and adapt to the preferences of potential clients, Salesforce has seen a marked improvement in sales effectiveness and customer satisfaction. Additionally, DISC-informed leadership development empowers managers to build stronger, more cohesive teams by understanding and leveraging the diverse styles of their employees.

L'Oréal: Promoting Collaboration and Inclusion through DISC

L'Oréal, the world's leading beauty company, has embraced DISC as a tool for building stronger, more collaborative teams. DISC-based workshops have become a cornerstone of their team-building efforts, promoting better communication, understanding, and appreciation of diverse perspectives. This emphasis on inclusion has created a more welcoming workplace where employees from all backgrounds feel valued and empowered to contribute their unique talents.

Visa: Enhancing Customer Service and Conflict Resolution

with DISC

Visa, a global leader in digital payments, has integrated DISC into its customer service and conflict resolution training. By understanding the diverse personality types of their customers, Visa's customer service representatives can tailor their interactions to better meet individual needs, resulting in higher satisfaction and loyalty. Additionally, DISC-informed conflict resolution training equips employees with the skills to navigate challenging situations and find win-win solutions, promoting a more harmonious workplace.

Moderna: Driving Innovation and Talent Acquisition with DISC

Moderna, a pioneer in mRNA therapeutics, has incorporated DISC into its innovation processes and talent acquisition strategies. By understanding the diverse perspectives and communication styles of team members, Moderna has created a more collaborative and inclusive environment where creativity thrives. Additionally, DISC assessments are used in the recruitment process to identify candidates whose behavioral styles align with Moderna's culture and values, leading to a better fit and higher employee engagement.

The Predictive Index (PI): DISC-Powered Onboarding for Engagement and Retention

The Predictive Index (PI), a talent optimization company, puts its own medicine to work by making DISC assessments a cornerstone of its onboarding process. New hires complete a DISC assessment before they even start, allowing PI to craft personalized onboarding experiences tailored to each individual's unique style. This results in faster ramp-up times, increased engagement, and higher retention rates.

TTEC: From Onboarding to Leadership Development with DISC

TTEC, a global customer experience leader, has integrated DISC into multiple aspects of its talent management strategy. From personalized onboarding that accelerates new hire learning to customized training and coaching programs that cater to individual needs, DISC helps TTEC maximize employee potential. DISC insights are also used to identify high-potential leaders and provide targeted development opportunities, ensuring a strong pipeline of talent for the future.

These real-world examples demonstrate that DISC is not just a theoretical framework – it's a practical tool that can be applied across a wide range of organizational functions to drive meaningful results. Whether you're looking to boost sales performance, enhance collaboration, improve customer service, or stimulate innovation, DISC can be a valuable asset in your toolkit.

Team DISC Profiles and Management Strategies

By aggregating the DISC profiles of team members, managers gain valuable insights into the overall dynamics of their teams. This information can help identify potential strengths, blind spots, and areas for improvement. Armed with this knowledge, managers can tailor their onboarding, communication, and leadership approaches to maximize team performance. For example, a team with a high concentration of "D" styles might benefit from a more directive leadership approach, while a team with a predominance of "S" styles might thrive under a collaborative and supportive leader.

DISC and Company Culture

Every company has a unique culture, and that culture can either amplify or diminish the impact of certain DISC styles. For instance, a highly competitive and results-driven culture might naturally appeal to individuals with a Dominant style, while a more collaborative and supportive culture might attract those with a Steady style. Understanding the interplay between DISC and company culture can help organizations create a more inclusive and welcoming environment for all employees, regardless of their behavioral preferences.

Disc: Your Onboarding Compass, Your Team's North Star

In this chapter, we've embarked on a journey through the DISC landscape, unearthing its potential to revolutionize how we welcome new talent. By tuning into the unique frequencies of each DISC style, we've discovered a symphony of personalized onboarding experiences that empower individuals to hit the ground running.

Picture this: a workplace where every new hire feels seen, heard, and valued from day one. Where communication flows effortlessly, tasks are perfectly aligned with individual strengths, and teams hum with collaboration and mutual respect. That's the magic of DISC-aware onboarding.

Here's a quick recap of our DISC discoveries:

- **Personalization is Key:** One size does *not* fit all. Tailoring onboarding to each individual's DISC style is the secret sauce for success.
- **Communication is Queen (or King):** Effective communication, customized to each style, builds trust, clarifies expectations, and ignites collaboration.
- **Task Alignment is a Superpower:** When tasks play to individual strengths, engagement and productivity soar.
- **Relationships Thrive on DISC:** Understanding DISC styles unlocks the secrets to building stronger connections and a more cohesive team.
- **Conflict Prevention is a Proactive Game:** By recognizing potential clashes early on, we create a harmonious workplace where everyone feels safe to contribute their unique talents.

But DISC isn't just a one-hit wonder; it's a long-term investment in your company's success. It's a compass guiding your onboarding journey, ensuring that every new hire feels empowered to reach their full potential. It's a north star for your team, illuminating a path towards greater collaboration, productivity, and overall employee satisfaction.

So, what are you waiting for? Embrace DISC, empower your HR team and managers, and watch as your onboarding process transforms into a personalized adventure that celebrates the unique brilliance of each individual. It's time to create a workplace where everyone feels valued, engaged, and ready to make their mark.

But the DISC journey doesn't end with onboarding. Just as we all have unique ways of learning and communicating, we also have distinct motivations and ways of feeling valued. In the next chapter, we'll turn our attention to the power of recognition and rewards, exploring how a DISC-informed approach can unleash the full potential of your team, one well-deserved pat on the back at a time.

Quiz: Match The Disc Style To The Onboarding Task

For each question, choose the option that best reflects the preference of the DISC style in bold.

1. **Dominant (D):**
    a. A detailed step-by-step training manual.
    b. A high-visibility project with a tight deadline.
    c. A team-building lunch with their new colleagues.
    d. A mentorship program with a seasoned professional.
2. **Influential (I):**
    a. A solo assignment with clear, measurable goals.
    b. A chance to present their ideas to a large group.
    c. A quiet workspace where they can focus on learning independently.
    d. A structured schedule with predictable tasks.
3. **Steady (S):**
    a. A fast-paced environment with constant change.
    b. A task that requires them to take charge and make decisions quickly.
    c. A collaborative project with a supportive team.
    d. A complex problem-solving assignment with minimal guidance.
4. **Conscientious (C):**
    a. A vague assignment with open-ended goals.

b. A social event with lots of networking opportunities.
c. A task that involves a lot of public speaking.
d. A detailed analysis of data with clear instructions.

5. **Dominant (D):**
    a. Being praised for their accuracy and attention to detail.
    b. Receiving a handwritten thank-you note from their manager.
    c. Being recognized for their leadership and initiative.
    d. Being given the freedom to work independently.

6. **Influential (I):**
    a. A private office with minimal distractions.
    b. A chance to mentor a new colleague.
    c. A team-building activity like an escape room or trivia night.
    d. A task that involves detailed research and analysis.

7. **Steady (S):**
    a. A surprise office party with a lot of noise and excitement.
    b. A solo project with a tight deadline and high stakes.
    c. A collaborative brainstorming session with their team.
    d. A complex technical training course with minimal interaction.

8. **Conscientious (C):**
    a. A task that involves a lot of ambiguity and requires quick decisions.
    b. A social mixer with new colleagues.
    c. A presentation to senior management.
    d. A chance to learn a new software program at

their own pace.
9. **Dominant (D):**
    a. A task that involves following strict procedures and guidelines.
    b. A role that requires a lot of patience and empathy.
    c. A project that allows them to take charge and make decisions.
    d. A task that involves a lot of collaboration and consensus-building.
10. **Influential (I):**
    a. A quiet workspace where they can work independently.
    b. A task that involves a lot of repetitive tasks and detailed work.
    c. An opportunity to present their ideas to a large audience.
    d. A role that requires a lot of technical expertise and attention to detail.
11. **Steady (S):**
    a. Being micromanaged and closely monitored.
    b. A task that requires them to work independently with little guidance.
    c. Being given a clear roadmap and regular check-ins with their manager.
    d. A task that involves a lot of public speaking and networking.
12. **Conscientious (C):**
    a. A task that requires quick decision-making based on limited information.
    b. A job shadowing experience with a colleague in a different department.
    c. An opportunity to attend a conference or training session.
    d. A task that involves a lot of social interaction and relationship building

13. **Dominant (D):** Which feedback style would they most appreciate?
    a. A detailed report highlighting their strengths and weaknesses, with specific suggestions for improvement.
    b. A heartfelt thank-you note recognizing their contributions to the team.
    c. A public announcement highlighting their achievements and impact on results.
    d. A private conversation where they can discuss their progress one-on-one.
14. **Influential (I):** What type of learning environment would be most effective for them?
    a. A self-paced online course with minimal interaction.
    b. A structured workshop with hands-on exercises and group discussions.
    c. A series of one-on-one coaching sessions with a mentor.
    d. A fast-paced, interactive environment with opportunities to present and share ideas.
15. **Steady (S):** What kind of work environment would they thrive in?
    a. A fast-paced, competitive environment with constantly changing priorities.
    b. A collaborative, team-oriented environment with a focus on shared goals.
    c. An independent work environment where they can focus on tasks without interruption.
    d. A highly structured environment with clear procedures and guidelines.
16. **Conscientious (C):** How would they prefer to receive constructive feedback?
    a. In a casual, informal setting, such as over lunch or coffee.

THE DISC ADVANTAGE

    b. In a group setting with their colleagues, where they can learn from others.

    c. In a private meeting with their manager, where they can ask questions and receive detailed explanations.

    d. Through a written report with specific data and examples.

17. **Dominant (D):** What type of training would be most beneficial for them?

    a. A leadership development program focusing on strategic thinking and decision-making.

    b. A communication skills workshop focusing on empathy and active listening.

    c. A team-building workshop focusing on collaboration and conflict resolution.

    d. A technical training program focusing on the latest industry trends and best practices.

18. **Influential (I):** How would they prefer to be recognized for their contributions?

    a. With a monetary bonus or gift card.

    b. With a public acknowledgement in a company-wide meeting or newsletter.

    c. With a handwritten note from their manager expressing gratitude for their work.

    d. With an opportunity to lead a new project or initiative.

19. **Steady (S):** What kind of onboarding buddy or mentor would be most helpful for them?

    a. A dominant (D) colleague who can push them out of their comfort zone.

    b. A conscientious (C) colleague who can provide detailed information and guidance.

    c. An influential (I) colleague who can

energize and inspire them.
    d. A steady (S) colleague who can offer a supportive and understanding ear.
20. **Conscientious (C):** What type of first-week assignment would best suit them?
    a. A quick project with a tight deadline and immediate results.
    b. A task that involves networking and building relationships with stakeholders.
    c. A collaborative project with a large team and diverse perspectives.
    d. A task that involves researching and analyzing data to solve a specific problem.

Answer Key And Explanations:

1. **Dominant (D): b)** A high-visibility project with a tight deadline. Dominant individuals thrive on challenges, taking charge, and seeing tangible results.
2. **Influential (I): b)** A chance to present their ideas to a large group. Influential individuals enjoy the spotlight, sharing ideas, and inspiring others.
3. **Steady (S): c)** A collaborative project with a supportive team. Steady individuals value teamwork, cooperation, and a sense of belonging.
4. **Conscientious (C): d)** A detailed analysis of data with clear instructions. Conscientious individuals appreciate structure, accuracy, and the opportunity to apply their expertise.
5. **Dominant (D): c)** Being recognized for their leadership and initiative. Dominant individuals value recognition for their achievements and impact on results.
6. **Influential (I): c)** A team-building activity like an escape room or trivia night. Influential individuals enjoy social interaction and building relationships with their colleagues.
7. **Steady (S): c)** A collaborative brainstorming session with their team. Steady individuals thrive in a team environment and enjoy working together towards a common goal.
8. **Conscientious (C): d)** A chance to learn a new software program at their own pace. Conscientious individuals appreciate the opportunity to master new skills and knowledge thoroughly.
9. **Dominant (D): c)** A project that allows them to take charge and make decisions. Dominant individuals thrive in positions of authority and enjoy making

decisions.
10. **Influential (I): c)** An opportunity to present their ideas to a large audience. Influential individuals enjoy public speaking and inspiring others with their ideas.
11. **Steady (S): c)** Being given a clear roadmap and regular check-ins with their manager. Steady individuals value structure, predictability, and a supportive manager.
12. **Conscientious (C): c)** An opportunity to attend a conference or training session. Conscientious individuals value learning and development opportunities to enhance their expertise.
13. **Dominant (D): c)** A public announcement highlighting their achievements and impact on results. Dominant individuals appreciate public recognition for their accomplishments and impact on the organization.
14. **Influential (I): d)** A fast-paced, interactive environment with opportunities to present and share ideas. Influential individuals thrive in dynamic learning environments with opportunities for social interaction and idea sharing.
15. **Steady (S): b)** A collaborative, team-oriented environment with a focus on shared goals. Steady individuals value teamwork, cooperation, and a sense of belonging to a group.
16. **Conscientious (C): c)** In a private meeting with their manager, where they can ask questions and receive detailed explanations. Conscientious individuals appreciate a formal setting where they can ask questions and receive thorough feedback.
17. **Dominant (D): a)** A leadership development program focusing on strategic thinking and decision-making. Dominant individuals are natural leaders and value opportunities to enhance their leadership skills.

18. **Influential (I): b)** With a public acknowledgement in a company-wide meeting or newsletter. Influential individuals enjoy being recognized and celebrated in front of their peers.
19. **Steady (S): d)** A steady (S) colleague who can offer a supportive and understanding ear. Steady individuals value supportive relationships and a sense of camaraderie with their colleagues.
20. **Conscientious (C): d)** A task that involves researching and analyzing data to solve a specific problem. Conscientious individuals enjoy applying their analytical skills and knowledge to solve complex problems.

CHAPTER 10: PERFORMANCE MANAGEMENT: DISC AS A GUIDE FOR GROWTH AND DEVELOPMENT

Cracking The Code To High Performance: The Disc Advantage

Think back to the last time you led a team project. Did everyone jump on board with the same enthusiasm? Did everyone communicate in the same way? Of course not! We're all a unique blend of traits, motivations, and communication styles. And that's where DISC comes in.

In earlier chapters, we explored the DISC model, diving into the four distinct styles – Dominant, Influential, Steady, and Conscientious – each with its own set of superpowers and quirks. We learned that DISC isn't about labeling people, but about understanding the beautiful tapestry of personalities that make up our teams. It's about decoding the unique ways each of us prefers to communicate, collaborate, and even handle conflict. Armed with this knowledge, we can build stronger, more cohesive teams where everyone feels heard and valued.

But hold on, there's more! DISC isn't just a one-hit wonder for team building. It's a secret weapon for supercharging performance management. Traditionally, we've thought of performance management as a numbers game – hitting targets, tracking metrics, and checking boxes. But let's be real, those numbers only tell part of the story. Behind those spreadsheets and graphs are real people with dreams, ambitions, and challenges.

DISC helps us see the human behind the numbers. It gives managers an understanding of what makes each employee tick. What motivates them? How do they best receive feedback? What kind of recognition makes them feel truly appreciated? By tapping into this knowledge, we can create personalized performance management plans that truly ignite passion and drive results.

Imagine a workplace where performance reviews aren't dreaded annual events but become exciting opportunities for growth and development. Picture a culture where feedback is both insightful and empowering, and where recognition feels genuine and motivating. That's the power of DISC-informed performance management.

So, get ready to ditch the cookie-cutter approach and embrace a performance management system that celebrates individuality. In this chapter, we'll dive into how you can use DISC to transform every aspect of performance management – from setting goals that spark ambition to delivering feedback that truly resonates. We'll even show you how DISC can turn those dreaded performance reviews into meaningful conversations that inspire growth and unlock the hidden potential of your team.

Ditch The Cookie-Cutter Performance Reviews: It's Time To Get Personal With Disc!

Performance reviews...those annual rituals that can leave both employees and managers feeling a bit...blah. You know the drill: generic assessments, awkward conversations, and a sense that it's all just a formality. But what if we told you there's a way to ditch the cookie-cutter approach and transform performance reviews into a personalized growth experience?

By understanding the unique ways each DISC style approaches goals, receives feedback, and craves recognition, you can tailor the entire review process to maximize engagement, motivation, and those all-important results.

Picture this:

- Goal-setting sessions that feel like brainstorming sessions, where everyone's ideas are valued and everyone walks away with a clear path forward.
- Feedback conversations that leave employees feeling empowered and inspired to grow, not deflated and demotivated.
- Development plans that align with individual passions and aspirations, igniting a fire of intrinsic motivation.

Sounds pretty good, right? Let's dive into how DISC can make this a reality.

Setting Goals: The DISC Way to Ignite Motivation and Achieve Results

Setting goals is the bedrock of effective performance management. It's about creating a clear path to success, aligning individual efforts with organizational objectives, and providing a roadmap for growth and development. But here's the thing: goals aren't one-size-fits-all. What motivates one person might not inspire another. That's where DISC comes in to craft goals that truly resonate.

Each DISC style brings a unique perspective to goal setting:

- **Dominant (D):** These go-getters thrive on a challenge. They crave ambitious goals that push their limits and showcase their leadership. Give them the autonomy to shine and watch them soar!
- **Influential (I):** Tap into their collaborative spirit by developing team-based goals. Let them brainstorm and share their big ideas – they light up when they can inspire others with their vision.
- **Steady (S):** Show appreciation for their reliability and value their need for clarity and structure. Craft practical goals that contribute to the team's success, and they'll be your most dependable players.
- **Conscientious (C):** Acknowledge their attention to detail and love for data. Provide specific, measurable targets that align with their expertise, and they'll unleash their inner data ninja to achieve them.

So, how do you tailor goals for each style?

- **D:** Get them involved in the goal-setting process, challenge them to aim high, and give them the autonomy to shine.
- **I:** Make it a collaborative effort, let them brainstorm and share their big ideas, and celebrate their wins publicly.
- **S:** Paint a clear picture of the impact their goals will have on the team, provide consistent support, and show your appreciation for their dependability.
- **C:** Get specific, provide measurable targets, and let them unleash their inner data ninja.

By understanding these nuances, you can tailor goal-setting conversations to each individual, creating a sense of ownership and excitement that fuels motivation and drives results. Imagine a goal-setting process that feels less like a top-down mandate and more like a collaborative journey, where everyone feels heard, valued, and invested in their own success.

Feedback: More Than Just a Pat on the Back

Feedback is a gift, but only if it's given in a way that the recipient can truly unwrap and appreciate. Dominants (D) want it straight, no chaser. Influencers (I) crave positivity and recognition. Steadys (S) need sincere appreciation and support, while Conscientious (C) folks value detailed analysis and constructive criticism.

Here's how to hit the right note with each style:

- **D:** Be direct, focus on results, and offer solutions they can own.
- **I:** Be enthusiastic, highlight their strengths, and offer opportunities for collaboration and visibility.
- **S:** Be genuine, express your appreciation, and provide specific guidance.
- **C:** Be thorough, back up your feedback with data, and offer opportunities for improvement.

Growth and Development: Fueling the Fire

A personalized development plan is like rocket fuel for employee growth. Dominants (D) crave leadership challenges. Influencers (I) shine in communication workshops. Steadys (S) thrive in team-building exercises, while Conscientious (C) individuals love to geek out on technical training.

So, stoke the flames of growth with these tailored approaches:

- **D:** Leadership programs, high-visibility projects, mentorship.
- **I:** Communication workshops, presentation skills training, networking events.

- **S:** Conflict resolution training, team-building activities, interpersonal skills development.
- **C:** Technical training, industry conferences, access to learning platforms.

Cracking The Recognition Code: A Disc Approach

Recognition and rewards are vital elements of a happy, high-performing team. But let's face it, not everyone gets excited about the same things. A gold star might mean the world to one person, while another might prefer a quiet "thank you" and a chance to learn something new. That's where DISC comes in – providing understanding what truly motivates each member of your crew.

In the diverse world of personalities, what gets one person jumping for joy might leave another feeling underwhelmed. Think about it:

- **Dominant (D) dynamos** thrive on the thrill of victory. They crave public recognition, shiny trophies (or promotions!), and challenging projects that let them lead the charge. Forget the gushy compliments, they want to know they crushed it!
- **Influential (I) social butterflies** are all about the positive vibes. They love verbal praise, basking in the limelight, and celebrating with their team. A heartfelt "great job!" and a chance to share their accomplishments with others fuel their fire.
- **Steady (S) team players** value genuine appreciation and connection. A handwritten thank-you note or a thoughtful gift speaks volumes to them. They may shy away from the spotlight, preferring quiet acknowledgement and opportunities to contribute to the team's success.
- **Conscientious (C) detail gurus** are all about precision and expertise. Specific, detailed feedback that recognizes their hard work and technical skills is their jam. They also get a kick out of opportunities to learn and grow, so

professional development is a big win.

Understanding these unique preferences isn't just a nice gesture – it's the key to unlocking peak performance. When you speak each employee's language of appreciation, you create a culture where everyone feels seen, heard, and valued for their individual contributions.

So, how do you build a recognition program that works for everyone?

Here's Your Cheat Sheet: Deciphering the DISC Recognition & Reward Code

Let's make recognizing your team as easy as pie (or maybe a customized reward they'll actually enjoy!). Here's your quick guide to making everyone feel valued and motivated:

The Recognition Buffet: A DISC-Inspired Feast of Appreciation

Let's make recognizing your team as exciting as a culinary adventure! Forget the stale one-size-fits-all approach and instead, create a vibrant buffet of recognition options that cater to the unique tastes and preferences of each DISC style. This personalized approach not only makes employees feel valued but also ignites their motivation and engagement.

Variety is the Spice of Recognition:

Imagine this: a recognition menu brimming with diverse flavors to satisfy every palate. It's not just about the standard "Employee of the Month" plaque (though those are great for some!). Think outside the box and offer a range of options that appeal to different DISC personalities:

- **Public Recognition:** For your **Dominants (D)** and **Influentials (I)** who thrive on the spotlight, consider company-wide announcements, awards ceremonies, or opportunities to present their work to a larger audience.

- **Private Appreciation:** Your **Steadys (S)** prefer a quieter approach. A heartfelt handwritten note, a personalized gift, or a one-on-one conversation expressing your gratitude can make a lasting impact.
- **Tangible Rewards: Dominants (D)** and **Conscientious (C)** individuals often appreciate bonuses, promotions, or other tangible rewards that reflect their hard work and dedication.
- **Growth Opportunities:** For your **Conscientious (C)** team members, offer professional development courses, conferences, workshops, or mentorship programs. They crave knowledge and the chance to expand their skillset.
- **Experiential Rewards:** Team outings, social events, or even extra time off can be a hit with **Influentials (I)** and **Steadys (S)** who value camaraderie and work-life balance.

The key is to offer a variety of options so everyone feels valued and recognized in a way that resonates with them.

Personalize: The Secret Sauce to Appreciation

Now that you have a diverse menu of recognition options, it's time to add the secret sauce: personalization. Once you understand what makes each person tick, you can tailor rewards that hit the bullseye every time.

Here's a quick guide to personalizing recognition for each DISC style:

- **Dominant (D):** Give them challenging assignments that showcase their leadership skills, publicly acknowledge their achievements in a company-wide meeting, or offer a bonus or promotion that reflects their impact.
- **Influential (I):** Let them lead a team-building activity, present their work to a wider audience, or shower them with verbal praise and recognition in a social setting.
- **Steady (S):** Write them a heartfelt thank-you note, get them a personalized gift that speaks to their hobbies

or interests, or simply express your appreciation for their dependability and teamwork in a private conversation.
- **Conscientious (C):** Offer detailed feedback on their work, provide opportunities for professional development or further training, or acknowledge their technical expertise in front of their peers.

Specificity: Beyond "Good Job"

Generic praise like "good job" is like giving someone a blank greeting card – it lacks the personal touch. Instead, get specific and focus on the unique contributions each person makes. For example, tell your Dominant employee how their decisive leadership led to a specific outcome, or acknowledge your Conscientious team member's meticulous attention to detail that saved the day.

By tailoring your recognition to each individual's DISC style and preferences, you create a culture of appreciation that promotes motivation, engagement, and high performance. Remember, recognition isn't just about rewards; it's about making each person feel truly valued and understood.

Timeliness: The Power of "In-the-Moment" Appreciation

Recognition is most impactful when it's timely. Waiting for the annual performance review is like giving a birthday present six months late – the excitement fizzles, and the impact diminishes. Instead, imagine a workplace where appreciation is a regular part of the culture, not just an annual event.

When you celebrate wins in real-time, you're not just saying "good job." You're sending a powerful message: "I see you, I value you, and I appreciate your contributions." This immediate recognition reinforces positive behaviors, fuels motivation, and strengthens the connection between effort and reward.

Here are some simple ways to integrate timely recognition into your daily routine:

- **Weekly Shout-outs:** Kick off your team meetings or company newsletters by acknowledging outstanding contributions or celebrating individual achievements. This creates a culture of appreciation and encourages healthy competition.
- **Monthly Awards:** Establish a "star employee" award or recognize exceptional work in specific categories. This adds a sense of excitement and anticipation, motivating employees to strive for excellence.
- **Spontaneous Appreciation:** Never underestimate the power of a simple "thank you," a surprise coffee run, or a small gift. These spontaneous acts of kindness show that you're paying attention and genuinely value your team's efforts.

By making recognition a regular, ongoing practice, you create a positive feedback loop that fuels engagement, productivity, and overall job satisfaction. Remember, the most meaningful recognition isn't just about the grand gestures, but about the consistent appreciation that shows your employees they're valued and seen.

Peer Recognition: The Power of Applause from Your Peers

Recognition isn't just a top-down affair. Imagine the energy and camaraderie that would spark if your employees regularly acknowledged and celebrated each other's wins. By building a culture of peer-to-peer recognition, you create a vibrant ecosystem where everyone feels valued, supported, and motivated to contribute their best.

A simple "thank you" from a colleague can often mean more than a formal award from a manager. It's a genuine expression of appreciation from someone who understands the challenges and triumphs of everyday work. Plus, it creates a ripple effect of positivity, encouraging others to join in and celebrate each other's successes.

There are countless ways to encourage peer recognition:

- **Online Platforms:** Implement a platform where employees can easily give shout-outs, share kudos, or award virtual badges to their colleagues. This can add a fun, gamified element to recognition, making it more engaging and accessible.
- **Informal Shout-outs:** Encourage team members to verbally acknowledge each other's contributions in meetings, emails, or even casual conversations. A simple "great job on that presentation!" or "I really appreciate your help with this project" can go a long way.
- **Recognition Rituals:** Create fun and engaging rituals, like a weekly "high-five" meeting where team members share what they appreciate about their colleagues.
- **Rewards and Incentives:** Consider offering small rewards for employees who actively participate in peer recognition programs. This could be a gift card, an extra day off, or even a fun team outing.

The benefits of peer-to-peer recognition are undeniable:

- **Boosted Morale:** When employees feel appreciated by their colleagues, it creates a sense of belonging and camaraderie.
- **Increased Motivation:** Knowing that their work is valued by their peers can inspire individuals to go above and beyond.
- **Enhanced Collaboration:** Peer recognition nourishes a collaborative spirit, encouraging team members to support and celebrate each other's successes.
- **Stronger Relationships:** Regular acts of appreciation build stronger relationships and trust between colleagues.

By embracing peer recognition, you not only empower your employees to celebrate each other but also create a positive and supportive work environment where everyone feels valued for their unique contributions. It's a win-win for both individuals and the organization as a whole.

Disc Strategies For Recognizing Unsung Heroes

Not all projects are created equal. Some are high-profile, exciting, and ripe with opportunities for recognition and reward. Others, however, involve tackling tough challenges, turning around underperforming areas of the organization, or working behind the scenes on essential but unglamorous tasks. Recognizing and rewarding employees in these situations requires a nuanced understanding of their motivations, frustrations, and individual needs.

This is where DISC becomes an invaluable tool. By understanding the unique preferences and drivers of each DISC style, you can tailor your recognition and reward strategies to resonate with employees facing less-than-ideal circumstances. This personalized approach can boost morale, develop resilience, and ultimately increase the likelihood of success, even in the face of adversity.

Let's explore how to effectively recognize and reward different personality types engaged in challenging projects:

Dominant (D):

- **Acknowledge the Challenge:** Dominants thrive on challenges, so highlight the project's difficulty and the importance of their leadership in tackling it. Acknowledge their resilience and problem-solving abilities.
- **Emphasize Impact:** Even if the project is underperforming, focus on the measurable impact they've made, such as improving efficiency, streamlining processes, or mitigating risks.
- **Offer Autonomy and Authority:** Allow them to take ownership of the turnaround strategy, giving them the autonomy to make decisions and implement solutions.

- **Reward with High-Visibility Opportunities:** Recognize their efforts with promotions, leadership roles in other areas of the business, or opportunities to present their work to senior executives.

Influential (I):

- **Celebrate Small Wins:** Influencers thrive on positive reinforcement. Celebrate milestones, even small victories, to keep their enthusiasm high.
- **Create Opportunities for Collaboration:** Encourage them to build relationships with stakeholders, share their ideas, and promote a positive team environment.
- **Offer Public Recognition:** Acknowledge their efforts in team meetings, company newsletters, or social media posts.
- **Reward with Social Incentives:** Consider team-building activities, social gatherings, or opportunities to network with industry leaders.

Steady (S):

- **Show Sincere Appreciation:** Steadys value genuine appreciation and recognition. Write a heartfelt thank-you note, acknowledge their contributions in private conversations, or give them a small, personalized gift.
- **Emphasize Team Unity:** Highlight the importance of their role in the team's success, even if the overall project is facing challenges.
- **Provide Stability and Support:** Offer additional resources, training, or mentorship to help them overcome obstacles and feel supported.
- **Reward with Team-Based Incentives:** Consider rewards that benefit the entire team, such as team lunches, off-site activities, or flexible work arrangements.

Conscientious (C):

- **Provide Detailed Feedback:** Conscientious

individuals crave specific feedback. Acknowledge their meticulousness, accuracy, and attention to detail, even if the results haven't yet manifested in overall project success.
- **Recognize Expertise:** Highlight their technical skills and knowledge, showcasing how their contributions are crucial to the project's long-term success.
- **Offer Learning Opportunities:** Provide access to relevant training programs, conferences, or workshops that can enhance their skills and knowledge.
- **Reward with Development:** Consider tuition reimbursement, professional certifications, or opportunities to work on special projects that align with their interests.

Additional Strategies:

- **Transparent Communication:** Clearly communicate the challenges and expected timelines of the project, so employees understand the context and have realistic expectations.
- **Celebrate Effort and Progress:** Recognize and reward not just the final results, but also the effort, dedication, and progress made along the way.
- **Link Rewards to Long-Term Goals:** Tie rewards to the eventual success of the project, even if it takes time to achieve, to keep employees motivated and invested.

By tailoring your recognition and reward strategies to the unique motivations of each DISC style, you can create a more positive and supportive environment for employees working on challenging projects. This can lead to increased engagement, resilience, and ultimately, a higher likelihood of achieving project success.

General Errors:

Even with the best intentions, recognizing and rewarding

employees in challenging projects can be tricky. Leaders may inadvertently fall into common traps that not only fail to motivate but can actually backfire, leading to disengagement and resentment. By understanding these potential pitfalls, you can avoid them and create a more positive and supportive environment for your team.

- **Ignoring the Project's Nature:** Leaders may fail to acknowledge the unique challenges and potential frustrations associated with difficult or unglamorous projects. This can lead to feelings of being undervalued and unappreciated.
- **One-Size-Fits-All Recognition:** Using generic rewards or praise that doesn't resonate with individual preferences can backfire, making recognition feel insincere or irrelevant.
- **Focusing Only on Results:** Leaders may neglect to recognize effort, dedication, and progress, especially when immediate results are lacking. This can demotivate employees who are working hard but haven't yet seen a turnaround.
- **Lack of Transparency:** Not communicating the challenges and expected timelines of the project can lead to confusion, frustration, and unrealistic expectations among employees.

DISC-Specific Errors:

- **Dominant (D):**
    - Micromanaging their work, not allowing them to take ownership or make decisions.
    - Failing to recognize their leadership and problem-solving abilities.
    - Offering rewards that don't align with their desire for visibility and advancement.
- **Influential (I):**
    - Ignoring their need for social interaction and

positive affirmation.
- Providing feedback that is overly critical or focuses solely on areas for improvement.
- Offering rewards that don't allow them to showcase their skills or network with others.
- **Steady (S):**
  - Overlooking their need for stability and support, particularly in challenging situations.
  - Giving public recognition that makes them uncomfortable or embarrassed.
  - Offering individual rewards that don't align with their team-oriented values.
- **Conscientious (C):**
  - Not providing detailed, specific feedback on their work.
  - Failing to acknowledge their expertise and attention to detail.
  - Offering rewards that aren't related to professional development or skill enhancement.

By being mindful of these potential pitfalls and tailoring recognition and reward strategies to the unique needs of each DISC style, leaders can create a more positive and supportive environment for employees working on challenging projects, ultimately increasing the chances of success.

Show, Don't Just Tell: Real-World Examples Of Disc In Action

Theory is great, but seeing how these concepts play out in the real world is where the rubber meets the road. Let's dive into some inspiring examples of companies that have successfully harnessed the power of DISC to transform their recognition and reward programs, boosting employee engagement, motivation, and overall performance.

Example: TechCo's DISC-Tailored Rewards

TechCo, a fast-growing software company, was struggling with employee engagement and retention. Recognizing the diverse needs of its workforce, TechCo implemented a DISC-based recognition program. After employees completed a DISC assessment, they were presented with a personalized menu of rewards tailored to their style.

- Dominants (D) could choose from opportunities to lead high-profile projects, attend leadership conferences, or receive performance-based bonuses.
- Influentials (I) were offered the chance to present their work at company meetings, receive public recognition from executives, or participate in team-building workshops focused on communication and collaboration.
- Steadys (S) were given options like personalized gifts, handwritten notes of appreciation from their manager, or opportunities to mentor new hires.
- Conscientious (C) individuals could select from professional development courses, technical training programs, or access to specialized industry publications.

The results were impressive. Employee satisfaction and motivation soared, and turnover rates decreased significantly.

Employees felt seen and valued for their unique contributions, leading to a more positive and productive work environment.

Example: HealthPlus' DISC-Informed Management Training

HealthPlus, a large healthcare organization, recognized that effective teamwork and communication were crucial for delivering high-quality patient care. To enhance these areas, HealthPlus invested in DISC training for its managers.

The training equipped managers with the knowledge and skills to:

- Identify the DISC styles of their team members.
- Tailor their communication style to effectively interact with each style.
- Recognize and reward employees in ways that resonated with their individual preferences.
- Address conflicts and challenges by understanding the underlying communication dynamics.

By implementing DISC-informed management practices, HealthPlus saw significant improvements in teamwork, communication, and overall patient care outcomes. Managers reported feeling more confident in their ability to motivate and engage their teams, while employees felt more understood and appreciated.

Example: RetailCo's Personalized Appreciation Events

RetailCo, a national retail chain, wanted to create more inclusive and engaging employee appreciation events. To achieve this, they used DISC to personalize the experience.

Instead of hosting a generic company-wide event, RetailCo organized several smaller events tailored to different DISC styles. For example:

- Dominants (D) were invited to a competitive team-building event where they could showcase their skills and

win prizes.
- Influentials (I) were treated to a social gathering with food, drinks, and entertainment.
- Steadys (S) enjoyed a more intimate luncheon with personalized gifts and a heartfelt thank-you message from their manager.
- Conscientious (C) individuals were offered a workshop on a topic of professional interest, followed by a Q&A session with industry experts.

By personalizing their appreciation events, RetailCo created a more positive and memorable experience for all employees. This approach not only boosted morale but also cultivated a sense of belonging and appreciation for the unique contributions of each individual.

The Disc Journey Continues: Unlocking Alignment And Realignment

In this chapter, we've explored how DISC can transform performance management from a routine process into a personalized journey of growth and development. We've seen how understanding the unique motivations, communication styles, and preferences of each DISC type can revolutionize goal-setting, feedback delivery, and development planning. We've also examined the power of tailoring recognition and rewards to speak to each individual's language of appreciation, building a culture where everyone feels valued and empowered.

But the journey doesn't end here. In the next chapter, we'll take a deeper dive into how DISC can be leveraged to not only improve performance but also to ensure alignment between individuals and their roles. We'll explore how performance reviews can serve as catalysts for identifying potential mismatches between roles and DISC types, leading to meaningful conversations about career paths and transitions. We'll also share inspiring examples of successful realignments, highlighting the positive impact this can have on both employees and organizations.

By continuing to embrace DISC as a guide, you'll be equipped to create a workplace where individuals thrive, teams collaborate effectively, and the organization as a whole achieves sustainable success. The journey of personal and professional growth is ongoing, and DISC can be your compass, helping you navigate the complexities of human interaction and unlock the full potential of your workforce.

CHAPTER 11: PERFORMANCE MANAGEMENT: FUELING GROWTH, ALIGNMENT, AND REALIGNMENT (WITH DISC)

Introduction: Unleashing The Power Of Disc For Peak Performance

Ready to transform your performance management from "meh" to "magnificent"? The secret weapon you've been missing is right under your nose: DISC.

Your employees are a diverse orchestra, each with their own unique instrument and sound. Trying to conduct them with a one-size-fits-all approach is like asking a violinist to play the drums – it just doesn't work. DISC, however, allows you to become a maestro, understanding the nuances of each instrument and tailoring your approach to create a symphony of productivity and engagement.

In previous chapters, we dove into the four distinct DISC styles: Dominant, Influential, Steady, and Conscientious. Now, it's time to harness this knowledge to revolutionize the way you manage, motivate, and develop your team.

DISC: Your Personal Performance-Boosting Playbook

DISC isn't just a fun personality quiz; it's a practical tool that can unlock the hidden potential within your workforce. Here's how:

- **Speak Their Language:** No more generic feedback or cookie-cutter goals. DISC helps you tailor your communication style, ensuring your message lands with each employee in a way that resonates and inspires action.
- **Ignite Passion:** Ditch the boring objectives and ignite your employees' intrinsic motivation by crafting goals that align with their unique strengths and aspirations.
- **Feedback That Sticks:** Forget generic praise or criticism that goes in one ear and out the other. DISC-informed feedback speaks directly to each individual's needs and preferences, ensuring it's both motivating and constructive.
- **The Right People in the Right Seats:** Uncover hidden talents and address those nagging feelings of "wrong fit." DISC helps you align employees with roles that unleash their full potential, driving satisfaction and performance through the roof.

What's In Store:

Get ready to roll up your sleeves and put DISC to work! In this chapter, we'll dive into the nitty-gritty of:

- Conducting performance reviews that feel like a breath of fresh air

- Setting goals that truly motivate and inspire
- Delivering feedback that promotes growth, not resentment
- Strategically aligning talent to maximize individual and organizational success

By the end, you'll have a powerful toolkit to transform your performance management practices and create a workplace where every employee feels valued, engaged, and empowered to reach their peak potential.

Case Study: Unlocking Hidden Leadership Potential At Innovatetech

InnovateTech, a leading software development firm, faced a common challenge: a high-performing software engineer named Maria wasn't advancing into leadership roles, despite her technical expertise and consistent overachievement on individual projects.

The company decided to implement DISC assessments across their teams to gain deeper insights into their employees' strengths and work styles. Maria's results revealed a "D" (Dominant) personality type, characterized by a preference for autonomy, challenges, and decision-making authority. These traits, while valuable, were not fully leveraged in her current role.

Recognizing this potential mismatch, InnovateTech's management engaged in an open and honest conversation with Maria about her career aspirations. They discovered a hidden desire to lead projects and take on more responsibility, a desire that had been masked by her reserved demeanor and independent work style.

InnovateTech took a proactive approach, offering Maria the opportunity to lead a new product development team. Although initially hesitant, Maria embraced the challenge, leveraging her technical skills and newfound confidence to successfully guide the project to completion. This strategic realignment not only significantly enhanced InnovateTech's product development process but also unlocked Maria's previously untapped leadership potential. This case underscores the value of DISC assessments in uncovering hidden talents and aligning individuals with roles that maximize their strengths and contributions.

Disc-Informed Performance Reviews: The Art Of Tailored Communication And Goal Setting

Reimagine Performance Reviews: Unleash the Power of DISC!

Picture this: a performance review where your words resonate deeply, sparking genuine excitement and motivation in your employee. Not a soul-crushing, awkward encounter, but a dynamic dialogue that fuels growth and ignites a passion for excellence. This is the magic of DISC.

Performance reviews often get a bad rap – dreaded by both managers and employees alike. But what if they could be transformed into a personalized experience that empowers each individual to reach their full potential? With DISC as your secret weapon, you can turn those dreaded reviews into meaningful conversations that inspire, motivate, and drive exceptional results.

Master the Art of DISC-Fueled Communication

DISC helps decipher the unique language of each employee. Learn to speak their language, adapt your tone, and tailor your approach to resonate with their specific DISC style. Your message won't just be heard; it will be felt, understood, and internalized.

Set Goals That Spark a Fire

Forget about generic, cookie-cutter objectives. With DISC, you can set inspiring goals that tap into each employee's deepest motivations. Picture a Dominant type fired up by a challenge, an Influential type energized by a collaborative project, a Steady type thriving with a clear, supportive plan, and a Conscientious type meticulously crafting a detailed strategy. Now that's motivation!

Feedback That Transforms, Not Terrorizes

Feedback doesn't have to be a source of dread. DISC empowers you to transform it into a catalyst for growth. Tailor your delivery to each individual, offering constructive criticism in a way that is both motivating and respectful. Imagine a Dominant type appreciating your directness, an Influential type thriving on your positive reinforcement, a Steady type finding comfort in your empathetic approach, and a Conscientious type valuing your detailed and well-reasoned insights.

The DISC Advantage

By embracing DISC as an integral part of your performance management toolkit, you're not just conducting reviews – you're creating a personalized experience that encourages understanding, fuels motivation, and ultimately drives better results for both the individual and the organization. It's time to ditch the one-size-fits-all approach and unlock the true power of personalized performance management with DISC.

Individualized Goals: Fueling Motivation and Growth Through DISC

Forget generic goals that gather dust on a shelf. With DISC, you'll transform goal-setting into an exhilarating journey, tailored to ignite each employee's unique passions and strengths. Imagine a workplace where every goal is a stepping stone towards personal and professional fulfillment. That's the power of DISC in action!

Dominant (D) – The Trailblazers: For these ambitious go-getters, think big and bold. They crave challenges that push their limits and opportunities to leave their mark. Picture them exceeding sales targets, turning around a deteriorated client relationship, leading high-stakes product launches, or securing major client wins. Fuel their fire by emphasizing the impact of their achievements and dangling the carrot of recognition, advancement, and expanded responsibilities.

Influential (I) – The Collaboration Champions: These social dynamos thrive on connection and collaboration. Their ideal goals involve teamwork and the chance to shine in the spotlight. Think organizing company-wide events, leading mentorship programs, or crafting marketing campaigns that captivate audiences. Emphasize the opportunity to build relationships, make a visible impact, and rally the troops toward a shared vision.

Steady (S) – The Reliable Anchors: For these supportive team players, stability and harmony are key. Goals that highlight their role in maintaining a smooth-running ship will resonate deeply. Think boosting customer satisfaction, streamlining processes, or mentoring colleagues to success. Let them know their contributions are valued, provide clear expectations, and watch them flourish in a predictable, supportive environment.

Conscientious (C) – The Detail Detectives: These analytical minds thrive on precision and accuracy. Think in-depth market analysis, meticulous project plans, or process optimization. Give them the autonomy to dive deep, provide the resources they need, and acknowledge their meticulous approach to problem-solving.

Why It Matters:

By tailoring goals to each DISC style, you're not just setting targets; you're igniting a spark. Employees feel seen, understood, and empowered to reach their full potential. This personalized approach doesn't just boost individual performance; it cultivates a culture of engagement, ownership, and shared purpose that drives your entire organization towards lasting success.

Remember, one size doesn't fit all when it comes to goals. Embrace the power of DISC to create a goal-setting process that truly motivates and inspires every member of your team.

DISC-Informed Feedback: Transforming Feedback into Fuel for Growth

Feedback isn't just about pointing out areas for improvement; it's a powerful tool to ignite growth and unleash potential. But here's the secret: One size does *not* fit all. Just like your employees have unique personalities, they also have distinct ways of receiving and processing feedback. That's where DISC comes in, turning feedback into a personalized experience that motivates, inspires, and truly resonates.

Dominant (D): Straight Talk for Straight Shooters: These action-oriented individuals crave directness and honesty. Skip the fluff and get straight to the point. When praising them, acknowledge their drive, decisiveness, and accomplishments. Need to offer constructive criticism? Focus on tangible results and concrete actions, providing solutions and strategies for improvement. Think: "Your initiative skyrocketed sales, but consider delegating to empower your team."

Influential (I): A Cheerleading Approach: These social butterflies thrive on positive reinforcement and recognition. Shower them with praise for their infectious enthusiasm and collaborative spirit, while gently nudging them towards greater focus. Imagine saying, "Your energy is contagious! Let's channel it into these top priorities for even greater success."

Steady (S): The Empathy Connection: Steady types value support and understanding. When offering feedback, approach them with empathy and focus on their contributions to the team. Recognize their loyalty, dependability, and willingness to go the extra mile. Constructive criticism? Offer it gently, focusing on how their actions impact the team and providing reassurance and guidance for growth. A simple, "Your dedication is invaluable. Let's explore ways to boost your confidence in sharing your ideas in meetings" can go a long way.

Conscientious (C): Data-Driven Dialogue: These detail-oriented individuals value thoroughness and logical reasoning. Offer them detailed, data-driven feedback that acknowledges their accuracy and commitment to quality. Suggest ways to improve efficiency or streamline processes with phrases like, "Your attention to detail is impeccable. Let's explore tools to free up your time for more high-level tasks."

The DISC Difference:

By tailoring goals and feedback to each DISC style, you're not just conducting performance reviews; you're orchestrating a symphony of growth and development. For your ambitious Dominant types, it's about setting the stage for a virtuoso performance, challenging them to reach new heights and acknowledging their drive for results. Your Influential team members crave the spotlight, so let them shine by supporting collaboration and recognizing their ability to inspire others. For the steady and dependable Steady types, create a harmonious environment with goals that emphasize stability and feedback that celebrates their teamwork. And for those detail-oriented Conscientious types, provide the intricate sheet music they need to thrive, with clear expectations and data-driven feedback that acknowledges their precision and expertise.

This approach is more than just a checklist; it's a deep dive into the unique strengths and motivations of each individual, nurturing an environment of trust and understanding. When employees feel seen, valued, and heard, they're empowered to reach their full potential, both individually and as part of a high-performing team. This dynamic creates a ripple effect that strengthens team dynamics, culvates a collaborative culture, and ultimately drives your organization towards greater success.

But performance reviews are just the beginning. In the next section, we'll take this personalized approach even further, exploring how DISC can be your compass for guiding career growth and development.

Case Study: Cultivating Collaboration And Empowering Teams At Harmony Health

Harmony Health, a rapidly expanding healthcare provider, faced a common challenge: a valued employee, Emma, was excelling in her customer service role but was becoming overwhelmed as the company grew. Her performance, though still strong, showed signs of strain.

Recognizing the need to address the situation, Harmony Health utilized DISC assessments to gain deeper insights into their employees. Emma's assessment revealed a strong "S" (Steady) style, highlighting her preference for stability, collaboration, and supportive environments. This insight, coupled with her proven track record of service excellence, sparked an idea.

Harmony Health's leadership team recognized that Emma's natural strengths in building relationships and promoting collaboration could be invaluable in a leadership role. They offered her the opportunity to lead a small team of customer service representatives, a move that aligned with her DISC profile and presented a new avenue for growth.

Initially hesitant about transitioning to a leadership role, Emma embraced the challenge, drawing upon her innate ability to create a positive and supportive work environment. Under her guidance, the team flourished. Communication improved, collaboration increased, and customer satisfaction ratings soared.

This case study illustrates the transformative power of DISC assessments. By understanding Emma's "S" style, Harmony Health not only addressed her individual needs but also tapped into her hidden leadership potential, benefiting both the employee and the organization. It underscores the importance of recognizing and nurturing talent, even in unexpected places, to create a more engaged, productive, and fulfilled workforce.

Realignment Strategies: Unlocking Hidden Potential And Supercharging Careers

Your organization is a puzzle. Each employee is a unique piece, and the DISC model reveals where each piece fits best. But sometimes, even the most talented employees might find themselves in the wrong spot, their strengths underutilized and their potential untapped.

That's where strategic realignment comes in – it's not about fixing problems, but about unlocking hidden potential and developing a sense of fulfillment. By recognizing when an employee's DISC style clashes with their current role, you can proactively create a pathway for them to shine.

Let's decode some common mismatches:

- **Dominant (D) individuals:** These trailblazers might feel like caged birds in roles that lack autonomy and decision-making power. They crave challenges, so give them the reins and watch them soar!
- **Influential (I) individuals:** These social butterflies thrive on connection. If they're stuck in solitary confinement, their wings will wilt. Give them opportunities to shine in collaborative, client-facing roles where their enthusiasm can spread like wildfire.
- **Steady (S) individuals:** These team players crave stability and support. Throw them into a chaotic environment, and they'll likely flounder. Instead, place them in roles that value collaboration, consistency, and clear expectations, and watch them build rock-solid teams.
- **Conscientious (C) individuals:** These detail-oriented masterminds thrive on structure and clarity. If they're lost in a sea of ambiguity, their potential will remain untapped. Give them the tools and information they need

to analyze, plan, and execute with precision, and watch them work their magic.

By spotting these mismatches early on, you're not just preventing frustration and turnover; you're opening doors to new possibilities. You're giving your employees the chance to rediscover their passion, leverage their strengths, and make a real impact.

DISC Assessment Tools: Your Treasure Map to Talent Optimization

Ready to embark on a treasure hunt? Your employees are the treasure, and DISC assessments are your map. In the realm of talent management, there's no shortage of tools to help you uncover hidden gems within your workforce.

DISC assessments aren't just personality quizzes; they reveal the inner workings of your employees' minds. They illuminate work preferences, communication styles, potential growth areas, and even pinpoint those "aha!" moments where a role and an individual's strengths align perfectly.

But just like a treasure map, there's more than one path to the gold. A multitude of DISC assessment tools exist, each with its own unique strengths and features:

- **Everything DiSC Workplace:** This popular choice is like a multi-tool for your team, offering a comprehensive profile of each individual's DISC style, work preferences, and communication style. It's a fantastic option for those seeking a user-friendly, actionable tool to promotes individual and team development.
- **DiSC Classic 2.0:** This deep-dive assessment is like a magnifying glass, revealing the intricate details of each person's DISC style, including their underlying motivations, values, and fears. If you're looking for a comprehensive understanding of how personality impacts workplace behavior and relationships, this one's

for you.
- **The Five Behaviors of a Cohesive Team:** This team-focused assessment is like a blueprint for building a high-performing team. Based on the DISC model, it uncovers your team's collective strengths and weaknesses, helps identify potential conflicts, and paves the way for smoother collaboration.

But wait, there's more! The treasure chest of DISC assessments goes on and on. You'll find specialized tools for leadership development, sales teams, customer service, and more. There are even assessments that focus on conflict resolution, stress management, and emotional intelligence. It's a whole DISC buffet!

Charting Your Course:

So, how do you choose the right assessment for your organization? Consider it your treasure map checklist:

- **X Marks the Spot:** What are your goals? Are you looking to enhance individual performance, create dream teams, or identify future leaders? Your treasure map should point you in the right direction.
- **The Cost of Adventure:** DISC assessments come with varying price tags. Determine your budget to ensure your treasure hunt doesn't break the bank.
- **Time is of the Essence:** How quickly do you need results? Some assessments are quick and easy, while others require a bit more time and exploration.

By carefully evaluating your needs and exploring the vast landscape of DISC assessment tools, you'll discover the perfect map to unlock your team's full potential and steer your organization towards lasting success.

Initiating Realignment Conversations: Unlocking Hidden Potential, One Conversation at a Time

Discovering a mismatch between an employee's DISC style and their role is like finding a hidden treasure chest—full of untapped potential! But opening that chest requires a delicate touch. It's not about criticizing or judging; it's about embarking on a collaborative journey to uncover hidden strengths and passions.

The realignment conversation is a career coaching session where you, the leader, become a guide, helping your employee navigate the bridge between their current reality and their dream destination. By approaching this conversation with empathy, transparency, and genuine excitement about their possibilities, you can transform a potential roadblock into a launching pad for their career.

Reframing the Narrative: From Mismatch to Opportunity

The key is to shift the focus. Instead of dwelling on the mismatch as a problem, reframe it as an exciting opportunity for growth and fulfillment. Help your employee see the mismatch not as a dead end, but as a fork in the road, leading to new and exciting possibilities.

A Step-by-Step Guide to Realignment Conversations

Ready to embark on this journey of discovery? Here's your step-by-step guide to navigating these crucial conversations:

1. **Set the Stage:** Choose a comfortable, private setting where your employee feels safe and at ease. This isn't a quick chat at the water cooler; it's a dedicated conversation that deserves your full attention.
2. **Express Appreciation:** Start by acknowledging their contributions and expressing your appreciation for their value to the organization. Let them know you're invested in their success and want to see them thrive.
3. **Share Observations:** Gently introduce your observations about the potential mismatch between

their DISC style and current role. Be specific, provide examples, and explain how their natural talents might be better suited for a different environment.
4. **Explore Possibilities Together:** This is where the magic happens! Brainstorm potential realignment options *together*. Discuss lateral moves, role adjustments, training opportunities, or even career pathing. The goal is to ignite their imagination and uncover possibilities they may not have considered.
5. **Co-Create a Plan:** Once you've identified a promising path, collaborate on a plan outlining the next steps, timelines, and resources needed for a smooth transition. This ensures the employee feels ownership and agency in shaping their career.
6. **Provide Ongoing Support:** The journey doesn't end with the conversation. Check in regularly to offer support, address any challenges, and celebrate their progress as they embark on this exciting new chapter.

Remember, realignment isn't about fixing problems; it's about unlocking potential. By guiding your employees towards roles that truly ignite their passion and play to their strengths, you'll create a workforce that is not only more engaged and fulfilled but also more productive and valuable to your organization.

Nurturing Growth: Unleashing Potential with Personalized Development Plans

Imagine a workplace where every employee feels empowered, challenged, and equipped to reach their full potential. This isn't a pipe dream; it's the reality you can create with DISC-informed development plans. Forget about generic training sessions that leave employees yawning. By understanding their unique DISC styles, you can craft personalized development paths that truly resonate and ignite their passion for growth.

Dominant (D) – The Leadership Expedition:

These natural-born leaders crave challenges and opportunities to make their mark. Send them on a leadership expedition with strategic thinking workshops, project management boot camps, or even executive coaching. Toss in a few stretch assignments that push their limits, and watch them conquer new heights with gusto.

Influential (I) – The Communication Cruise:

For these social butterflies, communication is their superpower. Embark on a communication cruise, equipping them with top-notch presentation skills, persuasive techniques, and team-building expertise. Don't forget to schedule a few networking events to expand their sphere of influence.

Steady (S) – The Collaboration Camp:

These team players thrive in harmonious environments. Send them to collaboration camp, where they can master conflict resolution, hone their active listening skills, and become collaborative problem-solving ninjas. A little mentoring can go a long way in building their confidence and unlocking their full potential.

Conscientious (C) – The Expertise Exploration:

These detail-oriented masterminds crave knowledge and mastery. Send them on an expertise exploration with technical skills training, data analysis workshops, and project planning bootcamps. Equip them with the latest tools and methodologies, and watch them transform into efficiency experts.

Reap the Rewards:

By investing in personalized development plans, you're not

just developing employees; you're building a stronger, more agile, and more innovative organization. Decreased turnover, increased engagement, and a vibrant company culture are just a few of the treasures that await you on this journey.

Case Study: Realigning Talent For Maximum Impact At Connectco

ConnectCo, a dynamic marketing and communications agency, faced a common challenge: a talented employee, David, was underperforming in his data-heavy, analytical role. Despite his best efforts, his performance reviews consistently highlighted a mismatch between his strengths and the demands of the position. While David received praise for his creativity and exceptional communication skills, his attention to detail and data analysis were consistently lacking.

Recognizing the need to address this issue, ConnectCo turned to DISC assessments to gain a deeper understanding of David's work style. The results revealed that David's "I" (Influential) style was better suited for a customer-facing role, where he could leverage his natural strengths in communication and relationship-building.

Taking a proactive approach, ConnectCo transitioned David to a marketing position, aligning his talents with the demands of the role. This strategic realignment proved to be a resounding success. David thrived in his new position, spearheading successful marketing campaigns, building strong relationships with clients, and exceeding his performance targets. By recognizing and addressing the mismatch between David's DISC style and his initial role, ConnectCo not only improved his performance and job satisfaction but also significantly boosted their marketing efforts and overall client satisfaction.

Unleash The Disc Advantage: Your Secret Weapon For Organizational Success

This chapter has revealed DISC as a powerful tool, not just for understanding individual personalities, but for igniting a transformation in your entire organization. DISC is a turbocharger for your talent management engine, boosting performance, engagement, and ultimately, your bottom line.

Recap: The DISC Difference

- **Engagement on Fire:** By tuning into each employee's unique DISC style, you'll create a workplace where people feel seen, valued, and eager to contribute their best.
- **Goals That Hit the Mark:** Say goodbye to generic objectives and hello to laser-focused goals that tap into individual motivations and strengths. Watch productivity soar as employees chase after targets that truly excite them.
- **Feedback That Fuels Growth:** DISC-informed feedback isn't just about criticism; it's a personalized roadmap for growth. Employees will embrace your guidance, knowing it's tailored to their specific needs and aspirations.
- **Talent in the Right Place:** Forget square pegs in round holes. DISC helps you align talent with roles that spark joy and unleash their full potential, leading to a more harmonious and productive workplace.
- **Bottom Line Boost:** Engaged employees, targeted goals, and optimized talent alignment – it's a recipe for success that translates directly into a healthier bottom line.

The Call to Action: Your DISC Transformation Awaits

Don't let this knowledge gather dust on the shelf! Embrace DISC as a strategic asset, empowering your managers and HR team with the tools to decode your workforce's unique needs and motivations. By investing in DISC assessments and training, you're not just making a smart business move; you're embarking on a journey towards a more vibrant, innovative, and profitable organization.

Looking Ahead: Taking the Pulse of Your Culture with DISC

Ready to zoom out and get the big picture? It's time to go beyond individual personalities and take a deep dive into the heart and soul of your organization – your company culture. Just like a doctor uses tools to assess a patient's health, DISC assessments can be your diagnostic tool for measuring the pulse of your culture.

In the next chapter, we'll swap our magnifying glass for a wide-angle lens, exploring how to evaluate your culture from every angle. We'll explore both quantitative and qualitative methods, uncovering the secrets behind employee engagement, collaboration, and overall well-being.

But here's the twist: We're not just taking a snapshot; we're creating a dynamic movie. DISC allows us to track changes over time, pinpointing areas where your culture is thriving and where it might need a little TLC. We'll uncover hidden strengths, expose potential blind spots, and arm you with the knowledge you need to cultivate a vibrant, high-performing culture that attracts and retains top talent.

CHAPTER 12: MEASURING AND MONITORING CULTURE (WITH DISC)

Measuring And Monitoring Culture (With Disc)

Is your company culture a well-oiled machine or a ticking time bomb? Think of it as your organization's unique personality – the collective values, beliefs, and behaviors that shape how your people interact and get things done. But unlike a person's personality, which can be a bit of a mystery, your company culture can be measured, tracked, and sculpted with intention.

This chapter is your guide to becoming a cultural detective, armed with the DISC assessment tool to decode the hidden patterns within your workplace. We'll uncover why measuring culture isn't just a nice-to-have, but a strategic imperative for success. After all, a thriving culture isn't just about good vibes; it's the secret sauce behind high employee engagement, soaring productivity, groundbreaking innovation, happy customers, and ultimately, a fatter bottom line.

Ignoring your culture is like ignoring a leaky pipe – it might seem minor at first, but left unchecked, it can wreak havoc. We'll show you how measuring culture empowers you to make smart, data-backed decisions, pinpoint areas ripe for improvement, and prove the ROI of your culture-building efforts.

So, what happens if you *don't* take the time to measure? Imagine plummeting morale, a revolving door of departing employees, a toxic work environment that repels top talent, and a tarnished reputation that scares away customers. Not a pretty picture, right? By proactively measuring and monitoring your culture, you can catch these issues early and steer your organization back on course.

Beyond DISC: The Quest for a Complete Picture

While DISC is a powerful tool, it's not the whole story. To truly understand your cultural health, you need to pair those insights with cold, hard data. In the following sections, we'll dive into the world of surveys, performance metrics, and other measurement techniques, showing you how to weave together a tapestry of information that reveals the full picture of your organization's cultural landscape.

Quantitative Methods For Assessing Cultural Health

A. Employee Surveys & Feedback: The Heartbeat of Your Organization

Want to know what's *really* going on inside your company? Employee surveys are your direct line to the heart and soul of your workforce. They're not just about collecting data; they're about listening to the voices that shape your culture, uncovering hidden gems of insight, and discovering areas where a little TLC is needed.

Standard Surveys: Your Cultural Checkup

These comprehensive surveys are your company's annual checkup. They cover everything from employee engagement (how connected and enthusiastic your team is) to satisfaction (how happy they are overall), alignment with company values (how well their beliefs match the leader's), and the effectiveness of teamwork, communication, and leadership.

These surveys use a mix of tools to get the full picture:

- **Likert Scales:** These "strongly agree" to "strongly disagree" ratings give you a quantifiable measure of attitudes and opinions.
- **Open-Ended Questions:** This is where the juicy details emerge! Employees can share specific examples and nuanced feedback that numbers alone can't capture.
- **Employee Net Promoter Score (eNPS):** This simple question – "How likely are you to recommend us as a great place to work?" – can be surprisingly revealing. It's a powerful predictor of employee loyalty, future behavior, and even your company's reputation.

Pulse Surveys: Your Cultural EKG

Need a real-time pulse check on your company's health? Pulse surveys are your go-to tool. These short, frequent bursts of questions can gauge employee sentiment on specific issues or track the impact of recent changes. They act as an early warning system, alerting you to potential problems before they snowball into full-blown crises.

Pulse surveys also give your employees a voice, letting them know their opinions matter. And when you respond promptly to their feedback, you build trust and show that you're committed to creating a positive work environment.

DISC-Based Feedback: Cracking the Code of Communication

Want to take your surveys to the next level? Sprinkle in some DISC-inspired questions to unlock even deeper insights. DISC reveals how different communication styles and personality types interact, shaping your team dynamics and overall culture.

By asking questions like "How well do different communication styles on your team collaborate?" or "Does your manager's communication style resonate with your own DISC style?", you can pinpoint potential friction points and discover opportunities to improve communication and collaboration.

Analysis and Action: Turning Data into Gold

Don't let those survey responses gather dust! Analyzing the data is where the real magic happens. Look for trends, patterns, and areas that need attention. Are employees disengaged? Is there a disconnect between what your company says it values and what employees actually experience? The answers to these questions are goldmines of opportunity.

Once you've got a clear picture, it's time for action. Develop targeted plans to address the issues you've uncovered. This could involve training programs, leadership development initiatives, or even a complete overhaul of your communication strategy. Remember, the key is to close the feedback loop by sharing the survey results and your action plan with your employees. This builds trust and shows that you're serious about creating a workplace where everyone can thrive.

B. Performance Metrics: Your Company's Cultural Vital Signs

Think of your company's performance metrics as its vital signs – a window into its overall health. While they won't diagnose a cultural flu outright, they can reveal a whole lot about how your culture is impacting your bottom line. These metrics aren't just numbers on a spreadsheet; they're clues that can help you decode whether your culture is a wellspring of success or a hidden obstacle.

The Pulse Points of Your Cultural Health

- **Productivity:** Is your company a well-oiled machine, cranking out products, closing deals, and exceeding targets? Or is it more like a sputtering engine, struggling to keep pace? Productivity metrics – sales revenue, units produced, projects completed – can tell you a lot about whether your employees are engaged, motivated, and aligned with your company's goals.
- **Absenteeism:** When employees are MIA more often than not, it's not just about lost productivity. It could be a red flag for low morale, burnout, or even a toxic work environment. Are your people feeling valued and supported? Or are they dreading coming to work each day?
- **Turnover (in General or by Position):** High turnover is like a canary in the coal mine for your company culture. When people are jumping ship, especially from specific roles, it's time to ask some tough questions. Are they dissatisfied with their managers? Do they feel like there's no room for growth? Is the workload unbearable?

- **Customer Satisfaction:** Happy employees tend to create happy customers. If your customer satisfaction scores are tanking, it might be time to look inward. Does your culture prioritize customer needs? Do your employees feel empowered to go the extra mile for clients? Your internal culture can have a huge impact on your external relationships.
- **Safety:** In industries where safety is critical, accidents and near-misses can be devastating. A spike in these incidents could signal a culture where safety takes a backseat to production, or where employees are afraid to speak up about hazards. A truly safe workplace is built on a foundation of trust, communication, and a shared commitment to well-being.
- **Diversity & Inclusion Metrics:** A diverse and inclusive workplace isn't just a feel-good initiative; it's a business imperative. Tracking representation of different demographics and measuring how included employees feel can tell you whether your D&I efforts are bearing fruit. Remember, diversity breeds innovation, creativity, and ultimately, a stronger company culture.

Connecting the Dots: From Numbers to Narratives

Here's the fascinating part: your company's performance metrics and its culture are deeply intertwined. A healthy, supportive culture can supercharge your company's performance, creating a ripple effect of positive outcomes. Think engaged employees, skyrocketing productivity, delighted customers, and a reputation that attracts top talent.

But the reverse is also true. A decline in your KPIs could be a smoke signal for underlying cultural issues. A mass exodus of employees, a string of missed deadlines, or plummeting customer satisfaction ratings – these are all clues that something might be amiss with your culture.

By digging into the data and connecting the dots between

your metrics and your cultural landscape, you can pinpoint exactly where your culture is working for you and where it's holding you back. Armed with this knowledge, you can focus your efforts on the most impactful interventions, ensuring that your culture becomes a driving force for success, not a roadblock to it.

Remember: Correlation doesn't always equal causation. A drop in sales might be due to a market downturn, not necessarily a cultural issue. But by keeping a close eye on your KPIs and gathering additional feedback from your employees, you can get to the root of the problem and take action.

C. DISC Assessments (Team-Level): Your Team's Unique Fingerprint

Think of your team as a band: each member brings their own unique sound, and the magic happens when those sounds blend together harmoniously. DISC assessments help you decipher the musical score of your team, revealing the dominant notes and hidden harmonies that shape your cultural symphony.

While individual DISC profiles are like solo performances, showcasing each person's communication style and preferences, combining them at the team level creates a vibrant tapestry of interactions. It's like a fingerprint, unique to your team, revealing its collective strengths, challenges, and hidden potential.

Imagine a team brimming with "D" (Dominant) styles. They might be a powerhouse of quick decisions and bold moves, but their symphony might lack the soothing notes of patience and collaboration. On the other hand, a team heavy on "S" (Steadiness) styles might play a harmonious tune of teamwork and support, but could struggle to hit the high notes of innovation and risk-taking.

Understanding this team-level DISC profile isn't just about

labeling your team members; it's about uncovering the hidden patterns that drive their behavior and interactions. This knowledge is your key to unlocking a more productive and harmonious workplace.

Here's how you can use DISC to fine-tune your team's performance:

- **Play to your strengths:** Identify the natural talents and tendencies of your team, then leverage them to their fullest potential. Got a team full of "I" (Influence) types? They're your brainstorming gurus, so let them loose on creative problem-solving!
- **Harmonize communication:** By understanding each team member's preferred communication style, you can tailor your approach to resonate with everyone. This means fewer misunderstandings, smoother collaboration, and a happier, more productive team.
- **Resolve discord:** When conflict arises, DISC can help you pinpoint the root cause. Are two clashing "D" styles vying for control? Or is a cautious "C" style feeling overwhelmed by a fast-paced "I"? By understanding the underlying motivations, you can mediate disagreements and restore harmony.
- **Track your progress:** As your team evolves, so will its DISC profile. By monitoring these changes, you can gauge the effectiveness of your team-building efforts, leadership development programs, or other interventions. It's like getting regular checkups for your team's health, ensuring it's always performing at its best.

Remember, team-level DISC analysis isn't about pigeonholing individuals or forcing them to conform. It's about celebrating diversity, understanding how different styles interact, and creating an environment where everyone feels valued and empowered to contribute their unique talents. By viewing your team through the lens of DISC, you can orchestrate a symphony of collaboration, innovation, and success.

Qualitative Methods For Assessing Cultural Health: The Stories Behind The Numbers

Numbers can tell you a lot, but they don't always reveal the full story. When it comes to understanding your company's culture, the real magic happens when you dive deeper, beyond the spreadsheets and graphs. Qualitative methods are your backstage pass to the human side of your organization, revealing the stories, emotions, and experiences that shape your workplace.

A. Qualitative Feedback: Get the Inside Scoop

Think of interviews and focus groups as your company's very own reality show, without the manufactured drama. These unscripted conversations give your employees a chance to share their unfiltered perspectives, giving you an insider's look at what makes your culture tick (or fizzle).

- **Interviews:** Forget those boring, scripted questions. Interviews are your chance to have real, meaningful conversations with your people. Ask open-ended questions that invite them to tell their stories, share their triumphs and challenges, and reveal what makes them tick. You might be surprised by what you uncover – hidden frustrations, unexpected successes, and the real reasons why people stay (or leave) your company.
- **Focus Groups:** Think of these as group therapy for your company culture. By bringing together a diverse group of employees, you can spark dynamic conversations and uncover shared experiences. This can help you identify common pain points, celebrate collective wins, and discover new ways to encourage collaboration and engagement.
- **Digging Deeper:** Don't just scratch the surface

– probe deeper into the things that really matter to your employees. Ask about their day-to-day experiences, their alignment with company values, their thoughts on leadership, the effectiveness of teamwork, their career aspirations, and their overall assessment of your cultural health. These conversations can reveal hidden gems of insight that you'd never find in a survey.

- **DISC-Specific Feedback:** While you're at it, don't forget to get the scoop on how DISC is playing out in your workplace. Is it helping employees understand and connect with their colleagues? Are leaders using DISC insights to promote a more inclusive and collaborative environment? The answers to these questions can help you gauge the effectiveness of your DISC initiatives and identify areas where you can fine-tune your approach.

By embracing qualitative feedback, you're not just collecting data – you're building trust, showing your employees that their voices matter, and creating a culture of open communication.

B. Observation: Your Cultural Detective Work

Don't underestimate the power of your own two eyes! In the world of culture assessment, observation offers a front-row seat to the daily drama (or harmony) of your workplace.

An organization's leaders are cultural detectives, sleuthing out the subtle cues and unspoken dynamics that shape your company's personality. They're not just evaluating spreadsheets and project outcomes; they're tuning into the interpersonal vibes, the unspoken communication patterns, and the way decisions get made.

Encourage your leaders to ditch their desks and wander around, engaging in casual conversations, sitting in on meetings, and observing how teams interact. Are people collaborating like a well-oiled machine? Do they radiate trust and respect for each other? Is communication flowing freely, like a lively dinner conversation? These positive signs are the telltale signs of a healthy, thriving culture.

But just like any good detective, your leaders need to be on the lookout for red flags too. Is there an undercurrent of disengagement? Do you sense a lack of trust? Are cliques forming, or is there a cutthroat vibe in the air? Are behaviors contradicting the values your company proudly proclaims? These warning signs can be subtle, but they're crucial to catch before they escalate.

Here's where DISC comes in handy. Your organization's leaders will spot potential conflicts brewing between different personality styles, understand why certain teams are thriving while others are floundering, and tailor their leadership approach to meet each individual's unique needs.

For instance, imagine a leader trained in DISC observes a team dominated by "S" (Steadiness) styles struggling with a sudden shift to a fast-paced, high-pressure project. Recognizing that "S" styles value stability and routine, the leader can proactively step in, offering extra support, clear communication, and a steady hand to guide the team through the transition.

By empowering your leaders to become skilled observers, you're tapping into a wealth of real-time cultural data that's impossible to capture through surveys or metrics alone. This front-line intel can complement your other assessment methods, giving you a 360-degree view of your culture's strengths, weaknesses, and hidden opportunities for growth.

C. Cultural Audits: A Deep Dive into Your Company's DNA

Want to truly know your company? It's time for a cultural checkup – a deep dive into the DNA that makes your organization tick. A cultural audit is like a comprehensive physical exam for your workplace, going beyond the surface to reveal the hidden strengths, weaknesses, and quirks that make your company unique.

Think of it this way: just as a financial audit ensures your books are in order, a cultural audit examines the values, beliefs, and behaviors that shape your workplace. It's a chance to peel back the layers and uncover the underlying forces that drive how your employees interact, collaborate, and contribute to your overall success.

What's in a Cultural Audit?

- **Artifacts:** These are the visible signs of your culture, like your mission statement hanging in the lobby, your company dress code (or lack thereof!), and even the language used in emails. Artifacts are like clues that hint at your company's personality, but they don't always tell the whole story.
- **Values:** Every company has values, but are they just words on a website, or do they actually guide your actions? A cultural audit digs into both your *espoused* values (what you say you believe) and your *enacted* values (what you actually practice). If there's a mismatch, it can lead to some serious cultural dissonance.
- **Behaviors:** Forget the official company line; a cultural audit is all about how people *really* act. Are they a team of collaborators or a pack of lone wolves? Do they embrace innovation or play it safe? Do they feel empowered to speak up, or do they fear the consequences? By observing meetings, casual conversations, and how people react under pressure, you can reveal the true nature of your culture.
- **Communication Patterns:** How does information flow through your company? Is it a free-flowing river of ideas, or does it get stuck in departmental dams? Who are the real influencers, the ones who shape opinions and drive decisions? A cultural audit can map out these communication highways, helping you identify

bottlenecks and ensure everyone's voice is heard.
- **Decision-Making Processes:** Who calls the shots, and how do they do it? Are decisions based on careful analysis and data, or are they driven by gut instincts and personal agendas? A cultural audit can shed light on whether your decision-making aligns with your values and goals.

Why Bother with a Cultural Audit?

- **Uncover Hidden Issues:** Like a skilled detective, a cultural audit can unearth problems that might be lurking beneath the surface. It can reveal a lack of trust between teams, unhealthy competition, or a disconnect between management and employees. The sooner you find these issues, the sooner you can address them.
- **Get an Outsider's Perspective:** Sometimes it takes a fresh pair of eyes to see things clearly. Cultural audits often involve bringing in external experts who can provide unbiased insights and challenge your assumptions.
- **Celebrate Your Strengths:** It's not all doom and gloom! A cultural audit also highlights what your company is doing right. Recognizing your strengths is just as important as identifying weaknesses, allowing you to build on your successes.
- **Create a Roadmap for Change:** The data you gather during a cultural audit is pure gold. It gives you a roadmap for making meaningful changes, whether that means investing in leadership training, revamping your communication strategy, or creating new policies that align with your values.
- **Invest in Your Future:** A healthy culture is like a magnet for top talent, a catalyst for innovation, and a source of pride for your employees. By investing in a cultural audit, you're not just fixing problems; you're investing in a brighter future for your organization.

There are various ways to conduct a cultural audit, from

surveys and interviews to observations and document reviews. The key is to involve a diverse group of employees at all levels, so you get a true reflection of your company's unique personality.

D. Social Network Analysis: Your Company's Social X-Ray

Ever wished you could see the invisible connections that make your company tick? Social Network Analysis (SNA) is like an X-ray for your organization, revealing the hidden pathways of communication, influence, and collaboration. It's like mapping out the social ecosystem of your workplace, showing you who talks to whom, how information flows (or gets stuck), and who's the life of the party (or the wallflower).

How Does SNA Work? It's Like Magic, But with Data

SNA uses special software to gather data from all sorts of sources: emails, chats, meeting invites, even those random Slack threads about the latest office snack debate. It then weaves this data into a visual map, with each person represented as a dot (or "node") and their connections as lines (or "links"). Think of it like a high-tech constellation, where the stars are your employees and the lines are their relationships.

This map isn't just a pretty picture; it's a goldmine of insights. Here's what it can reveal:

- **Communication Flow:** Is information zipping through your company like a well-oiled machine, or is it getting stuck in departmental silos? SNA can pinpoint the traffic jams and detours, helping you streamline communication and ensure everyone gets the memo.
- **The Hidden Influencers:** We all know the official leaders, but who are the *real* movers and shakers? SNA can uncover the hidden influencers – the people whose opinions and actions hold sway, even if they don't have a fancy title. These folks can help drive change and boost morale.

- **The Water Cooler Gang:** Every office has its cliques and informal networks. SNA can map out these social circles, showing you where the real action is happening. This knowledge can help you nurture collaboration, tap into the power of these networks, and even prevent toxic gossip from spreading.
- **The Lone Wolves:** On the flip side, SNA can also identify those who are feeling isolated or left out of the loop. This can be a major red flag for disengagement and potential turnover. By understanding these patterns of isolation, you can build bridges and create a more inclusive environment.

Why Should You Care About SNA?

In a nutshell, SNA gives you the power to:

- **Turbocharge communication:** By understanding how information flows, you can optimize your communication channels, ensuring everyone gets the right info at the right time.
- **Break down silos:** Support collaboration by connecting people across departments and encouraging them to share ideas and knowledge.
- **Target your efforts:** Use the insights from SNA to create tailored interventions that address specific cultural issues, like low trust, poor communication, or resistance to change.
- **Make smarter decisions:** Say goodbye to gut feelings and anecdotal evidence. SNA gives you hard data to back up your cultural assessments and improvement plans.

By harnessing the power of social network analysis, you're not just mapping out your company's social structure; you're creating a roadmap for a more connected, collaborative, and high-performing culture.

E. Additional Qualitative Methods: Unearthing Hidden Gems

& Sharing the Spotlight

Think you've uncovered everything about your company culture? Think again! These additional qualitative methods are like hidden treasure chests, waiting to be unlocked and reveal valuable insights into your organization's soul.

Suggestion Box/Anonymous Feedback: Ever heard the phrase "honesty is the best policy"? Well, it applies to your company culture too. Give your employees a safe space to speak their minds, free from judgment or fear of repercussions. A suggestion box – whether it's an old-school wooden box or a sleek online form – can become a treasure trove of candid feedback, innovative ideas, and even constructive criticism. By encouraging anonymous feedback, you create an environment of trust and transparency, allowing hidden truths to surface and spark meaningful change.

Storytelling/Case Studies: Stories have the power to ignite emotions, inspire action, and bring your company values to life. Tap into this power by collecting and sharing stories about how your employees experience and embody your culture. These stories could highlight acts of kindness, innovative solutions, or moments of triumph over adversity. They might be gathered through casual conversations, dedicated storytelling workshops, or even a company-wide "culture story" contest.

Once collected, these stories can be shared in a variety of ways, from internal newsletters and company-wide meetings to social media campaigns and external publications. Imagine the impact of sharing a story about a team that went above and beyond to help a customer, or an employee who embodies your company's commitment to innovation. These stories become powerful reminders of what your company stands for, inspiring others to live those values and creating a shared sense of pride and purpose.

By incorporating these additional qualitative methods into your cultural assessment toolkit, you'll gain a deeper, more nuanced understanding of your organization. You'll uncover hidden issues, celebrate successes, and create a culture that resonates with your employees and drives your business forward.

Case Study: The Customer Success Conundrum At Techco

Background:

TechCo, a mid-sized technology company renowned for its innovative products and agile environment, was grappling with a persistent problem: an alarmingly high turnover rate within its Customer Success Manager (CSM) position. While the company boasted a cutting-edge culture overall, the CSM role seemed to be a revolving door. In the past year, the turnover rate for CSMs had skyrocketed to 35%, significantly higher than the 15% industry average. This constant churn was not only expensive, requiring frequent recruitment and onboarding, but it was also impacting customer satisfaction and retention.

The Challenge:

TechCo's HR department was tasked with identifying the root cause of this CSM turnover crisis. They suspected that cultural factors were contributing to the problem, but they needed concrete evidence to pinpoint the specific issues and formulate effective solutions.

The Approach:

To gain a deeper understanding of the CSM experience, TechCo embarked on a comprehensive investigation, combining various data sources:

1. **Targeted Exit Interviews:** HR conducted in-depth exit interviews specifically with departing CSMs, delving into their reasons for leaving, their day-to-day experiences, and their perceptions of the role and the company culture. These interviews revealed common pain points, including excessive workload,

a lack of clear career progression within the CSM track, and feeling undervalued compared to other departments.

2. **Employee Surveys (CSM-Focused):** TechCo designed a survey specifically for current CSMs, addressing their job satisfaction, relationship with their managers, perceived support from other teams, and their overall assessment of the company culture. The survey results echoed the concerns raised in the exit interviews and highlighted additional issues, such as inadequate training and resources, unclear performance expectations, and a disconnect between the company's stated values and the realities of the CSM role.
3. **Performance Metrics Analysis:** HR analyzed CSM-specific performance metrics, including customer satisfaction ratings, renewal rates, and upsell/cross-sell success. They found a correlation between declining customer satisfaction and the tenure of CSMs, suggesting that newer CSMs were struggling to meet customer needs effectively.
4. **DISC Assessments:** TechCo also utilized DISC assessments to analyze the communication styles and preferences of CSMs. They discovered a significant mismatch between the dominant DISC style of CSMs (often "I" or "S," valuing relationships and support) and the prevalent communication style of their engineering counterparts (often "D" or "C," prioritizing directness and data). This mismatch could lead to frustration, misunderstandings, and a feeling of being unheard for the CSMs.

The Solution:

Armed with this comprehensive data, TechCo implemented a series of targeted interventions:

1. **Workload Management:** They redefined the CSM role, reassigning certain tasks to other departments to reduce the overall workload. They also hired additional CSMs to ensure a more manageable client-to-manager ratio.
2. **Career Path Development:** TechCo established a clear career path for CSMs, outlining potential progression routes within the customer success department or even into other areas of the company. They also provided training and mentorship opportunities to support CSMs' professional growth.
3. **Improved Onboarding and Training:** They revamped the onboarding process for new CSMs, providing more extensive training on product knowledge, customer relationship management skills, and internal processes. They also created resources and tools to support CSMs in their day-to-day work.
4. **Communication and Collaboration Enhancement:** TechCo organized regular cross-functional meetings between CSMs and engineering teams to improve communication and collaboration. They also provided training on DISC to help employees understand and adapt to different communication styles.

The Results:

Within six months of implementing these changes, TechCo saw a dramatic drop in CSM turnover, from 35% to 12%. Customer satisfaction ratings also improved significantly, and the company experienced a higher rate of customer renewals and successful upsells.

Key Takeaways:

This case study demonstrates the importance of taking a

targeted, data-driven approach to address high turnover in specific roles. By combining various data sources and focusing on the unique challenges of the CSM position, TechCo was able to identify and address the root causes of their turnover problem, ultimately creating a more positive and supportive environment for their CSMs, which translated into improved customer outcomes and overall business success.

Using Disc Assessments To Track Cultural Changes: Your Culture's Dynamic Fingerprint

DISC is more than just a personality test; it's a dynamic tool that acts like a cultural seismograph, detecting subtle shifts and tremors in your organization's landscape. By analyzing how DISC profiles change over time, both at the team and individual levels, you gain a deeper understanding of your company's evolving personality.

This isn't about pigeonholing people into rigid categories. It's about recognizing the dynamic interplay of communication styles, collaboration patterns, and potential conflicts that shape your cultural ecosystem. Are your teams becoming more collaborative or more competitive? Are communication styles shifting towards directness or diplomacy? Are there underlying tensions that could erupt into full-blown conflict?

By keeping a finger on the pulse of your DISC data, you can catch these subtle shifts early on, like a canary in a coal mine warning of potential hazards. This allows you to proactively address issues, fine-tune your team-building efforts, and nurture a culture that's adaptable, resilient, and constantly evolving for the better.

A. Team Dynamics: Charting the Course through Ever-Changing Waters

Your team is a vibrant coral reef, teeming with diverse life forms, each with its own unique role and rhythm. Just like a reef, your team's dynamics are constantly shifting and evolving, shaped by the currents of personalities, goals, and challenges. DISC assessments are your trusty compass in this ever-changing landscape, helping you navigate these currents and steer your team towards smoother waters.

By blending individual DISC profiles, you can create a snapshot of your team's collective personality – its unique "reef print." But this snapshot is not a static picture. As new "fish" join the reef or old ones swim away, the team's DISC profile can shift, signaling subtle changes in how your team communicates, collaborates, and handles conflict. A sudden influx of driven "D" (Dominant) types might create a more competitive current, while a growing presence of supportive "S" (Steadiness) types could signal a desire for calmer waters and greater collaboration.

Monitoring these shifts is like checking your compass regularly. It allows you to spot early warning signs of cultural drift – the subtle undercurrents that can lead to choppy waters, such as increased conflict, disengagement, or declining productivity. Catch these warning signs early, and you can steer your team back on course before a storm brews.

Imagine a team that was once a harmonious haven, full of collaborative "S" and enthusiastic "I" (Influence) types. But then, a new "D" style leader enters the scene, shaking things up with their take-charge attitude and focus on results. Suddenly, the once-calm waters become turbulent, with some team members feeling overwhelmed by the newfound pressure and others struggling to adapt to the new leadership style.

This is where your DISC compass becomes invaluable. By understanding these shifts, you can proactively intervene, using your knowledge of each style's strengths and weaknesses to tailor team-building activities and communication strategies. Maybe your "C" (Conscientious) folks need a little help opening up and expressing their feelings, or perhaps your "I" types need some structure to channel their boundless energy.

By adapting your approach to fit the unique personality of your team, you can create a thriving ecosystem where everyone feels valued, understood, and empowered to contribute their best. Your team will become more than just a collection of individuals; it will become a cohesive unit, navigating the ever-changing waters of the workplace with confidence and resilience.

B. Onboarding and Offboarding: Using DISC to Find Your Perfect Puzzle Pieces

Imagine your company culture as a vibrant jigsaw puzzle. Each piece represents a unique individual with their own set of skills, experiences, and – most importantly – personality. DISC assessments can help organizational leaders find the perfect puzzle pieces that fit seamlessly into the existing cultural picture.

Think of it like a matchmaking service for your team. By understanding a candidate's DISC style during the hiring process, you're not just evaluating their resume; you're getting a sneak peek into their communication style, work preferences, and how they might vibe with your existing crew. This allows you to make smarter hiring decisions, avoiding those awkward moments when a new hire feels like a fish out of water.

When you strategically match DISC styles to your team's dynamics and overall company culture, you're setting the stage for a beautiful picture of harmony and productivity. New hires will feel like they belong, hit the ground running, and be less likely to jump ship – a win-win for everyone involved.

But DISC doesn't stop at onboarding. It's also your trusty detective when it comes to figuring out why people leave. By analyzing the DISC profiles of departing employees, you can uncover hidden clues about potential cultural mismatches.

For example, if you notice an exodus of "S" (Steadiness) types, it might be a sign that your culture is a bit too chaotic for their liking. They crave stability, support, and collaboration, so if your workplace is all about cutthroat competition and high-pressure deadlines, they might feel like they're drowning.

Armed with this knowledge, you can take proactive steps to refine your onboarding process, tailor training programs to different DISC styles, and create a more inclusive environment where everyone feels valued and supported. Think of it as adjusting the lighting and temperature in your office to create the perfect environment for your unique blend of personalities.

By using DISC to fine-tune your onboarding and offboarding processes, you can create a workforce that's not just a collection of random pieces, but a masterpiece of collaboration, innovation, and success.

C. Leadership Development: Sculpting Your Cultural Champions with DISC

Ever heard the saying, "People don't leave bad jobs, they leave bad bosses"? The truth is, leaders have an outsized impact on your company culture. They're not just managers; they're the architects of your workplace environment, setting the tone for how employees interact, collaborate, and thrive.

That's where DISC comes in. It's like shining a spotlight on your leaders' unique styles, revealing their strengths, blind spots, and how they influence the cultural ecosystem around them. Imagine your leadership team as a cast of characters in a play:

- The "D" (Dominant) director, boldly making decisions and driving results.
- The "I" (Influence) star, captivating the audience with their enthusiasm and vision.
- The "S" (Steadiness) ensemble player, promoting collaboration and harmony.
- The "C" (Conscientiousness) stage manager, ensuring every detail is perfect.

Understanding this cast of characters is key to directing a show-stopping performance. Are your leaders all "D" types, creating a high-pressure, results-driven environment that leaves little room for collaboration? Or maybe your "S" style leaders are so focused on harmony that they struggle to make tough decisions or challenge the status quo.

DISC gives you the director's notes you need to fine-tune your leadership symphony. By recognizing each leader's unique style, you can pinpoint areas for growth and craft personalized development plans that truly make a difference.

Imagine coaching your "D" director to dial down the intensity and cultivate more empathy, or helping your "S" stage manager find their voice and become a more assertive decision-maker. The result? A more well-rounded leadership team that can tackle any challenge and inspire their teams to greatness.

But DISC isn't just about developing existing leaders; it's about nurturing future talent. By identifying high-potential individuals with diverse DISC styles, you're building a leadership bench that's ready to tackle the ever-changing demands of the modern workplace. This diverse mix of personalities can spark innovation, lead to better decision-making, and create a culture where everyone feels valued and heard.

Investing in leadership development through DISC is a long-term play, but the payoff is huge. By cultivating a team of self-aware, adaptable, and collaborative leaders, you're creating a cultural powerhouse that can drive employee engagement, boost performance, and ultimately catapult your company to the top of its game.

Case Study: Streamlining Collaboration At Pharmadev

Background:

PharmaDev, a pharmaceutical development firm known for its cutting-edge research and rigorous drug development processes, was experiencing a growing sense of disconnect among its employees. The company's expansion had led to the formation of distinct silos between research, clinical trials, regulatory affairs, and marketing departments. This fragmentation hindered collaboration, slowed down project timelines, and threatened to stifle innovation.

The Challenge:

PharmaDev recognized the need to break down these silos and promote a more collaborative culture. However, they lacked a clear understanding of the underlying communication patterns and relationships that were perpetuating the problem. They needed a way to visualize the social dynamics of the organization and identify targeted interventions.

The Approach: Social Network Analysis

PharmaDev decided to leverage Social Network Analysis (SNA) to map the company's social ecosystem. They partnered with an external consultant specializing in SNA to collect and analyze data from various sources, including emails, internal messaging platforms, meeting schedules, and project collaboration tools.

Key Findings:

The SNA revealed several critical insights into PharmaDev's organizational structure:

- **Departmental Silos:** The network map clearly

showed distinct clusters of communication within each department, with limited interaction between them. This confirmed the initial suspicion of silos and highlighted the urgency of supporting cross-functional collaboration.
- **Hidden Experts:** The analysis identified several "hidden experts" – individuals with deep knowledge and expertise who were not in formal leadership positions but were highly sought after for advice and consultation within their specific areas. These individuals could be valuable resources for knowledge sharing and mentoring.
- **Communication Bottlenecks:** SNA revealed key individuals who acted as gatekeepers of information, often delaying the flow of critical information between departments. This highlighted the need to streamline communication channels and empower employees to share information more freely.
- **Isolated Teams:** The analysis also identified entire teams that were isolated from the main communication networks, particularly those working on highly specialized projects. This isolation led to feelings of disengagement and lack of awareness of broader company goals.

Interventions:

Based on the SNA findings, PharmaDev implemented a multi-faceted approach to encourage collaboration:

- **Cross-Functional Task Forces:** They established task forces comprised of individuals from different departments to address specific challenges or projects. This encouraged collaboration, broke down barriers between silos, and supported a shared sense of ownership.
- **Expert Knowledge Sharing Platforms:** They created online platforms and forums where hidden experts could share their knowledge and expertise

with the wider organization. This facilitated knowledge transfer, encouraged learning, and promoted a culture of continuous improvement.
- **Communication Training:** They provided training to managers and employees on effective communication strategies, emphasizing the importance of clarity, transparency, and active listening. They also encouraged the use of collaborative tools and platforms to facilitate communication across departments.
- **Company-Wide Events:** They organized regular company-wide events, such as town halls, social gatherings, and team-building activities, to build informal interactions and build stronger relationships between employees from different departments.

Results:

After implementing these interventions, PharmaDev observed a significant improvement in collaboration and communication across the organization. Project timelines were shortened, bottlenecks were reduced, and employee engagement scores increased. The company also experienced a renewed sense of shared purpose and collective commitment to its mission.

Key Takeaways:

This case study demonstrates the power of social network analysis in uncovering hidden patterns of communication and collaboration within a pharmaceutical development firm. By understanding the social dynamics of the organization, PharmaDev was able to identify and address cultural issues, break down silos, and encourage a more connected and collaborative workforce. This, in turn, led to improved efficiency, innovation, and overall organizational performance.

Case Study: Navigating Cultural Currents At Golden Gate Investments

Background:

Golden Gate Investments, a prestigious financial services firm with a long-standing history of success, was facing a period of internal turbulence. Despite a strong reputation and consistent financial performance, employee morale was waning, turnover was on the rise, and a sense of stagnation had settled over the organization. Leadership recognized that a cultural shift might be necessary to reinvigorate the company, but they lacked a clear understanding of the underlying issues.

The Challenge:

Golden Gate Investments needed to gain a comprehensive understanding of its culture, both the positive aspects that had driven its past success and the potential challenges that were hindering its current growth. They sought to identify the root causes of employee dissatisfaction and develop a roadmap for cultural transformation.

The Approach: A Cultural Audit

To embark on this journey of self-discovery, Golden Gate Investments decided to conduct a cultural audit. They partnered with an external consulting firm specializing in organizational culture assessment to ensure an unbiased and thorough evaluation.

The Audit Process:

The cultural audit unfolded in several phases, each designed to peel back a different layer of the company's cultural onion:

> 1. **Document Review:** Consultants meticulously reviewed the company's mission, vision, and

values statements, as well as internal policies, employee handbooks, performance reviews, and communication materials. This provided a foundation for understanding the company's espoused values and formal structures.
2. **Employee Surveys:** A comprehensive survey was distributed to employees across all levels, from entry-level analysts to senior executives. The survey included both quantitative questions (using Likert scales) and open-ended questions to capture a wide range of opinions and experiences related to work environment, leadership, communication, decision-making, and overall satisfaction.
3. **Interviews and Focus Groups:** The consultants conducted in-depth interviews with a diverse group of employees, representing different departments, tenure levels, and demographic backgrounds. These interviews provided a platform for employees to share their personal experiences, insights, and concerns about the company culture. Focus groups were also held to promote open discussions and explore shared perspectives within specific teams or functions.
4. **Observation:** The consultants immersed themselves in the daily life of Golden Gate Investments, observing interactions in meetings, common areas, and social events. They paid close attention to communication patterns, leadership styles, and the overall atmosphere of the workplace.

Key Findings:

The cultural audit unearthed several critical insights:

- **Misalignment of Values:** While Golden Gate Investments proudly proclaimed values of integrity, client focus, and teamwork, the audit revealed that

employees felt these values were not consistently practiced. There was a perceived emphasis on individual achievement over collaboration, a risk-averse culture that stifled innovation, and a hierarchical structure that hindered open communication.
- **Communication Breakdown:** Communication was often top-down and lacked transparency. Employees felt their voices were not heard and that they were not included in decision-making processes.
- **Lack of Recognition:** There was a widespread feeling of underappreciation, with employees feeling that their hard work and contributions were not adequately recognized or rewarded.
- **Stifled Growth:** Many employees expressed frustration with the lack of opportunities for professional development and career advancement within the company.

Action Planning and Implementation:

Armed with these insights, Golden Gate Investments embarked on a comprehensive cultural transformation initiative:

- **Leadership Transformation:** The executive team underwent intensive leadership coaching and development programs to cultivate a more collaborative, inclusive, and empathetic leadership style. They committed to more transparent communication and actively sought employee feedback.
- **Empowerment and Autonomy:** The company introduced initiatives to empower employees at all levels, giving them more autonomy and decision-making authority. They also implemented cross-functional teams to encourage collaboration and break down silos.
- **Recognition and Rewards:** A revamped recognition and rewards program was introduced, celebrating

both individual achievements and team successes. The company also invested in professional development opportunities to support employees' growth and career aspirations.
- **Open Communication Channels:** The company established new channels for communication, such as regular town hall meetings, employee forums, and anonymous feedback mechanisms.

Results:

The cultural transformation at Golden Gate Investments yielded remarkable results. Employee engagement scores improved significantly, turnover rates dropped, and the company experienced a renewed sense of energy and optimism. Clients reported a more positive and collaborative experience, and the company's overall financial performance improved.

Key Takeaways:

This case study demonstrates the power of a cultural audit in uncovering hidden cultural issues and driving transformative change. By taking a holistic approach and investing in data-driven interventions, Golden Gate Investments was able to create a more positive, inclusive, and high-performing culture that benefited both employees and the company's bottom line.

Measuring And Monitoring Culture (With Disc)

Your company culture isn't a destination you reach and then kick back; it's a vibrant, ever-evolving journey. It's shaped by everything from leadership changes and market fluctuations to the diverse personalities and experiences of your employees.

Just like a living organism, your culture needs constant nourishment and care. That's why measuring and monitoring it isn't a one-time check-up, but an ongoing practice. Imagine it as a regular fitness routine for your workplace, ensuring it stays healthy, strong, and adaptable to whatever challenges come its way.

By regularly collecting data through surveys, interviews, observations, and DISC assessments, you become a cultural fitness coach. You can track your company's vitals, spot any areas that need a little extra attention, and celebrate the strengths that make your organization unique. This ongoing feedback loop empowers you to make informed decisions and guide your culture towards greater health and vitality.

Data is the key to unlocking the full potential of your culture. It's not just about crunching numbers; it's about gaining a deep understanding of your people, their needs, and their experiences. By combining the quantitative "big picture" insights from surveys and metrics with the rich, nuanced stories revealed through qualitative methods, you create a multi-dimensional portrait of your cultural landscape.

And with DISC, you can probe even deeper, understanding how the diverse personalities within your organization interact, communicate, and collaborate. This knowledge allows you to tailor your communication, leadership development, and team-building strategies to maximize engagement and create a more inclusive, high-performing workplace.

In this chapter, we've explored a wide range of tools and techniques for measuring and monitoring your culture, giving you a solid foundation for building a thriving workplace. But the journey is far from over. In the next chapter, we'll shift our focus from assessment to action, exploring strategies for adapting and evolving your culture to meet the challenges of a rapidly changing world.

We'll dive into how to navigate change while maintaining a positive culture, how to use DISC to create personalized development plans for your leaders and teams, and how to build a culture of continuous improvement that keeps your organization agile, resilient, and ready for whatever the future holds.

CHAPTER 13: THE CULTURE EVOLUTION: ADAPTING AND THRIVING (WITH DISC)

The Inevitability And Power Of Cultural Evolution

Ever think your company culture is like a framed motto on the wall, unchanging and timeless? Think again. Organizational culture isn't a static museum piece; it's a living, breathing organism, constantly evolving and adapting to the world around it. It's shaped by everything from the personalities of your employees to the latest market trends. Ignore this reality at your peril.

Shattering the Illusion of Static Culture

Forget the notion that your company culture is a rigid monolith, frozen in time like a dusty museum exhibit. The reality is far more dynamic and exciting! Your culture is a living, breathing organism, constantly evolving and adapting to the ever-changing world around it.

Internally, a whirlwind of forces is constantly at play, shaping and reshaping your culture. New leaders bring fresh perspectives, employees come and go, values shift, and the company itself grows and transforms. Externally, market trends, technological advancements, economic fluctuations, and societal changes all leave their mark on the cultural landscape.

Organizations that stubbornly cling to the illusion of a static culture are like dinosaurs refusing to adapt to a changing climate. They become rigid and unresponsive, missing out on valuable opportunities and ultimately facing extinction. Adaptability is the key to survival and thriving in today's fast-paced world, and that starts with recognizing the ever-evolving nature of your organizational culture.

The Imperative for Evolution

Buckle up, because the modern business world is a rollercoaster of rapid change, unexpected disruptions, and cutthroat competition. Organizations that refuse to evolve their culture are like passengers clinging to a broken seatbelt – they might hang on for dear life, but the ride is going to get a lot bumpier (and potentially much shorter).

Stagnation isn't just boring; it's toxic. A stagnant culture breeds disengagement like mold in a damp basement. Employee morale plummets, productivity tanks, and your top performers start eyeing the exit. But it doesn't stop there. Innovation, the lifeblood of any organization, is suffocated under the weight of outdated practices and rigid thinking. The result? Missed opportunities, frustrated customers, and a slow descent into irrelevance.

The Promise of Adaptable Cultures

Picture your organization as a chameleon, seamlessly blending into new environments and thriving amidst the ever-changing colors of the business landscape. That's the power of an adaptable culture. These agile organizations possess a resilience that allows them to not only weather storms of uncertainty but to emerge stronger on the other side.

Imagine a workplace that pulses with energy, where change is welcomed as an exciting adventure rather than a dreaded disruption. This is a magnet for top talent. The brightest minds crave an environment that champions learning, growth, and continuous improvement. They yearn for a company that doesn't just talk about innovation, but breathes it, empowering them to experiment, take risks, and ultimately, revolutionize the game.

In adaptable cultures, the impossible becomes possible. It's a playground for bold ideas, where experimentation is encouraged and failure is seen as a stepping stone to success. This is the fertile ground where innovation flourishes, giving birth to groundbreaking solutions and propelling the organization to new heights of achievement.

The Purpose of This Chapter

In this chapter, we're going beyond theory and equipping you with the practical tools and knowledge you need to not just survive, but thrive, in today's fast-paced business world.

We'll uncover the hidden forces that shape your company culture, from the subtle nuances of leadership styles to the seismic shifts of market trends. You'll learn to spot the warning signs of a stagnant culture and discover how to transform it into a dynamic engine of growth and innovation.

We'll arm you with a toolkit of proven strategies for assessing your current culture, identifying areas ripe for improvement, and implementing change initiatives that will propel your organization forward. But it doesn't stop there. We'll also show you how to harness the power of change to attract top talent, spark groundbreaking ideas, and build a resilient organization that can weather any storm.

By the end of this chapter, you'll be ready to embrace change as a catalyst for success, transforming your culture from a potential liability into a powerful competitive advantage.

Case Study: Johnson & Johnson's Credo-Based Culture: Navigating Crisis And Change With Unwavering Values

Challenge: The Tylenol Crisis and Beyond

Johnson & Johnson (J&J), a multinational healthcare company, faced a defining moment in 1982 when seven people died after consuming cyanide-laced Tylenol capsules. This crisis threatened not only the Tylenol brand but also J&J's reputation and the safety of countless consumers. However, J&J's response, guided by their longstanding Credo, became a textbook example of crisis management and cultural resilience.

Cultural Foundation: The J&J Credo

At the heart of J&J's culture is its Credo, a one-page document written in 1943 by then-chairman Robert Wood Johnson. The Credo outlines the company's responsibilities to its stakeholders, prioritizing the well-being of patients, employees, and communities above all else.

The Credo has been ingrained in J&J's culture for decades, serving as a guiding light for decision-making, employee behavior, and the company's overall approach to business. It's not just a document; it's a living, breathing ethos that shapes how J&J operates.

Navigating the Tylenol Crisis

When the Tylenol crisis hit, J&J executives turned to the Credo for guidance. They made the unprecedented decision to recall 31 million bottles of Tylenol, costing the company millions of dollars, but ultimately saving lives and protecting the public.

J&J's response was guided by the Credo's emphasis on putting the needs of patients first. They prioritized safety over profits, taking swift and decisive action to protect consumers. This decision, while costly in the short term, ultimately strengthened the company's reputation and reinforced its commitment to its values.

The Credo's Impact on Cultural Resilience

The Tylenol crisis was just one of many challenges that J&J has faced over the years. However, the Credo has consistently provided a framework for navigating these challenges and emerging stronger on the other side.

The Credo has built a culture of:

- **Responsibility:** Employees feel a sense of ownership and accountability for their actions and decisions.
- **Integrity:** J&J upholds high ethical standards in all aspects of its business.
- **Transparency:** The company communicates openly and honestly with its stakeholders.
- **Collaboration:** Employees work together across departments and divisions to solve problems and achieve common goals.
- **Adaptability:** J&J is willing to change and evolve to meet the needs of its stakeholders and the changing business landscape.

These cultural attributes, rooted in the Credo, have enabled J&J to adapt to changing market conditions, embrace new technologies, and navigate complex ethical dilemmas.

Key Takeaways for HR Professionals and Organizational Leaders:

- **The Power of Values:** Strong values can provide a foundation for cultural resilience and adaptability, helping organizations navigate challenges and emerge stronger.

- **Values-Based Decision Making:** When faced with difficult choices, turn to your core values for guidance.
- **Culture as a Strategic Asset:** Cultivate a strong culture that aligns with your values and business strategy. This can be a powerful source of competitive advantage.
- **Living the Values:** It's not enough to simply articulate values; they must be embedded in the company's culture and reflected in the everyday actions of its employees.
- **Leading with Integrity:** Leaders must embody the company's values and hold themselves and others accountable for upholding them.

J&J's story demonstrates that a strong values-based culture is not just a "nice to have." It's a critical asset that can help organizations navigate change, build trust with stakeholders, and achieve long-term success.

Understanding Culture As A Dynamic Ecosystem

Ditch the image of your company culture as a rigid, unyielding monolith. It's far more fascinating than that! It is a vibrant ecosystem, teeming with life and energy. Every element within this ecosystem—your leaders, your employees, your values, even your office layout—interacts and influences the others, creating a dynamic and ever-evolving landscape. Just like a rainforest or a coral reef, your culture is shaped by both internal and external forces, and its ability to adapt and thrive depends on its flexibility and resilience.

Culture as a Living Organism

Picture your organizational culture as as a lush, thriving ecosystem, teeming with life and energy. Every element within this intricate web—from the visionary leaders at the helm to the fresh-faced new hires—interacts and influences the others, creating a landscape that's as dynamic as it is complex.

Your leaders are the master gardeners of this ecosystem. Their values, behaviors, and choices shape the cultural climate, influencing everything from how teams collaborate to the overall vibe in the office. These shared values and beliefs are the fertile soil from which your culture grows. They might be proudly displayed in your mission statement or subtly woven into the daily rhythms of your workplace.

Each employee brings their own unique personality, experiences, and perspectives to the mix, adding color and richness to the tapestry. The way your team communicates—whether it's buzzing through the grapevine or flowing through formal channels—shapes how information travels, decisions are made, and relationships blossom. Even the structure of your organization, with its hierarchy and decision-making processes, can either cultivate a fertile ground for collaboration or create stifling silos that hinder growth.

But it's not just the internal workings of your company that shape your culture. Imagine a sudden earthquake shaking the ground beneath your feet, or a torrential downpour flooding the landscape. That's what external forces like shifting market trends, disruptive technologies, and evolving societal norms can do to your cultural ecosystem. They demand adaptation, forcing you to reevaluate your values, strategies, and ways of working.

Understanding your culture as this living, breathing ecosystem is the key to navigating these seismic shifts. By recognizing the intricate dance between internal and external forces, you can proactively shape your culture, cultivating an environment that not only weathers the storm but thrives in the face of change.

The Perils of Stagnation

It's tempting to treat a successful company culture like a prized antique, something to be polished and preserved in its original state. But this is a dangerous illusion. Cultures, like the world around them, are not meant to be frozen in time. They're living, breathing organisms that must constantly evolve to stay relevant and thrive.

Imagine a pond that never gets fresh water. It stagnates, becoming a murky breeding ground for complacency and resistance to change. New ideas struggle to take root, innovation dries up, and the once-thriving ecosystem loses its luster. The same is true for organizations that cling to the past.

When a company's culture stagnates, it's like a slow leak in a tire. Employee engagement deflates, top talent jumps ship, and productivity grinds to a halt. What was once a vibrant workplace becomes a stifling environment where creativity and initiative wither away.

But the consequences of stagnation are far more insidious than just low morale. Companies that refuse to adapt are like dinosaurs facing an asteroid – they're doomed to extinction. In today's lightning-fast business landscape, clinging to outdated norms is a recipe for disaster. You risk missing out on game-changing trends, groundbreaking technologies, and the ever-evolving needs of your customers. Just ask Kodak and Blockbuster how that worked out for them.

These cautionary tales should send chills down the spine of any leader who values long-term success. They are stark reminders that adaptability isn't just a nice-to-have, it's the survival instinct that separates thriving companies from those that fade into oblivion. So, don't let your culture become a relic of the past. Embrace change, cultivate adaptability, and watch your organization flourish in the face of any challenge.

The Power of Adaptability

Forget rigid, inflexible cultures - they're dinosaurs in the fast-paced world of modern business. Enter the adaptable culture, the chameleon of the corporate jungle. These vibrant organizations don't just survive change; they thrive on it, continuously evolving and shifting to stay ahead of the curve. They're not afraid to reinvent themselves, to experiment, to take risks. And that's why they're the ones who win.

At the heart of these agile powerhouses is a growth mindset, a belief that every challenge is a learning opportunity and every individual can evolve. This fuels a culture of continuous learning, where curiosity is king and experimentation is not just encouraged, it's expected. Employees feel empowered to push boundaries, try new things, and stretch their skills.

But innovation doesn't happen in a vacuum. It needs a safe haven to take root and flourish. That's where psychological safety comes in. In adaptable cultures, people feel secure enough to speak their minds, challenge the status quo, and even stumble without fear of repercussions. This atmosphere of trust and open communication is the fertile soil where the seeds of groundbreaking ideas are sown.

Imagine a workplace where information flows like a river, where feedback is valued as a gift, and collaboration isn't just a buzzword, it's a way of life. That's the power of open communication. In these environments, everyone's voice is heard, respected, and contributes to the collective wisdom of the organization.

But what truly sets adaptable cultures apart is empowerment. Employees aren't just cogs in a machine; they're the engine that drives the organization forward. They're given the autonomy and responsibility to make decisions, take ownership of their work, and shape the company's future. This sense of ownership doesn't just boost morale, it fuels a passion for innovation that propels the organization to new heights.

By embracing the ever-changing nature of culture, you'll unlock a world of possibilities. Encourage a growth mindset, create a psychologically safe haven, champion open communication, and empower your people. By doing so, you'll transform your culture into a dynamic force that propels your organization towards enduring success.

Case Study: Ibm's Cloud Ascent: How A Legacy Giant Transformed Its Culture For The Digital Age

Challenge: The Legacy of Hardware and Software

IBM, founded in 1911, was a pioneer in the computer industry, dominating the market for decades with its mainframe computers and software solutions. However, the rise of cloud computing in the 21st century threatened to disrupt IBM's traditional business model. The company needed to adapt to this new technological landscape or risk becoming obsolete.

Cultural Transformation: Embracing Agility and Collaboration

Under the leadership of CEO Ginni Rometty, IBM embarked on a bold transformation to become a cloud-first company. This required a significant cultural shift, moving away from the traditional hierarchical structure and siloed approach to one that emphasized agility, collaboration, and customer-centricity.

Key elements of IBM's cultural transformation included:

- **Embracing Agile Methodologies:** IBM adopted agile development practices across the organization, breaking down projects into smaller, more manageable chunks and working in iterative cycles. This allowed teams to respond more quickly to changing customer needs and market demands.
- **Promote Collaboration:** IBM broke down silos between departments and encouraged employees to work together across disciplines. They created cross-functional teams, established open communication channels, and implemented collaboration tools to facilitate knowledge

sharing and innovation.
- **Customer-Centricity:** IBM shifted its focus from selling products to providing solutions that meet the specific needs of its customers. They invested in design thinking methodologies, customer journey mapping, and other tools to gain a deeper understanding of customer pain points and develop tailored solutions.
- **Investing in Talent:** IBM recognized the need to attract and retain talent with expertise in cloud computing, artificial intelligence, and other emerging technologies. They launched new training programs, partnered with universities, and hired aggressively in these areas.
- **Acquisitions and Partnerships:** IBM made strategic acquisitions (e.g., Red Hat) and partnerships to accelerate its cloud transformation and expand its capabilities in this space.

Results: A Cloud Powerhouse

IBM's transformation has been a resounding success. The company is now a leading provider of hybrid cloud solutions, helping businesses of all sizes to modernize their IT infrastructure and leverage the power of cloud computing. IBM's cloud revenue has grown significantly, and the company has been recognized for its leadership in this space by industry analysts.

Key Takeaways for HR Professionals and Organizational Leaders:

- **Embrace Disruption:** Don't be afraid to challenge the status quo and embrace disruptive technologies that can transform your industry.
- **Align Culture with Strategy:** Ensure that your organizational culture supports your business strategy. If your strategy requires agility and collaboration, your culture must support those values.
- **Invest in Your People:** Provide your employees with

the training and development opportunities they need to adapt to new technologies and ways of working.
- **Embrace Collaboration:** Break down silos and encourage cross-functional collaboration to encourage innovation and agility.
- **Be Customer-Centric:** Focus on understanding and meeting the needs of your customers, rather than simply selling products.

IBM's journey demonstrates that even large, established companies can successfully transform their cultures to embrace new technologies and thrive in a changing market. By prioritizing agility, collaboration, and customer-centricity, organizations can position themselves for continued growth and success in the digital age.

A Framework For Ongoing Culture Assessment And Improvement With Disc

A Multi-Faceted Assessment Approach

Assessing your company culture is similar to piecing together a vibrant mosaic. Each tile—representing a different aspect of your workplace—contributes to the overall picture. DISC assessments are a valuable tool, offering a glimpse into the personalities and dynamics that shape your organization. But to truly understand the intricate patterns and nuances of your culture, you need a more comprehensive view.

A multi-faceted assessment approach is like using a magnifying glass, revealing details that might otherwise go unnoticed. Regular DISC assessments for both individuals and teams provide a baseline understanding of communication styles, decision-making approaches, and potential areas of growth. By tracking changes over time, you can identify any shifts that might signal a need for adjustment.

But don't stop there. Dive deeper with culture surveys, a direct line to the hearts and minds of your employees. These surveys are your chance to ask the tough questions: Are employees engaged? Do they feel heard? Are they proud to be part of your organization? By conducting these surveys regularly, you'll gain a pulse on employee sentiment, spot emerging trends, and measure the impact of your cultural initiatives. Remember, anonymity and confidentiality are key to getting honest, unfiltered feedback.

Next, assemble a culture committee—a diverse group of passionate employees who represent the different facets of your organization. This committee isn't just a talking shop; it's a task force dedicated to analyzing survey data, uncovering areas for improvement, and crafting action plans that resonate with the entire company. They're the guardians of your culture, ensuring it remains vibrant, healthy, and aligned with your values.

But why stop there? Your toolbox is overflowing with additional assessment tools like 360-degree feedback, engagement surveys, and pulse surveys. Each tool adds another layer of depth and nuance to your understanding of the cultural landscape.

By weaving together the insights from all these tools, you create a rich tapestry that truly reflects the unique character of your organization. Armed with this knowledge, you'll be able to pinpoint areas for improvement with laser precision, implement targeted interventions, and cultivate a culture that sparks engagement, ignites innovation, and drives long-term success. Your cultural mosaic will be a masterpiece, a testament to the power of understanding and shaping the human dynamics that make your organization thrive.

Unleashing the Power of Data: Igniting Cultural Transformation

Gathering data about your organizational culture is like discovering a treasure map. It's a crucial first step, but the real adventure begins when you decode those insights and embark on a transformative journey.

By delving into the treasure trove of data from DISC assessments, culture surveys, and other tools, you can uncover hidden patterns and trends that illuminate the path forward. Look for the connections between specific DISC styles and cultural issues, like a detective piecing together clues.

Are your meticulous "C" style employees feeling overshadowed in meetings dominated by the assertive "D" styles? Do your steady "S" styles feel overwhelmed by a whirlwind of change?

These insights are the keys to unlocking targeted

interventions that tackle specific cultural challenges head-on. Armed with data, you can craft customized solutions that speak directly to different personality types, cultivate a more inclusive and harmonious workplace.

Imagine communication breakdowns are hindering collaboration. With data as your guide, you can implement training programs on active listening, conflict resolution, or feedback – all tailored to resonate with each DISC style. If your leadership team lacks diversity in communication styles, leadership development programs can bridge the gap, building understanding and appreciation.

Data-driven insights can even guide you in making structural or process changes that ignite collaboration and innovation. Is your decision-making overly bureaucratic, stifling creativity? Streamline those processes, empowering employees to take charge and drive initiatives forward.

In essence, data transforms abstract concepts into a roadmap for action. By embracing a data-driven approach to cultural change, you can move beyond generic solutions and create tailored interventions that truly address the unique needs and challenges of your organization.

Fueling Growth with Feedback: Cultivating a Continuous Improvement Culture

Continuous feedback is the lifeblood of your organization – a constant flow of energy that fuels growth, innovation, and adaptability. To thrive in a dynamic world, your organization needs to embrace a culture where feedback flows freely and openly, sparking a vibrant exchange of ideas and perspectives.

Imagine a workplace where everyone, from frontline employees to the C-suite, feels empowered to share their thoughts, ideas, and concerns. That's the kind of environment that supports continuous improvement. Let everyone know that feedback isn't just welcomed, it's actively sought after. It's the secret ingredient that drives your organization's evolution.

To nurture this open dialogue, offer diverse feedback channels that cater to different communication styles. Regular one-on-one meetings create a safe space for candid conversations, while team meetings and retrospectives become collaborative brainstorming sessions. For those who prefer to express themselves anonymously, suggestion boxes or online forums can be a game-changer. And don't forget the power of employee surveys and pulse checks – these provide a panoramic view of organizational sentiment, revealing trends and areas that need attention.

But collecting feedback is just the beginning. The true magic happens when you take action on that feedback. It's not enough to just listen; you need to show your employees that their voices matter. By responding to their insights, addressing their concerns, and incorporating their ideas into decision-making, you create a sense of ownership and empowerment that reverberates throughout the organization.

Remember, a culture of continuous feedback is more than just gathering information. It's about promoting an environment where everyone feels heard, valued, and empowered to contribute to the organization's success. By nurturing this culture, you're building a powerful engine for change, driving continuous improvement, and ensuring your organization stays agile and resilient in a constantly evolving world.

Case Study: Fujifilm's Radical Reinvention

Challenge: The Digital Disruption

Fujifilm, founded in 1934, was once a global giant in the photographic film industry. However, the advent of digital photography in the late 20th century posed an existential threat to their core business. As the demand for film plummeted, Fujifilm faced a critical juncture: adapt or perish.

Cultural Adaptation: A Paradigm Shift

Rather than clinging to the past, Fujifilm embarked on a bold transformation. They recognized that their expertise in chemical processes and materials science could be applied to a variety of other industries. This led to a radical diversification strategy, expanding into areas such as cosmetics, pharmaceuticals, and medical devices.

Key elements of Fujifilm's cultural adaptation included:

- **Innovation and Risk-Taking:** Fujifilm built a culture that encouraged employees to experiment, explore new ideas, and take calculated risks. They created an environment where failure was not seen as a setback, but as a learning opportunity. This allowed the company to quickly identify and capitalize on new market opportunities.
- **Employee Empowerment:** Fujifilm empowered employees at all levels to contribute to the reinvention process. They encouraged employees to share their ideas, take ownership of projects, and collaborate across departments. This created a sense of shared purpose and collective responsibility for the company's future.
- **Agility and Flexibility:** Fujifilm adopted a more agile and flexible approach to decision-making and execution. They decentralized decision-making authority, allowing teams to respond quickly to market changes and customer

needs.
- **Strategic Partnerships:** Fujifilm formed strategic partnerships with other companies to accelerate their entry into new markets and leverage complementary expertise. This allowed them to quickly gain a foothold in unfamiliar industries.

Results: A Diversified Powerhouse

Fujifilm's bold transformation paid off handsomely. Today, the company is a global leader in healthcare, materials, and imaging solutions. Their diverse portfolio includes medical devices, pharmaceuticals, regenerative medicine, cosmetics, and advanced materials used in a wide range of industries.

Fujifilm's success is a testament to the power of cultural adaptability. By embracing change, empowering employees, and developing a culture of innovation and risk-taking, they were able to transform their business and thrive in a rapidly changing environment.

Key Takeaways for HR Professionals and Organizational Leaders:

- **Anticipate Disruption:** Be proactive in identifying potential disruptions to your industry or business model.
- **Embrace Change as an Opportunity:** Don't resist change; view it as a chance to reinvent and grow.
- **Support a Culture of Innovation:** Encourage experimentation, risk-taking, and continuous learning.
- **Empower Your Employees:** Give employees the autonomy and resources they need to contribute to the change process.
- **Be Agile and Flexible:** Adapt your decision-making processes and organizational structures to respond quickly to market changes.
- **Seek Strategic Partnerships:** Collaborate with other organizations to accelerate your transformation and

leverage complementary expertise.

Fujifilm's story is a powerful reminder that even the most established companies can reinvent themselves in the face of disruption. By encouraging a culture that embraces change and empowers employees to innovate, organizations can not only survive but thrive in an ever-changing world.

Thriving Amidst The Waves: Navigating Change While Preserving A Positive Culture

Change is a constant companion in the world of organizations. It's like the tides – sometimes gentle, sometimes turbulent, but always present. Whether it's a shift in the market landscape, the adoption of cutting-edge technology, or a bold new strategic direction, change can stir up a whirlwind of emotions in employees, ranging from exhilaration and anticipation to apprehension and resistance.

Change: Your Adventure Awaits, Not a Threat to Fear

Change often gets a bad rap, seen as a disruption, something to dread. But what if we flipped the script? What if we saw change not as a threat, but as a thrilling opportunity?

It's no secret that change can stir up a cocktail of emotions. Fear, uncertainty, resistance – they're all part of the experience. But here's the key: acknowledging those emotions and tackling them head-on is the secret sauce to success. Leaders who shine a light on the reasons behind the change, paint a vivid picture of the future, and offer a helping hand during the transition? They're the ones who turn change into a positive force.

Shift the focus to the incredible possibilities change brings – growth, innovation, a chance to shine brighter than ever before. When employees see change as an adventure, a chance to learn, evolve, and make a real impact, their resistance melts away.

Leaders: The Captains of the Change Voyage, Nurturing a Positive Culture

When it comes to navigating the uncharted waters of change and keeping the culture ship afloat, leaders are the true captains. Their actions and words echo throughout the entire organization, setting the course for everyone on board.

Leading by example isn't just a buzzword – it's the compass that guides the way. Leaders who walk the talk, embodying the behaviors and attitudes they expect from their crew, are the ones who inspire trust and confidence. They're transparent about the storms ahead, adaptable to changing winds, and always there to lend a helping hand.

Communication? It's the lifeline that keeps everyone connected during the voyage. Leaders who share the "why" behind the change, paint a picture of the exciting destination, and address concerns openly are the ones who create a shared sense of purpose. Celebrating progress along the way? That's like throwing confetti on the deck – it boosts morale and keeps the energy high.

But that's not all. Leaders also need to create a safe haven where everyone feels comfortable voicing their worries, asking questions, and experimenting with new ways of doing things. Active listening, empathy, and a willingness to take feedback on board? Those are the keys to building trust and psychological safety.

Oh, and don't forget about your change agents – those passionate crew members who champion the change and spread enthusiasm throughout the ship. Identify them, empower them, and watch them set the sails for a brighter future.

DISC-Informed Change Management: A Personalized Approach

Understanding the diverse ways individuals respond to change is crucial for effectively managing transitions and minimizing disruption. The DISC model, which categorizes individuals into four primary styles (Dominance, Influence, Steadiness, and Conscientiousness), offers a valuable framework for tailoring your change management strategies.

Dominant (D): These individuals thrive on challenge and control. When navigating change, they need to be given opportunities to lead and take ownership. Engage them early in the process, solicit their input, and provide them with clear roles and responsibilities. Focus your communication on the results and impact of the change, emphasizing how their contribution will drive success.

- **Practical Tip:** Create a steering committee or task force led by "D" style individuals to spearhead the change initiative. This allows them to take charge, make decisions, and see tangible progress.

Influence (I): "I" styles are fueled by enthusiasm and collaboration. To get them on board with change, involve them early and often. Create opportunities for them to brainstorm ideas, share their excitement with others, and be part of a team effort. Emphasize the positive aspects of the change and how it will benefit the team and the organization.

- **Practical Tip:** Organize team-building activities or social events related to the change initiative. This will allow "I" styles to connect with others, share their enthusiasm, and build a sense of community around the change.

Steadiness (S): "S" styles value stability and security. Change can be unsettling for them, so it's important to provide reassurance and support. Communicate clearly and often, emphasizing how the change will benefit the team and the organization while minimizing disruption to their routines and relationships.

- **Practical Tip:** Create a detailed timeline outlining the steps of the change process and the expected impact on each team member. Offer one-on-one meetings or group sessions to address concerns and provide individualized support.

Conscientious (C): "C" styles are driven by logic and accuracy. To gain their support, provide them with detailed information and data that clearly explains the reasons for the change and the expected outcomes. Emphasize how the change will improve processes, increase efficiency, or enhance quality.

- **Practical Tip:** Create a comprehensive FAQ document or presentation that addresses common questions and concerns about the change. Offer opportunities for "C" style individuals to ask questions and provide input.

By understanding the unique needs and preferences of each DISC style, you can tailor your communication, involvement, and support strategies to ensure that everyone feels heard, understood, and empowered to embrace change. This personalized approach will not only smooth the transition but also create a more inclusive and collaborative change management process.

Supercharging Your Culture: Extra Tools for Thriving Through Change

While tailoring your change management strategy to individual DISC styles is a game-changer, there are even more tricks up your sleeve to keep your culture sparkling during transitions.

Transparency is your secret weapon. Imagine an open-book policy where everyone understands the reasons behind the change, the exciting possibilities it holds, and even the potential bumps in the road. This honesty builds trust and calms those change jitters.

Want to make change a team sport? Get your employees in on the action! Surveys to hear their thoughts, focus groups to gather feedback, workshops to brainstorm solutions – when people feel involved, they become invested in the change's success.

Don't forget the power of a good celebration! Remember to pause and acknowledge even the smallest victories along the way. These little wins fuel the momentum, keep spirits high, and remind everyone that progress is happening, even when the journey is long.

Let's talk about failure – it's not the end of the world! In fact, it's a fantastic learning opportunity. Embrace a culture where missteps are seen as stepping stones to innovation. This creates a safe space for experimentation, where employees feel empowered to try new things, learn from both successes and stumbles, and ultimately, find creative solutions.

Last but not least, remember to drop anchor amidst the change. When things get turbulent, people need something to hold onto. By consistently reinforcing your organization's core values and principles, you provide a sense of stability and continuity. These shared values become a guiding light, leading your team through the storm and reminding everyone of the deeper purpose that binds you together.

Tech: The Double-Edged Sword of Cultural Evolution – Mastering the Digital Landscape

Technology isn't just a tool; it's a force that reshapes how we work, connect, and learn. In the context of cultural evolution, it's a game-changer, but one with both exciting possibilities and potential pitfalls.

The Upside:

- **Supercharged Communication and Collaboration:** Technology breaks down barriers, allowing real-time communication across distances and encouraging collaboration among diverse teams.
- **Knowledge at Your Fingertips:** Learning becomes a 24/7 adventure with online courses, virtual workshops, and a wealth of information accessible with a few clicks.

- **Flexibility and Work-Life Balance:** Remote work, flexible schedules, and virtual meetings offer employees greater autonomy and control over their work lives.

The Potential Downside:

- **Information Overload:** The constant barrage of emails, notifications, and messages can overwhelm employees and hinder productivity.
- **Digital Distractions:** Social media, instant messaging, and other online temptations can easily derail focus and disrupt workflow.
- **Erosion of In-Person Connection:** Over-reliance on virtual communication can lead to a decline in face-to-face interactions, potentially weakening relationships and hindering team cohesion.

Strategies for Success:

- **Mindful Technology Use:** Encourage employees to set boundaries, manage notifications, and prioritize meaningful interactions.
- **Digital Detox Initiatives:** Offer opportunities for employees to disconnect from technology and recharge, whether through designated "unplugged" times or company-sponsored retreats.
- **Break Down Silos and Forge Connections:** In multi-office organizations, physical distance can breed siloed teams and weaken connections. But technology offers a solution: replace impersonal emails with engaging video calls and instant messages and use video tech for expanded team gatherings.
- **Invest in Digital Skills Training:** Equip your workforce with the skills needed to navigate the digital landscape effectively and responsibly.

By understanding the dual nature of technology and implementing strategies to maximize its benefits while minimizing its drawbacks, you can cultivate a thriving digital culture where technology serves as a catalyst for growth, innovation, and employee well-being.

Embracing The Dance Of Cultural Evolution: Your Journey Continues

In this whirlwind tour of organizational culture, we've witnessed its vibrant, ever-changing nature. It's not a static monument, but a living, breathing entity, constantly evolving and adapting. This evolution isn't just a choice; it's the secret to thriving in today's unpredictable business world.

Let's take a moment to recap the gems we've unearthed. Stagnation? That's the villain of the story, stifling innovation and scaring away talent. But embracing change? That's the superhero, swooping in to fuel growth and progress. Organizations with adaptable cultures, those that cultivate a "learn and grow" mindset, encourage bold experimentation, and empower their people – they're the ones who not only survive storms but emerge stronger than ever.

The DISC model has been our trusty sidekick on this adventure, helping us decode the fascinating world of individual and team dynamics. With DISC assessments as our guide, we can tailor communication strategies, pinpoint areas for growth, and cultivate a workforce that's more connected and effective.

But remember, DISC is just one tool in our toolbox. To truly understand your culture, we need a multifaceted approach – culture surveys, feedback loops, and more. By analyzing the data from these different sources, we can pinpoint areas for improvement and craft custom solutions to tackle specific cultural challenges.

And let's not forget our trusty companion: continuous feedback. By creating a culture where feedback flows freely, is cherished, and acted upon, you ensure your culture stays in sync with your organization's goals and values. This ongoing dialogue empowers your employees, making them co-creators in the exciting journey of cultural evolution.

The Cultural Evolution Imperative: Thriving in the Winds of Change

In the ever-shifting currents of the business world, clinging to a rigid culture is like anchoring yourself in a hurricane. It's the agile, the adaptable, the organizations that embrace change as a mantra for success who not only weather the storms but ride the waves to triumph. A vibrant and responsive culture isn't just a perk; it's the lifeblood that attracts top-tier talent, sparks innovation, and builds resilience when challenges strike. Investing in your culture isn't just shaping your workplace today; it's laying the groundwork for your organization's future success.

Ready to embark on this exciting journey of cultural evolution? It all starts with a thoughtful, deliberate approach, led by HR pros and organizational leaders who are eager to roll up their sleeves and become champions of change.

First, take a moment for some soul-searching. Leaders, your style and biases have a ripple effect. Reflect on how you influence the current culture and model the behaviors and attitudes you want to see thrive.

Next, ignite a growth mindset throughout your organization. Picture a workplace buzzing with curiosity, where learning is the norm, experimentation is encouraged, and taking calculated risks is applauded. When your people feel empowered to push their boundaries and contribute their unique talents, innovation explodes.

Open and transparent communication? It's the glue that holds everything together. Share the "why" behind the changes, the hurdles you're facing, and the progress you're making. Regular updates, forums for open dialogue, and shared celebrations of milestones build trust and a sense of shared purpose.

Remember, your employees are the heart of your culture. Give them a voice in this journey. Invite their feedback through surveys, focus groups, or even casual chats. Really listen to their concerns and ideas, and show them you value their input by taking action. When people feel heard and appreciated, they become passionate advocates for the evolving culture.

Invest in your team's growth like you would a prized stock. Offer training programs, resources, and mentorship opportunities to help them acquire new skills, adapt to change, and reach their full potential. Remember, your people are your greatest asset, and their growth fuels your organization's progress.

Don't forget to celebrate! Acknowledging and rewarding progress, big or small, is a powerful motivator. And build a culture that sees failure not as a setback, but as a stepping stone to success. Encourage experimentation and risk-taking, knowing that missteps are simply valuable learning experiences.

While technology can be a fantastic tool for communication and collaboration, use it wisely. Balance digital interactions with real-world connections, prioritize building genuine relationships, and be mindful of information overload and distractions.

Remember, cultural evolution is an ongoing adventure. Regularly check your progress, gather feedback, and adjust your course as needed. By staying in tune with the ever-changing needs of your organization and its people, your culture will remain a vibrant, dynamic force, driving your organization towards lasting success.

Final Thoughts

Your organizational culture isn't a snapshot frozen in time; it's a vibrant tapestry, constantly woven and rewoven by the hands of your people and the winds of change. This journey of cultural evolution is not a one-time project with a finish line, but a continuous expedition with thrilling twists and turns along the way.

But fear not, for you hold the compass to navigate this adventure. With a clear vision of your ideal culture, leadership that exemplifies the way forward, and an unwavering commitment to progress, you can harness the transformative power of evolution to propel your organization to new heights.

Remember, change is not a threat, but a spark that ignites growth. Cultivate a growth mindset that embraces challenges and sees opportunities in every setback. Empower your employees to take ownership, unleash their creativity, and contribute their unique perspectives to the collective tapestry. And above all, create a space where open communication and honest feedback flow freely, nurturing a vibrant community where every voice is heard and valued.

The path may be winding, and there will be obstacles to overcome. But with a steadfast focus on your vision, a willingness to adapt to the ever-shifting landscape, and a thirst for learning from every experience, you can confidently steer your organization towards a future filled with promise.

Just as a tree must shed its leaves in autumn to burst forth with new life in spring, your organization must be willing to let go of outdated norms and practices to make way for innovation and renewal. Embrace the exhilarating process of cultural evolution, for it is in this constant state of becoming that true resilience and enduring success are forged.

As you embark on this extraordinary journey, know that you have a map to guide you. The tools and strategies outlined in this book are your trusted companions, illuminating the path towards a vibrant culture where individuals thrive and the organization flourishes.

May your journey be one of continuous growth, profound learning, and the enduring satisfaction of knowing that you are not merely adapting to change, but actively shaping a brighter future for your organization.

ABOUT THE AUTHOR

Matthew Snyder is a seasoned leader and entrepreneur passionate about building high-performing teams and revitalizing communities. As the founder and President of ManageMax, he's dedicated to helping business owners unlock the full potential of their teams through personality-driven leadership.

Matthew's expertise is a product of his resilience and adaptability. He successfully navigated the Michigan housing crisis, leading financial institutions and government agencies through complex challenges. His journey is a testament to the power of these qualities and a relentless focus on cultural alignment.

With an MBA from Carnegie Mellon and a CFA Charter, Matthew brings a unique blend of analytical rigor and real-world experience to his work. He's learned firsthand the importance of understanding individual strengths, fostering collaboration, and empowering teams to achieve their goals.

In this book, Matthew shares practical, personality-driven strategies and insights that are the driving force behind an organization's success. Whether you're an organizational leader or a human resource professional, this guide will empower you with the tools to build a dream team that thrives.

To learn more about Matthew and the ManageMax team, visit https://managemax.properties/.

APPENDIX: TEMPLATE: CULTURAL MANIFESTO

Our Company Name

Our Cultural DNA

Mission: (A concise statement of your company's purpose and reason for being)

Values:

1. **[Value 1]:** (Definition and explanation)
2. **[Value 2]:** (Definition and explanation)
3. **[Value 3]:** (Definition and explanation) ... (Add more as needed)

Behaviors:

- (We believe in...)
- (We strive to...)
- (We celebrate...)
- (We challenge ourselves to...) ... (Add more as needed)

Our Cultural Commitments:

- **To Our Employees:** (What you promise to your employees in terms of support, development, and well-being)
- **To Our Customers:** (How your culture translates into exceptional service and value for your customers)
- **To Our Community:** (How your culture inspires you to give back and make a positive impact)

Our Culture in Action:

(Briefly describe a few examples of how your culture is lived out in everyday interactions and decision-making)

APPENDIX: LEADERSHIP SELF-ASSESSMENT TOOL – YOUR CULTURAL COMPASS

This assessment is designed to help you reflect on your leadership style and its alignment with the growth-oriented culture you envision for your organization. Remember, there are no right or wrong answers; the goal is to gain insights into your strengths and areas for development.

Instructions:
1. Read each question carefully.
2. Choose the answer that best reflects your typical behavior or approach.
3. Be honest with yourself – this is for your personal growth.
4. Reflect on your answers and identify any patterns or themes that emerge.

Questions:

Leading by Example:

1. How often do I actively participate in activities that demonstrate the values I want my team to embody (e.g., taking on challenging projects, seeking feedback, continuous learning)?
   o   Always
   o   Often
   o   Sometimes
   o   Rarely
   o   Never
2. When faced with a setback or failure, how do I typically respond?
   o   I view it as a learning opportunity and openly share lessons learned with my team.
   o   I acknowledge the setback but quickly move on to the next challenge.
   o   I dwell on the failure and may try to assign blame.
   o   I avoid taking responsibility and may try to downplay the impact.
3. How comfortable am I with taking calculated risks and encouraging my team to do the same?
   o   Very comfortable
   o   Somewhat comfortable
   o   Neutral
   o   Somewhat uncomfortable
   o   Very uncomfortable

Communicating the Vision:

1. How often do I communicate the company's vision and values to my team?
   o   Regularly and through multiple channels
   o   Occasionally, in formal settings
   o   Infrequently

2. How transparent am I with my team about decisions that affect them?
      - Very transparent – I proactively share information and explain my reasoning.
      - Somewhat transparent – I share information when asked or when necessary.
      - I share information on a need-to-know basis.
      - I rarely share information unless absolutely necessary.
   3. When communicating with my team, how do I typically frame mistakes or setbacks?
      - As learning opportunities for growth and improvement
      - As challenges to be overcome
      - As problems to be solved
      - As individual failures
      - As reasons for blame or punishment

Fostering Growth and Development:

   1. How often do I provide my team members with opportunities for learning and development?
      - Regularly and proactively
      - Occasionally, based on requests or performance reviews
      - Infrequently
      - Rarely
      - Never
   2. How involved am I in mentoring or coaching my team members?
      - Very involved – I actively seek out opportunities to mentor and coach.
      - Somewhat involved – I mentor or coach when asked or when needed.
      - I provide guidance when requested but don't

actively seek out opportunities.
- I rarely mentor or coach unless required.
- I do not engage in mentoring or coaching.
3. How do I typically respond when a team member makes a mistake?
- I see it as a learning opportunity and offer support and guidance.
- I offer constructive feedback and help the team member develop a plan to avoid similar mistakes in the future.
- I express disappointment but focus on finding a solution.
- I criticize the mistake and may express frustration.
- I reprimand the team member and may consider disciplinary action.

Creating a Positive and Supportive Environment:

1. How often do I recognize and celebrate my team's successes?
- Regularly and in a variety of ways
- Occasionally, in formal settings
- Infrequently
- Rarely
- Never
2. How comfortable are my team members sharing their ideas and concerns with me?
- Very comfortable – They feel safe to speak their minds openly.
- Somewhat comfortable – They share their thoughts but may hesitate on sensitive topics.
- They share information only when asked or when necessary.
- They rarely share their thoughts or feelings openly.
- They feel unsafe or uncomfortable sharing their thoughts or feelings.
3. How would I describe my overall approach to

leadership?
- ○ Collaborative and empowering
- ○ Supportive and encouraging
- ○ Directive and results-oriented
- ○ Authoritarian and controlling
- ○ Laissez-faire and uninvolved

Reflection and Action Planning:

1. After completing this assessment, take some time to reflect on your answers.
2. Identify areas where your current leadership style aligns with the desired culture and areas where it may not be fully aligned.
3. Develop a plan of action to address any areas where you see room for improvement. This might involve seeking out additional training or development opportunities, experimenting with different leadership approaches, or seeking feedback from your team.

Remember: This brief assessment is just a starting point and is intended to get you thinking. There are many detailed personality and leadership style tools available if you want to explore this subject further. For purposes of this book, the focus is to help you understand how your leadership can potentially be a road block to your company's cultural success and teaches you to identify that and realign with the company culture you want to build. The most important step is to use these insights to intentionally shape your leadership style and create a culture where growth, innovation, and risk-taking thrive.

APPENDIX: UNCOVERING YOUR COMPANY'S CULTURAL DNA: A SURVEY & INTERVIEW GUIDE

Introduction

This guide is designed to help you gain a deeper understanding of your organization's culture. It combines a survey with an interview component to gather both quantitative and qualitative data, providing a more holistic view of your workplace environment.

Instructions

1. **Survey:** Begin by having employees complete the survey. Encourage honest and open responses. Assure them that their feedback will remain anonymous and confidential.

2. **Interviews:** Select a diverse group of employees from different departments and levels to participate in interviews. Use the interview questions to delve deeper into their responses and gain additional insights.
3. **Analysis:** Analyze the survey results and interview transcripts to identify patterns, themes, and areas for improvement. Compare your findings with your desired culture to identify gaps and misalignments.
4. **Action:** Use the insights gained from this assessment to develop a plan for strengthening your company culture.

Survey

Please rate the following statements on a scale of 1 to 5, where:

- 1 = Strongly Disagree
- 2 = Disagree
- 3 = Neutral
- 4 = Agree
- 5 = Strongly Agree

Collaboration

1. I feel comfortable sharing my ideas and opinions with my colleagues.
2. My team members are supportive and willing to help each other.
3. Collaboration is encouraged and rewarded in our company.
4. Cross-functional collaboration is easy and efficient.
5. Our teams have a strong sense of camaraderie and shared purpose.

Innovation

1. I am encouraged to experiment and take risks in my work.

2. New ideas are welcomed and valued in our company.
3. I have the resources and support I need to pursue innovative projects.
4. Our company fosters a culture of continuous learning and improvement.
5. We are quick to adapt to changing circumstances and market trends.

Customer Focus

1. I understand the needs and expectations of our customers.
2. We actively seek and use customer feedback to improve our products/services.
3. Customer satisfaction is a top priority for our company.
4. I feel empowered to go above and beyond to meet customer needs.
5. We strive to build long-term relationships with our customers.

Communication

1. Communication within our organization is open and transparent.
2. I feel comfortable sharing my concerns and feedback with my manager.
3. Leaders communicate regularly and effectively with employees.
4. We have effective channels for both formal and informal communication.
5. I feel well-informed about company news, updates, and changes.

Employee Well-being

1. Our company cares about the physical and mental health of its employees.
2. Work-life balance is encouraged and supported.

3. I feel valued and appreciated for my contributions.
4. The company provides opportunities for professional development.
5. I feel a sense of community and belonging within the workplace.

Leadership

1. Our leaders embody the values of the company.
2. Leaders are accessible and approachable.
3. I trust our leadership team to make sound decisions.
4. Our leaders inspire and motivate me to do my best work.
5. I feel confident in the direction our leadership is taking the company.

(Continue with other relevant dimensions, such as decision-making, ethics, etc.)

Open-Ended Questions

1. What are the three most important values that define our company culture?
2. What are some of the biggest challenges you face in our current culture?
3. If you could change one thing about our culture, what would it be and why?
4. Tell me about a time when you felt most proud to work here. What made it so special?
5. Describe a situation where you saw our company's values in action.

(Optional: Include demographic questions (e.g., department, tenure) if you want to analyze results by different groups)

Interview Guide

(Use the Open-Ended Questions from the survey as a starting point for your interviews. Then, use probing questions to delve deeper into their responses and gain additional

insights.)

Probing Questions:
- Can you elaborate on that?
- Tell me more about how you felt in that situation.
- What were the specific actions or behaviors that led you to that conclusion?
- Can you give me a concrete example of what you mean?
- How do you think that impacts our overall culture?

Remember: The goal is to foster a genuine conversation and create a safe space for employees to share their honest perspectives. Use these questions as a starting point, but allow the discussion to flow naturally and adapt your approach based on the individual's responses.

APPENDIX: ORGANIZATIONAL CULTURE SELF-ASSESSMENT

Please rate the following statements on a scale of 1 to 5, where:
- 1 = Strongly Disagree
- 2 = Disagree
- 3 = Neutral
- 4 = Agree
- 5 = Strongly Agree

Dimension: Collaboration

1. Employees regularly share information and resources with each other.
2. There is a high level of trust and respect among team members.
3. Cross-functional collaboration is encouraged and rewarded.
4. Employees feel comfortable challenging each other's ideas constructively.
5. Teamwork is valued more than individual

achievements.

Dimension: Innovation

1. New ideas are welcomed and encouraged at all levels.
2. Experimentation and risk-taking are tolerated, even if they don't always succeed.
3. Employees are given the time and resources to pursue innovative projects.
4. The company values continuous learning and improvement.
5. The organization is adaptable and open to change.

Dimension: Customer Focus

1. Employees understand the needs and expectations of customers.
2. Customer feedback is actively sought and used to improve products/services.
3. Customer satisfaction is a top priority for the organization.
4. Employees are empowered to go above and beyond to meet customer needs.
5. The company fosters long-term relationships with customers.

Dimension: Communication

1. Communication within the organization is open and transparent.
2. Employees feel comfortable sharing their opinions and concerns.
3. Leaders communicate regularly and effectively with employees.
4. Feedback is given and received constructively.
5. Information flows freely across departments and levels.

Dimension: Employee Well-being

1. The company cares about the physical and mental health of its employees.
2. Work-life balance is encouraged and supported.
3. Employees feel valued and appreciated for their contributions.
4. The organization provides opportunities for professional development.
5. There is a sense of community and belonging within the workplace.

Scoring Guidelines

- Calculate the average score for each dimension.
- Overall Culture Score: Average the scores of all dimensions.

Interpretation of Results:

- **4.0 – 5.0:** Strong culture in this dimension.
- **3.0 – 3.9:** Moderate culture in this dimension, with room for improvement.
- **1.0 – 2.9:** Weak culture in this dimension, requiring significant attention.

Additional Insights:

- Look for patterns: Are there specific dimensions where your organization excels or struggles?
- Compare with desired culture: How do these results align with your ideal culture?
- Identify areas for improvement: Use this assessment as a starting point for conversations and initiatives to strengthen your culture.

Note: This is a simplified self-assessment tool. For a more comprehensive analysis, consider using validated organizational culture surveys or consulting with a culture expert.

APPENDIX: THE CULTURAL WEB TOOL

Weaving the Cultural Web: A Practical Guide

The Cultural Web is a powerful tool for unraveling the complex tapestry of your organization's culture. It provides a framework for examining the stories, rituals, symbols, power structures, organizational structures, and control systems that collectively shape your workplace. By analyzing these interconnected elements, you can gain valuable insights into the hidden assumptions and patterns that drive behavior within your organization.

Step 1: Gather Information

This is the investigative phase. Your goal is to collect as much data as possible about each of the six elements of the Cultural Web. Here's how to approach it:

- **Stories:**
  - Listen actively to the stories that employees tell about the company's history, successes, failures, and legendary figures.
  - Pay attention to the tone and underlying message of these stories. What values are being celebrated? What kind of behavior is admired or frowned upon?
- **Rituals and Routines:**
  - Observe how people interact with each other on a daily basis. How do they greet each other? What are the typical communication styles?
  - Attend meetings, both formal and informal. What's the atmosphere like? Who speaks up? How are decisions made?
  - Note any recurring events or celebrations. What do they reveal about the company's values and priorities?
- **Symbols:**
  - Walk around the office space and take note of the physical environment. What kind of decor is used? Are there any visible awards, trophies, or mementos?
  - Pay attention to the dress code. Is it formal or casual? What does this say about the company's image and culture?
  - Analyze the language used in emails, presentations, and other forms of communication. Is it formal or informal? Are

there any specific jargon or buzzwords?
- **Power Structures:**
    - Identify the key decision-makers in the organization. Who has the authority to approve projects, allocate resources, and hire or fire employees?
    - Look beyond formal titles to identify informal sources of power and influence. Are there any individuals or groups who hold sway over others, regardless of their official position?
- **Organizational Structures:**
    - Review organizational charts and reporting relationships. How is the company structured into departments, teams, and divisions?
    - Observe how work flows through the organization. Who reports to whom? Who collaborates with whom? What are the communication channels?
- **Control Systems:**
    - Examine the performance evaluation process. How is performance measured and rewarded?
    - Analyze financial metrics, quality control procedures, and other systems used to monitor and control organizational performance.

Step 2: Identify Patterns and Uncover Assumptions

Once you've gathered a wealth of information, it's time to start making sense of it.

- **Identify Patterns:** Look for recurring themes, values, and beliefs that emerge across the different elements of the Cultural Web. For example, you might notice that many stories celebrate risk-taking and innovation, while the control systems focus heavily on minimizing errors and avoiding mistakes. This could indicate a potential tension between the company's stated values and its actual practices.

- **Uncover Assumptions:** Dig deeper to uncover the underlying assumptions that drive behavior. What do people believe about the company's purpose, its customers, its competitors, or even themselves? These assumptions may not be explicitly stated, but they can have a powerful influence on how people act and make decisions.

Step 3: Create a Visual Map

A visual representation of the Cultural Web can be a powerful tool for understanding the interconnectedness of its elements.

- **Diagram:** Create a diagram that depicts the six elements as interconnected nodes. Use arrows to show how the elements influence each other.
- **Highlights:** Highlight the key patterns, themes, and assumptions that you've identified. This will help you see the big picture and understand how the different elements of the culture interact to create the overall experience.

Step 4: Analyze and Interpret

Now it's time to reflect on your findings.

- **Strengths and Weaknesses:** What are the strengths of your current culture? What aspects need to be strengthened or changed?
- **Alignment with Goals:** How does your culture support or hinder your organization's goals? Are there any misalignments that need to be addressed?
- **Areas for Change:** Based on your analysis, identify specific areas where you can intervene to create a more positive and productive culture.

The insights you gain from the Cultural Web are only valuable if you use them to drive positive change. Here are some ways you can leverage the Cultural Web to transform your company culture:

- **Storytelling:** Share stories that exemplify the desired culture.
- **Rituals and Routines:** Create new rituals that reinforce desired behaviors.
- **Symbols:** Redesign the physical space, change the dress code, or update the company logo to reflect the desired

culture.
- **Power Structures:** Empower employees to make decisions and take ownership of their work.
- **Organizational Structures:** Restructure teams or departments to foster collaboration and communication.
- **Control Systems:** Align performance metrics and reward systems with the desired cultural values.

The Cultural Web: An Ongoing Process

Culture is not static; it's a dynamic force that constantly evolves. The Cultural Web is not a one-time exercise but an ongoing process of inquiry and reflection. By regularly revisiting the Cultural Web, you can stay attuned to your organization's evolving culture and ensure that it remains aligned with your goals and values.

Additional Tips for Using the Cultural Web

- **Engage Employees:** Involve employees in the process of analyzing and interpreting the Cultural Web. This will create a shared understanding of the culture and build support for change initiatives.
- **Challenge Assumptions:** Don't be afraid to question long-held beliefs and assumptions. The Cultural Web can help you uncover blind spots and identify areas where your culture may need to shift.
- **Be Patient:** Cultural change takes time. Don't expect to see immediate results. Focus on making incremental improvements and building momentum over time.

APPENDIX: THE O'REILLY CULTURE MODEL

The O'Reilly Culture Model – Your Compass for Cultural Transformation

The O'Reilly Culture Model provides a comprehensive framework for assessing your organization's culture across seven critical dimensions. By understanding your cultural profile, you can pinpoint strengths to leverage and areas for improvement, enabling you to create a workplace that resonates with employees and drives success.

Understanding the Seven Dimensions

1. **Results-Oriented:**
   - **What it means:** Emphasis on achieving goals, driving performance, and rewarding accomplishments.
   - **Signs of a strong results-oriented culture:** Clear goals and expectations, regular performance feedback, merit-based rewards, a focus on efficiency and productivity.
2. **Learning-Oriented:**
   - **What it means:** Commitment to continuous learning, development, and innovation.

- Signs of a strong learning-oriented culture: Encouragement of experimentation, knowledge sharing, training programs, a willingness to embrace new technologies and ideas.
3. **Enjoyment-Oriented:**
   - **What it means:** Value placed on a positive work environment, celebrating successes, and fostering strong relationships.
   - **Signs of a strong enjoyment-oriented culture:** Fun and collaborative atmosphere, social events, recognition of achievements, opportunities for team building.
4. **Authority-Oriented:**
   - **What it means:** The extent to which power and decision-making are centralized or decentralized.
   - **Signs of a high authority-oriented culture:** Clear hierarchy, top-down decision-making, formal communication channels, emphasis on rules and procedures.
   - **Signs of a low authority-oriented culture:** Empowered employees, collaborative decision-making, open communication, tolerance for risk-taking.
5. **Safety-Oriented:**
   - **What it means:** Focus on risk management, stability, and predictability.
   - **Signs of a strong safety-oriented culture:** Emphasis on safety protocols, risk assessment procedures, thorough planning, aversion to mistakes and failures.
6. **Order-Oriented:**
   - **What it means:** Emphasis on processes, structures, and procedures.
   - **Signs of a strong order-oriented culture:** Clearly defined roles and responsibilities, well-documented procedures, strict adherence to rules, emphasis on

efficiency and standardization.

7. **Purpose-Oriented:**
   o **What it means:** The degree to which employees feel a sense of meaning and purpose in their work.
   o **Signs of a strong purpose-oriented culture:** Clear mission and values, alignment between individual and company goals, opportunities for employees to contribute to something bigger than themselves.

Steps to Implement the O'Reilly Culture Model

1. **Conduct a Culture Assessment:**
   o Design a survey or questionnaire based on the seven dimensions. Include both Likert scale questions (e.g., "I feel my work has a significant impact on the company's success.") and open-ended questions (e.g., "What do you value most about our company culture?").
   o Distribute the survey or questionnaire to all employees or a representative sample.
   o Anonymize and analyze the responses to identify patterns and trends.

2. **Analyze Your Cultural Profile:**
   o Calculate average scores for each dimension.
   o Create a visual representation of your cultural profile, such as a radar chart or bar graph.
   o Identify your organization's strengths and weaknesses. Which dimensions are you strongest in? Which need improvement?

3. **Compare with Your Ideal Culture:**
   o Reflect on your organization's vision, mission, and strategic goals.
   o Define what your ideal culture would look like across each of the seven dimensions.
   o Compare your current cultural profile with your ideal profile. What gaps exist?

4. **Develop an Action Plan:**

- Prioritize the cultural dimensions that need the most attention.
- Create specific action items to address weaknesses and leverage strengths.
  - **For example:**
    - If your culture is lacking in enjoyment, you might implement team-building activities, social events, or recognition programs.
    - If your culture is overly authority-oriented, you might consider delegating more decision-making power to employees or fostering a more collaborative leadership style.
- Assign responsibility for each action item and set timelines for implementation.

5. **Implement, Monitor, and Iterate:**
   - Communicate your action plan to employees and explain how it will benefit them and the company.
   - Regularly track your progress and measure the impact of your interventions.
   - Be prepared to adapt your approach as needed based on feedback and results.

Printed in Great Britain
by Amazon

3dfda338-29a2-41bb-b95a-70f9e586e398R01